CW00552836

TRUTH AND WONDER

Truth and Wonder is an accessible introduction to Plato and Aristotle, showing their crucial influence for literary and cultural studies, modern languages and related disciplines. It focuses on both *what* Plato and Aristotle say about literature and *how* they say it, and so demonstrates the ways their philosophies still shape our reading, thinking and living.

In the clear and engaging style for which he has become known, Robert Eaglestone uses Plato and Aristotle's literary qualities to explain their thought. He presents Plato's ideas through the metaphors, stories and style of his dialogues, and Aristotle's ideas through the significance of narrative. *Truth and Wonder* draws on a wide range of thinkers including Hannah Arendt, Martin Heidegger, Jacques Derrida and Martha Nussbaum, and a number of canonical writers including Phillip Sidney, Percy Shelley, Ngũgĩ wa Thiong'o and Iris Murdoch with examples that will be familiar to students.

The ideas of Plato and Aristotle underlie much of Western culture, continue to inspire contemporary literary and philosophical work and shape the case for the central importance of the humanities today. *Truth and Wonder* is essential reading for students and researchers in the study of literature, theory and criticism as well as for those wishing to understand the foundations of the field. It will also be of interest to those studying philosophy, classics and political theory. Its accessible style and approach also mean it's a perfect starting point for any literary-minded person who wants to know more about these two foundational thinkers.

Robert Eaglestone is Professor of Contemporary Literature and Thought at Royal Holloway, UK, and has published widely on contemporary literature and literary theory, contemporary European philosophy and Holocaust and Genocide studies. He is the author of *Doing English* (fourth edition, 2017), editor of *Brexit and Literature* (2018) and co-editor, with Daniel O'Gorman, of *The Routledge Companion to Twenty-First Century Literary Fiction* (2018).

TRUTH AND WONDER

A Literary Introduction to Plato and Aristotle

Robert Eaglestone

Routledge
Taylor & Francis Group

LONDON AND NEW YORK

Cover image: *Ephemeris* and photograph © Darren Almond.

First published 2022
by Routledge
2 Park Square, Milton Park, Abingdon, Oxon OX14 4RN

and by Routledge
605 Third Avenue, New York, NY 10158

Routledge is an imprint of the Taylor & Francis Group, an informa business

British Library Cataloguing-in-Publication Data
A catalogue record for this book is available from the British Library

Library of Congress Cataloging-in-Publication Data
A catalog record has been requested for this book

ISBN: 978-0-367-56472-8 (hbk)
ISBN: 978-0-367-56471-1 (pbk)
ISBN: 978-1-003-09791-4 (ebk)

DOI: 10.4324/9781003097914

Typeset in Bembo
by Newgen Publishing UK

CONTENTS

CONTENTS

ACKNOWLEDGEMENTS

I'd like to thank my colleagues at Royal Holloway, University of London, with a special note of appreciation to the Library and their scan and deliver staff. At Routledge, I'd like to thank Polly Dodson and Zoe Meyer (hard to imagine more supportive editors) and the anonymous readers of the original proposal for their constructive comments, as well as Thara Kanaga and all at Newgen KnowledgeWorks. Special thanks to some friends and colleagues who have helped with this book in different ways: Jessica Chiba, Neil Gascoigne, Simon Glendenning, Lawrence Hemming, Ahuvia Kahane, Ben Knights, Gail Marshall, John Sellars, Dan Rebellato, Adam Roberts, Danielle Sands, Lyndsey Stonebridge, Aaron Turner and Robert Vilain. I want particularly to thank Angie Wilson for her explicit and extensive advice, and Doug Cowie and Nick Hoare, with whom I discussed many of these ideas, usually with beer. All errors and introductory oversimplifications are mine.

I also want to express my deepest appreciation for all the students who have taken *EN3106 Literature and Philosophy* with me since 1997: more than 20 years of discussing, reading, listening, what-if-you-think-about-it-like-this?-ing during which I learned quite as much, usually more, than they did.

Two more general thanks. I am very grateful to the late David Walford who introduced me with such care to German philosophy and to the work of Martin Heidegger. Thanks as well to R. R. Rockingham-Gill, who introduced me to a very different way of discussing philosophical matters, convivial and precise (I have tried to be both, but feel more confident in the former than the latter): he also introduced me to the word *philophilosophos* (see the end of the introduction).

Thanks also to Gina Alexander and the late Laidon Alexander and family, Abhishek Arun, Antonio Bricese, Matthew Broadbent, Pie and Mel Corbett, Jo Cotrell, Penny Crawford, Holly Crocker, Tommy Crocker, Ben Davies, Sarah Dimmelow, Brian Docherty, William and Jadwiga Eaglestone and family, Margaret Eaglestone, Malcolm and Jane Geere, Paul Ging, Sophie Goldsworthy, Rebecca Jinks, Elizabeth and Benedict Kelly and family, Judith Hawley, Simon Kövesi, Barry Langford, Katie and Tim Livesey and family, Jennifer Neville, Jen Panchal, Hilary Saunders, Jo Sockett, Gavin Stewart, Dan Stone, Richard and Sarah Tennant, Julian Thomas, Catherine Thomas, Lucie Wenigerova and all at KSE.

I am extremely grateful to Darren Almond for creating and for letting me use a wonderful piece from his *Ephemeris* series on the cover: I discuss it in the conclusion.

Most of all: thank you to my wife Dr Poppy Corbett and my children, Alex and Isabella Eaglestone, for their love (and useful comments on the manuscript: Bella, I took what you said about Thucydides to heart).

Everyone in the UK owes a debt of thanks to the NHS staff and care workers for all they have done during the pandemic. I have two more specific debts. The first is to the psychiatrists at the Phenomenology Reading Group at the London and Maudsley NHS Foundation Trust, with whom I have had the pleasure of working through *Being and Time* for a number of years. The second is to thank those who cared for my mother in her last years. I dedicate this book to my late parents, Alex and Clare Eaglestone.

INTRODUCTION

Plato and Aristotle *for* and *as* literature

This book is an introduction to Plato and Aristotle *for* the study of literature and *as* literature. I explain their ideas about poetry, drama and stories and I explore what reading their work as literature means. Truth and wonder are my starting points.

Truth is for Plato. Born in Athens, probably around 424/3 BCE, and dying there around 348/7 BCE, Plato is the most important founder of Western philosophy. His work consists of around 35 texts (scholars argue over the authenticity of some) in which the philosopher Socrates is usually the central character. Plato knew Socrates for probably about a decade, and it was Socrates who first inspired Plato to philosophy. Plato founded a school in Athens in 383 BCE and we still use its name to describe higher study: the Academy.[1]

Plato's dialogues are motivated by a search for what is true, beautiful, good and just. However, this pursuit leads Plato's characters to argue that stories, poems and plays are far from true and do not make us wise. In the dialogues, literature is talked about as a silly distraction, as a bad influence or as a dangerous disease for which we need a cure: poems, plays and stories stop you from becoming yourself and can harm the community. The main speaker from *The Sophist* attacks what previous thinkers have said because rather than explore the truth, each of them seems "to tell us a story, as if we were children" (*The Sophist* 242c). Most famously in *The Republic*, Socrates plans to ban the poets from his imagined city unless they follow very strict rules about what and how they write. This may seem mad or bad to us and is why Plato is often invoked as a hater of literature.

But Plato is a great writer of subtle genius. As we become even a little more familiar with the dialogues, we can see that they are complex, layered works of drama which call for literary understanding and analysis. Character, setting and narrative, metaphor and image, form and style are not divisible from the arguments and ideas. Plato never simply writes in his own voice to 'tell you what he thinks' nor does he arrive at final conclusions. This means there are ways of reading Plato's work that don't take this hatred of literature for granted. Plato's Socrates seems to suggest one thing *for* literature but reading the dialogues *as* literature might suggest something else, as we'll see.

DOI: 10.4324/9781003097914-1

Wonder is for Aristotle, Plato's most important interlocutor. He was born in Stagira in northern Greece around 384 BCE. He studied and taught mostly in Athens, first as a pupil then as a kind of rival to Plato. After a period away from Athens, he returned and set up his own school, the Lyceum. He fled the city as the political climate changed and died on the island of Euboea in 322 BCE. Aristotle is also a foundational thinker for Western philosophy and science. He writes at the start of his book *Metaphysics* that we all naturally desire to understand. The source of this desire, and so the beginning of philosophy and wisdom, is wonder. The early thinkers wondered "about the phenomena of the moon and ... the sun and the stars, and about the genesis of the universe" (*Metaphysics* 982b14–17). Aristotle thinks, too, that "the lover of stories is, in a way, a lover of wisdom, since a story is composed of wonders" (982b19–20). For Aristotle, literature helps us in our task of being good, having a fulfilled life and developing wisdom and understanding. Aristotle even wrote a kind of 'natural history' of literature and handbook for creative writing, the *Poetics*. Publishers report that, these days, this is Aristotle's best-selling work and it is where, unhelpfully I think, many literary people first encounter his thought directly.

Aristotle's work is not as approachable as Plato's. Very many of the books that Aristotle wrote for wider circulation, praised in the classical world for their style and beauty, are lost. What we have left are often described as his 'lecture notes': still an enormous body of work, but dense, frequently abrupt and hard to follow. However, even these are open to a kind of literary interpretation which draws out his ideas, tracing something like a story from his most fundamental inquiries into being itself, to how we are in the world, to his views on ethics, happiness and the mirrored patterns of our mind and the universe, and on to his discussions of language, in his book *Rhetoric*, and literature in the *Poetics*.

Reading Plato and Aristotle with literature in mind gives a specific kind of illumination to each. There are three further shared advantages. First, literature fuses plot, character, ideas, themes, form, style and it delights in subtext, ambiguity and allusion. Literature is a kind of bringing together. By contrast, philosophers often divide thought and writing into separate fields (ethics, logic, epistemology, political theory, aesthetics and so on) in order to seek tighter and finer distinctions and so to achieve a greater kind of clarity. Indeed, philosophers liberally throw around their rich wealth of "definitions, divisions, and distinctions" joked the Elizabethan courtier and poet Sir Philip Sidney in his witty defence of poetry.[2] The problem is that all these fields of enquiry are not really separate. For example, ideas about politics (how should the community work?) and art (what is valuable or beautiful?) are not divisible from epistemology (how do we know?), and, in turn, these are not really divisible from ideas about ethics (what is right and good?) and existence itself (what does it mean to be?). For Plato and Aristotle, these distinctions did not exist or were just beginning to take shape through their work: reading their work in a more holistic literary way gives a sense of this. Although sometimes we may need to divide our experiences and knowledges into these different and more technical fields, literary reading suggests that we need also to bring them back together to achieve a fuller understanding of ourselves and our world.

Second, literary reading also brings together our daily life and philosophy. It emphasises that seemingly abstract philosophical questions arise from and are important to the everyday. Plato shows this interaction by setting most of his dialogues in more-or-less typical day-to-day situations: a party, *another* party, a country walk, a chance encounter on the street, finding out more about a celebrity. Aristotle frequently reminds his audience that the point is not just to know about, say, virtue or health, but actually to be virtuous in our lives, to keep healthy.

Third, thinking about Plato and Aristotle *as* literature also helps us understand the ways in which their influence continues to evolve. There is a huge gulf between classical Athens and now, and it is naïve to say that this can be passed over or that they 'were like us'. Virginia Woolf wrote of classical antiquity that

> it is vain and foolish to talk of knowing Greek … since we do not know how the words sounded, or where precisely we ought to laugh, or how the actors acted, and between this foreign people and ourselves there is not only difference of race and tongue but a tremendous breach of tradition.[3]

Some of the most significant differences are ethical. For example, as Simone Weil writes of Aristotle, a "man who takes the trouble to draw up an apology for slavery cannot be a lover of justice".[4] Yet these Platonic and Aristotelian texts and ideas still speak to us, either because they are woven into our debates today about politics and community, or about what it is to live 'the good life', or because we discover in them strange, unexpected illuminations of our present moment. This is because they make up part of a tradition, certainly stretched, holed or breached, as Woolf suggests, but one which each generation has actively to revise, reweigh and re-evaluate, choosing, as they may, to reject, reshape or reclaim. This evolution of a tradition occurs whether you believe that scholars are still finding out new things about these works (using the growing resources offered by computing or new archaeological discoveries) or are reinterpreting them by the changing lights of every new generation.[5] The amazing story of how the works of Plato and Aristotle were lost, kept, rediscovered, translated and spread, which involves Greece and Rome, the Middle East, North Africa and Europe and believers in the Greek gods, Muslims, Christians, Jews, atheists and more, is also part of this tradition.[6] Literature, in its widest sense, is very good at dealing with this constant evolution of traditions. Theatres translate, adapt and perform ancient Greek dramas; authors across the globe and in all periods rewrite or reuse the classics, rework or challenge the canon.[7] Literature returns to the past, makes present and opens towards the future. Reading as literature allows us to approach Plato and Aristotle through capacious and flexible senses about traditions and their active revisioning, reshaping and rewriting.

Paths through Plato and Aristotle

Reading a writer or thinker for the first time is a bit like making your way through unfamiliar territory. The point of an introduction is to guide you along a path. Of course, this does not show you everything and the main reason it's useful is because after walking one path, it's easier to explore others, and, most importantly, make your own. Some introductions lead you down a single track after all, the author has spent years finding out where it leads. I take a slightly different, and maybe more characteristically literary approach. My main route is, obviously, the importance of Plato and Aristotle *for* and *as* literature, but I have tried to show a diversity of readings and meanings, suggesting forks in the path, other directions and new openings (some, for example, may find even the '*as* literature' contentious). My aim is to encourage you to explore these yourself, to become your own pathfinder.

I begin with introducing two key concepts for both Plato and Aristotle (Chapter 1) which are both historical and philosophical: *Polis* and *Logos* (very roughly, community and language). These two ideas, shifting in form and emphasis, will accompany us on our journey through these thinkers.

The first part of the book, 'What is truly written in the soul', introduces Plato by telling stories. I begin looking at the themes of Plato's thought in Chapter 2 through some of his most famous and influential narratives, metaphors and literary devices, including that of the dialogue form itself. This approach avoids a more simplistic account of his 'doctrines' and gives a powerful sense of what Plato (or Socrates, rather) is *for* rather than against (the *against* is what literary people often first hear about Plato). Then I look at four of his most important dialogues. Each has things to say about literature: *Phaedrus* and *Ion* are well-known to literary people; *The Republic* known in part (**books 2, 3** and **10** concern poetry, drama and representation) and *Protagoras* ought to be well known, for both its style and content. To counteract the way that arguments about literature are often taken out of context from *The Republic*, I introduce the whole long dialogue in Chapter 3: like a film, I contrast panorama shots with detailed close-ups for especially relevant moments. This approach also brings out some of the dialogue's narrative shape and recurring images. Chapter 4 looks at responses to *The Republic*. Some of these deal directly with the apparent authoritarianism and 'hatred of literature', but I also discuss the view that his texts as writing tell us something more subtle, and I look at the ways some creative writers have turned Plato against Plato. Taking up these ideas, Chapters 5 and 6 explore slightly divergent paths. Chapter 5 looks at *Phaedrus*, one of the most beautiful dialogues, and follows an extremely influential reading by the philosopher Jacques Derrida which claims to find a revealing inconsistency in Plato's argument about the nature of writing. Chapter 6 turns to *Ion* and

Protagoras to suggest that there is considerable nuance in Plato's work itself, enough to suggest a kind of literary interpretive approach within it. Both these discussions stem from some scintillating Platonic scholarship of the last 50 years or so.

Aristotle's work provides the most powerful response to Plato's. The second part of this book, 'The lover of stories is … a lover of wisdom', introduces Aristotle in a literary way (Chapter 7): the challenges of Aristotle for a literary reader are very different from those of Plato. The texts are often difficult to follow, there is simply so much to read, and, I think most importantly, it's hard to see what is really going on. Moreover, the obvious literary beginning, the *Poetics*, is far from the best place to start. My path begins with Aristotle's belief that life is about doing, and with his most fundamental question about being itself (what is 'is'?). These lead me to explain his ideas about the purpose of life, the meaning of this for happiness, fulfilment and how to live, and how what he calls the moral and intellectual virtues help us (Chapter 8). At each step, I draw out the importance for how we understand and use literature. This approach explains why the *Rhetoric*, a much misunderstood and ignored book, is so important (Chapter 9). In Chapter 10 I turn to the *Poetics*, offering a summary and a discussion of the importance of patterns, the role of the emotions and politics, and answer the question of what literature is for Aristotle. Then I focus on the pleasure of literature and the patterns of understanding, drawing out some key issues, *mimesis*, catharsis, tragedy and metaphor (Chapter 11). I conclude by returning to some of the themes of this book.

Why I wrote this book

Plato and Aristotle might be the most introduced philosophers in history. Teachers have written guides to their work for well over two millennia, first all around the eastern and central Mediterranean, then in North Africa and the Middle East, then in Europe and then throughout the world, on papyrus, clay tablets, parchment, vellum, paper, digital screens and soon on materials not yet invented or even imagined.

My professional justification for another introduction is simple. Plato and Aristotle have extremely important and thought-provoking, if not always comfortable, things to say about poetry, drama and stories for an interested audience. Conveniently but perhaps unsurprisingly, navigating what they say about literature and how they say it turns out to be a speedy passage into the vaster oceans of their philosophy. Literary scholars often tell us that Plato is against literature, but why, and what is he for? Answering these questions tells us a great deal about Plato's work. Similarly, while literary scholars often discuss the *Poetics*, usually in passing, they very rarely explore Aristotle's wider thought and its more fundamental implications for how to live and for understanding literature.[8] Putting the central concerns of Aristotle's thought and the *Poetics* together illuminates both.

Plato and Aristotle still have much to teach us. Many thinkers and critics who have inspired our contemporary ways of understanding literature, our current criticism and theory draw a great deal from Plato and Aristotle, as debates about old words like representation (akin to what the classical Greeks called *mimesis*) or newer terms like *logocentric* suggest. As Miriam Leonard and Paul Allen Miller argue, we need to uncover these classical foundations more fully in order to understand the ideas of these more recent thinkers, and so our own responses, more clearly.[9] Some thinkers who perhaps *ought* to inspire our study of literature more (say, Hannah Arendt, Hans-Georg Gadamer) draw on this classical heritage too. Understanding how and why makes these thinkers and the complex questions they ask (and that they beg) more comprehensible. There are also missed encounters. Many major contemporary philosophers who have turned to Plato or Aristotle to discuss literature (Martha Nussbaum, Alasdair MacIntyre, Bernard Williams) pass almost unnoticed in literary studies (and I introduce a little of what is significant about them here).

Finally, recent work on Plato and Aristotle shares a great deal with the contemporary study of literature: ideas about writing, meaning, narrating, form, style and content, ways of reading, as well as discussions about the role and significance of literature. So as these two vessels sail parallel courses, this seems an ideal opportunity to swap stories, exchange information and share supplies. That's how interdisciplinary dialogues happen (and I hope this book plays a small part in furthering the excellent work that already does this). One of my happy discoveries as an interloper in these waters is that much contemporary scholarship on Plato and Aristotle is not only lively and exciting but also reassuringly welcoming. It is characterised by clarity, humour, a sense of purpose and an eye for the newcomer. In this book, I aim to chart some of the tides and currents of that scholarship, and, when completed, I urge readers to board their own ships, cast off and put to sea.

My personal justification for embarking on this is also simple: fascination. 'To fascinate' originally meant 'to cast a spell' and Socrates is compared, in the dialogue *Meno*, to a witch. Sure enough, I have been bewitched by Socrates and Plato since I read the dialogue *Ion* one morning as a scruffy undergraduate sitting on a table in the foyer of the Arts Building at the University of Manchester. To be brought up a Catholic, as I was, is also to be brought up with one powerful legacy of Aristotle, for both good and bad. That, too, is fascinating: wondering about and puzzling through a complex, interwoven and developing tradition of thought with which one is always already involved. I've had the privilege to teach Plato and Aristotle, mainly to literature students, since 1995 and I was further prompted to write this introduction by a long project on Hannah Arendt, which led me to reread the classical heritage that she reworks.[10] The pandemic and lockdown, during which I wrote most of this book, as well as my own disposition, lead me to feel that it's better to offer some patient and sympathetic commentary that looks for links, rather than divisions, in our ways of seeing the world. I'm not a philosopher or a poet (or a political theorist or a classicist), but I take heart in Sir Philip Sidney's remark that no one is "so much a *philophilosophos*", a friend to the philosopher, as the person who thinks about the philosopher and the poet together.[11]

Notes

1 A short, but admirably dense, biography is Debra Nails, 'The Life of Plato of Athens' in *A Companion to Plato*, ed. Hugh H. Benson (Oxford: Blackwell, 2006), pp. 1–12.

2 Philip Sidney, *Sidney's 'The Defence of Poesy' and Selected Renaissance Literary Criticism*, ed. Gavin Alexander (London: Penguin, 2004), p. 14.

3 Virginia Woolf, 'On Not Knowing Greek' in *The Common Reader* (London: Hogarth Press, 1948), pp. 39–59, p. 39.

4 Weil goes on: the "age in which he lived has nothing to do with it. To accept as authoritative the ideas of a man who doesn't love justice constitutes an offence against justice, inevitably punished by a decrease in powers of discernment". Simone Weil, *The Need for Roots*, trans. Arthur Wills (London: Routledge, 2002), p. 241. The impact of enslavement on classical thought is not as widely discussed as it should be but see: Bernard Williams, *Shame and Necessity* (Princeton: Princeton University Press, 2008), ch. 5; Malcolm Heath, 'Aristotle on natural slavery', *Phronesis* 53:3, 2008, 243–70.

5 See: Nicholas Smith, 'Editorial Afterword: Platonic Scholars and Other Wishful Thinkers' in *Methods of Interpreting Plato and His Dialogues: Oxford Studies in Ancient Philosophy: Supplementary Volume*, eds. James C. Klagge and Nicholas D. Smith, 1992, pp. 245–60.

6 The generally agreed numbers by which quotations from Plato and Aristotle are cited are themselves a sign of this history. For Plato, they are called 'Stephanus numbers', marking a page and column from the 1578 edition of Plato, published by Henri Estienne. For Aristotle, the analogous system is called 'Bekker pagination' and uses the Prussian Academy of Sciences edition of the complete works of Aristotle (1831–1870), edited by the classical philologist August Immanuel Bekker.

7 See, for a range of examples of contemporary reworking of literature from classical antiquity, Jennifer Wallace, *Tragedy Since 9/11: Reading a World Out of Joint* (London: Bloomsbury, 2019); I discuss other examples from Ato Quayson, *Tragedy and Postcolonial Literature* (Cambridge: Cambridge University Press, 2021) in Chapter 8.

8 This is a point made tellingly by Stephen Halliwell, one of the very best analysts of Aristotle and classical literary theory. Fairmindedly, Halliwell also notes that some specialised Aristotelians think of the *Poetics* as "marginal". Stephen Halliwell, *Aristotle's Poetics*, 2nd ed. (London: Duckworth, 1998), pp. 2–3. See, for a recent exploration of the links between the *Poetics* and the rest of Aristotle's work, *The Poetics in Its Aristotelian Context*, eds. Pierre Destrée, Malcolm Heath, Dana L. Munteanu (London: Routledge, 2020).

9 See Paul Allen Miller, *Diotima at the Barricades* (Oxford: Oxford University Press, 2016) and Miriam Leonard, *Athens in Paris: Ancient Greece and the Political in Post-War French Thought* (Oxford: Oxford University Press, 2005).

10 I was far from alone in this: see, for example, 'Hannah Arendt and the Ancients', a special issue of *Classical Philology* 113:1 (2018).

11 Sidney, *Sidney's 'The Defence of Poesy'*, p. 22.

1

THREE WORDS

Polis and *Logos*

This chapter will introduce both the historical context for Plato and Aristotle and key ideas for this book: *polis* (city), *logos* (speech and reason) and their relationship ('and'). I'll explain roughly what these ancient Greek words mean, and why they were so important for Plato and Aristotle, and remain so for us.

Polis

Polis means city, city-state or community and it was the dominant form of Greek communal organisation in Plato's and Aristotle's time. *Polis* is the root of a range English words: metro*polis* (a city); *polity* (a state); *polite* (a way to behave); *politician* and *police* (important public roles); *politics* (the skill of governing, all the institutions that go with government). These various meanings hint at the interlinked ideas of communal identity, personal and social behaviour, public life, responsibilities and duties, authority, justice and government that cluster around *polis* for the ancient Greeks and still, though transformed, for us. I'm going to offer a very brief introduction to the classical *polis* and then turn to the specific history of Athens, where Plato and Aristotle (mostly) lived and worked. Their thought developed *in*, *with* and *about* the *polis*.

In his *Politics*, Aristotle wrote that "man is by nature a political animal" (*Politics* 1253a2–3). More, the *polis* is "by nature clearly prior to the family and to the individual since the whole is of necessity prior to the part" (*Politics* 1253a19–20). People are part of the *polis* as the limbs are part of the body. Shakespeare, among many others, continually returns to this metaphor of the 'body politic'. In the very first scene of *Coriolanus*, a nobleman, Menenius Agrippa tries to calm the rioting Roman population by invoking a fable from Aesop which tells of a "time when all the body's members/Rebell'd against the belly" (*Coriolanus* I.i. 52–3). The crowd immediately grasps the metaphor, understanding the "kingly-crowned head, the vigilant eye/The counsellor heart, the arm our soldier/Our steed the leg, the tongue our trumpeter" (*Coriolanus* I.i. 71–3) and listens as Menenius argues that the belly feeds the rest of the body. For Aristotle, somebody who is not part of a *polis* must be "either a beast or a

DOI: 10.4324/9781003097914-2

god" (*Politics* 1253a29), subhuman or divinely self-sufficient. (This is a point the angry Coriolanus makes when he arrives, spoiling Menenius's work by calling the rioters "curs", that is, untamed dogs, and so excluding them, in his patrician view, from the *polis*.)

Yet, for the Greeks of the fifth century BCE, the *polis* was a relatively new form of society. They shared a cultural memory of a golden heroic age, recounted principally in Homer's epic poems and by other myths.[1] Around 1600–1200 BCE, there had been a thriving Late Bronze Age civilisation throughout the eastern Mediterranean. Poems and stories recalled the heroes of this time, who fought mounted on chariots, and the rule of kings, simultaneously military and religious leaders who held secret knowledge. Their cities and kingdoms were centred on palaces, such as the one at Mycenae or at Knossos in Crete. Writing systems had developed to record the authoritative laws of the king and, more prosaically, his possessions (this many jars of oil; that much wheat and so on). Around 1200 BCE this civilisation collapsed: the reasons are unknown. In myth, it was claimed that the sons of Hercules had returned to claim their lands; scholars used to think that there was an invasion of the 'Dorians', a different strand of Greek people; some have blamed natural disasters, famine or plague. In his accessible book *1177 B.C.: The Year Civilization Collapsed* Eric Cline writes of a "system collapse that was caused by a series of events linked together": a catastrophic "domino effect" which brought down these early Greek civilisations and the whole highly interconnected region.[2]

In the centuries that followed, Greek society slowly redeveloped in a strikingly different way. Jean-Pierre Vernant envisages this change in the shape of the cities themselves. A fortified royal palace had been at the centre of the community: now a *polis* developed focused instead on the *agora*, the 'town square', "a public area where problems of general interest were debated". Walls had once only defended the palace now defended the whole city and where the palace had been, the community "erected temples that were open to public worship".[3] This shared *agora* and communal wall reflected a different sort of community that was finding ways of governing itself.

In the *polis*, property-owning men (not women or enslaved people) made communal decisions, responding to dialogue and discussion, rather than royal commands. This meant there was a growing awareness of the importance of justice (*dike*): fairness, order and equality before the law (for property-owning men, at least). In this context, new forms of political and legal speech grew up: persuasion and rhetoric. Writing, in a new script developed from Phoenicia, became used for the public propagation of laws and information, and so reading became part of education. Knowledge, which had been secret and exclusively royal or mystical, became more shared and public. This simultaneously encouraged a new openness and inquiry as well as the growth of cults which kept their wisdom secret, unwritten and for a select few. The word 'philosophy' means from 'lover of wisdom': some of this wisdom was hidden and 'philosophy' was sometimes considered a kind of cult.

These political shifts were reinforced by changes in military technology and strategy. In the *polis*, each property-owning man was required to provide his own armour and weapons. These citizen-soldiers were called 'hoplites' and fought in a communal, highly disciplined and tightly locked phalanx which demanded the virtue of *sophrosyne*, self-control, in order to hold formation under attack in battle.[4] This is a rather exciting speculation. More prosaically, it's clear that any growing community requires a degree of moderation and self-control. The ideals of *dike* and *sophrosyne*, as well as a sense of shared Greek identity, became added to the more heroic traditions and ideals that were passed down through epic poems and wisdom literature.

Poetry and drama were extremely important for the Greeks of Plato and Aristotle's time. At the core of their culture were the two epic poems of Homer: *The Iliad*, the story of Achilles's anger during the siege of Troy, and *The Odyssey*, the story of Odysseus's return home to the island of Ithaca and his wife Penelope after the Trojan War. Even though Homer was almost certainly not a single poet and these epics probably came to be written through the codification of an oral tradition in the eighth century BCE, they were foundational texts. It was through Homer that a person learned who they were supposed to be, how to behave and how society worked, which is why Homer was called 'the educator of Greece'. The other most influential poet was Hesiod: his *Theogony* described the origins of the world and the birth of the gods, and so provided a cosmology for the Greeks. His *Works And Days* is 'wisdom literature' and offers moral advice ("He does mischief to himself who does mischief to another, and evil planned harms the plotter most" (238); "Let the wage promised to a friend be fixed; even with your brother smile – and get a witness; for trust and mistrust, alike ruin men" (370) as well as information for farmers ("When the Pleiades … are rising, begin your harvest, and your ploughing when they are going to set" (380); "Poles of laurel or elm are most free from worms" (435).[5] Other poets were important too: Plato and Aristotle both refer to the work of Simonides, for example. The great works of Greek theatre were essential to religious and civic festivals and helped shape their audience's profoundest views on fate, fortune and the world. The most famous, the tragedies of Aeschylus, Sophocles and Euripides and the comedies of Aristophanes are performed, revived and rewritten today. Literature created the norms of behaviour and moulded lives and expectations: it was a central part of the education of young men.

Athens, the leading Greek *polis*, is the model for much of this account. "The multi-coloured variety of exuberant Athenian life" and its democracy has been idealised by many philosophers and artists over two and half millennia, but all the sources do show that Athens was characterised by discussion and argument, by a veneration of poets, and by a focus on the *agora* and public life.[6] Athens had a developed democracy, rule by the people (*demos*). Through a series of lotteries and ballots of the 50,000–60,000 property-owning men in Athens, 500 men were chosen as members of the council that ran the *polis*. Citizens were elected as judges, juries and to other public offices. The law became extremely significant: there were thousands of lawsuits each year. The use and abuse of politics and law looms large in the work of Plato and Aristotle and is often expressed through a concern about rhetoric. This democracy coexisted with deep divisions of gender and of class, between wealthy nobles and the poorer tradesmen and workers. The enslaved people were of the *polis* but both politically and existentially excluded from the *polis*. Aristotle, for example, did not count them "among human beings", Hannah Arendt writes. She continues: slavery's "fundamental offence was not that it took liberty away … but that it excluded a certain category of people even from the possibility of fighting for freedom"; then "it was forgotten that man had deprived his fellow-men of freedom" and so this crime "was attributed to nature".[7] Slavery was ubiquitous ("only the most impoverished citizen could not afford a slave at all") and so "affected the Athenians' conceptualisation of the universe at every level", shaping ideas about family, the state and the role of fate, for example.[8]

In any democracy, and certainly in Athens, voters are won over and juries persuaded by clever and convincing speeches. Throughout Greece, and in Athens in particular, there grew up a class of people who claimed to teach the virtues, skills and knowledge needed to succeed in the *polis*, focusing on the ability to argue well: the *sophists*. We still have this word. Calling someone 'sophisticated' can be double-edged; accusing someone of 'sophistry' – using cunning but deceptive arguments – is insulting. In fact, our image of these sophists is shaped by Plato's Socrates. He judged that they were only interested in winning arguments, cases and elections and not, as philosophers should be, seeking after truth and virtue for their own sake. You can judge the fairness of this view yourself in later chapters because, as we'll see, many of Plato's dialogues set Socrates against sophists like Protagoras, Gorgias, Hippias and Thrasymachus. Just as poetry and drama were important for knowing how to think and behave in 'polite society', the persuasive power of rhetoric was important for politics.

The internal politics of Athens were part of a wider history. Before Socrates was born, there had been a generation-long war between Persia and the many different Greek city-states. In 480 BCE, Athens had been sacked and occupied by Persian soldiers. The same year, Athenians led the alliance which effectively ended the Persian threat with a massive victory at the sea battle of Salamis. This was the beginning of an Athenian golden age. Funded by silver mines worked by enslaved people close to the city, Athens flourished and established a series of colonies across the Eastern Mediterranean.

The greatest Athenian politician of this period was Pericles (495–429 BCE) who led the city for around 30 years until his death. In 430 BCE, he gave a famous 'Funeral Oration', recorded by the historian Thucydides, which is often taken as a summation of this golden age: looking at it in a little detail tells us a great deal about the city and its values at this time. Pericles begins by saying that he would rather have the war dead honoured by their own deeds, because a speech risks praising too much or not enough and so is suspect, as all eloquence is. But custom demands he should speak. He praises their Athenian ancestors and the community they built: in Athenian democracy there is "equal justice to all" and yet "the claim of excellence is also recognized"; public service is a reward, not a privilege and does not depend on wealth; there are many "relaxations from toil" and because "of the greatness of our city the fruits of the whole earth flow in upon us; so that we enjoy the goods of other countries as freely as our own". The Athenian military meets "danger with a light heart but without laborious training, and with a courage which is gained by habit and not enforced by law". Importantly, the strength of the *polis* lies in "that knowledge which is gained by discussion preparatory to action": Athenians "have a peculiar power of thinking before we act, and of acting, too, whereas other men are courageous from ignorance but hesitate upon reflection". Athens, he declares (and not Homer, he implies), is the "school of Greece" showing others cities how to live. It is so great a city that it does not need "the praises of Homer or of any other panegyrist" and indeed, Pericles concludes that he does not have to praise the dead warriors any further because "in magnifying the city I have magnified them, and men like them whose virtues made her glorious".[9] The *polis*, the world of action and rhetoric, is where people show their greatness.

Thucydides's account of Pericles's speech is heavy with irony. The soldiers Pericles hubristically memorialised had died in the first year of the war between Athens and Sparta. The two had been allies against the Persians but were also rival powers, and by 431 BCE this turned to war. Thucydides's *History of the Peloponnesian War* covers most of the conflict which through a series of terrible communal decisions, bad planning and bad luck led to the utter ruination of Athens. This disaster forms the backdrop to Plato's thought.

The year after this oration, Thucydides records that a terrible plague hit the city: red, inflamed eyes, bleeding in the throat, vomiting, ulcers, diarrhoea and a feeling of burning and thirst (people climbed into water tanks but could not quench themselves), memory loss, death.

> The most terrible thing of all was the despair into which people fell when they realised they had caught the plague for they would immediately adopt an attitude of utter hopelessness and ... would lose their power of resistance.[10]

Thucydides caught the plague but survived: Pericles did not. New political leaders jockeyed for position, but lacked the foresight and integrity of Pericles and were led by the crowds (rather than lead them, as Pericles had done: he was so trusted that he could even berate the voters). The war began well but turned against Athens. Severely weakened by a badly planned and poorly supported invasion of Sicily (415–413 BCE), the government of Athens became unstable and there were two coups, in 411 and 404 BCE. In 411 BCE, after a military defeat at Syracuse, the party of the nobles overthrew the democracy, murdered their opponents, terrorised the city and installed an oligarchic government known as the Four Hundred. Riven by internal division, this collapsed the following year, and democracy was restored. Again, in 404 BCE, after the loss of the Athenian fleet and final defeat by the Spartans, democracy was abolished and Athens was subjected to the 'Rule of the Thirty' (sometimes called the 'Thirty Tyrants'), another a gang of nobles, supported by the Spartans. The "most avaricious and violent" was Critias, a member of Socrates's circle and a character in Plato's dialogues.[11] The Thirty put to death around 500 Athenians and forced more into exile. Their rule collapsed the next year and democracy was restored in a diminished form to a demoralised city.

Then in 399 BCE came one of the most notorious events in European intellectual culture. Socrates, Plato's inspirer and teacher, was charged with impiety and corrupting the youth of Athens. He was tried, found guilty and allowed to kill himself by drinking hemlock. This was a life-shaping event for Plato. His early work, the *Apology*, is Socrates's defence speech (or an imagined version of it) and three dialogues (*Euthyphro*, *Phaedo* and *Crito*) are set during the last days of Socrates. Many others refer implicitly to Socrates's trial and death.

Athens began to recover some of its former glory over the next 50 years or so, and, shifting alliances and treaties, competed again with Sparta and with Thebes to be the leading Greek *polis*. However, in 359 BCE Philip II became the king of Macedon in northern Greece, and began a rapid expansion. By the 340s, the dominance of Macedon became the key issue for Athenian politics, as politicians argued over how to best protect the city from his growing reach. Phillip defeated Athenian forces and their allies at the Battle of Chaeronea in 338 BCE and ended Athenian independence. His son Alexander became king in 336 BCE and led a Pan-Hellenic army against the Persians and on to conquer most of the world known to the Greeks. Plato lived and wrote in this period. Apart from three trips to Syracuse (in 384/3, 366, 361 BCE), all disastrous in different complex ways, he worked in and around Athens, founding the Academy in 383 BCE. His reputation as a philosopher was unparalleled. Some recent scholarship argues, by looking at his writing and the texts of Athenian debates, that his work aimed to shape not just philosophy but also politics, helping to ferment a 'culture war' and shift Athenian politics towards "elite expertise and forms of managerial, rather than direct, democracy".[12] As we'll see, Aristotle studied with him as a young man, but abandoned Athens on Plato's death in 348 BCE, returning later to found his own school as Macedonian power grew. Years later in 323 BCE, Aristotle left Athens again: he was charged with impiety but the real reason was that the Macedonian faction, with which he was associated, collapsed on Alexander's death. Socrates was on Aristotle's mind, too: he's supposed to have said that he left to prevent giving the Athenians "a second opportunity to sin against philosophy".[13]

The decline of Athens, the precarity of its politics, the death of Socrates, the city's revival and then capitulation to Macedonia form the historical context for Plato's and Aristotle's work. Perhaps the themes to which their thought keeps returning are no surprise: the contrast between a better, unchanging world and our worse, changeable one; justice and the good; the demands of war and conflict; the organisation of society and how to live in the *polis*; the power of language and argument; a concern for the way rhetoric, not reason, convinced people; the role of poetry and drama in shaping the person and the *polis*. This leads to the other concept I want to introduce, the idea of *logos*.

Logos

Just as Plato and Aristotle were developing an understanding of the *polis*, so they were – and we still are – developing an understanding of *logos*. *Logos* is one of the hardest and yet most basic concepts. Bernard Williams explains:

> Ancient Greeks, and particularly, perhaps, the notoriously litigious and political Athenians, were very impressed by the power of speech. It is significant that the common Greek word *logos* had semantic roots in both speech and reason; it can mean 'word', 'utterance', 'story', 'account', 'explanation', 'reason' and 'ratio' among other things. One of Plato's major and ongoing undertakings was to construct models of what it is for an utterance not just to tell a story but to give a reason.[14]

I am going to introduce *logos* in two ways: first, and most basically, as speech; second, as reasoning. Again, we still have shadows of the word in English: as speech, in, for example, eu*logy* (good words), tri*logy* (three 'speeches'), *logo* (an image connected to a company or institution); and as reasoning, most obviously in 'logic' but also in the suffix-ology, the naming of a science or field of knowledge.

The elementary meaning of *logos* is speech. But, as Aristotle says:

> Man is the only animal who has the gift of speech. And whereas mere voice is but an indication of pleasure or pain, and is therefore found in other animals (for their nature attains to the perception of pleasure and pain and the intimation of them to one another, and no further) the power of speech is intended to set forth the expedient and inexpedient, and therefore likewise the just and unjust.
>
> (*Politics* 1253a10–15)

The German philosopher Martin Heidegger, who was fascinated by the *logos*, explains that speech here doesn't mean making a sound or forming an individual word. Instead it means we might call bringing something to light, bringing something up in conversation, making "manifest 'what is being talked about' in discourse".[15] *Logos* is about intelligibility. A great deal is going on in this idea, though. Take as a very approximate illustration, a parent pointing out something to a child: 'that's a duck'. Think of all the child is learning here. For the child, this thing, this duck, is suddenly drawn out and different from other things. It has some defining features or qualities, a green head, feathers, a size you could just about hold in your hands, that it 'is' in some simple way. It also has a name and now exists in a web of language, connected in meaning with other things that can be named: some of these you can see (ponds, birds) but some can't be seen except in the mind's eye (childhood memories, stories about animals: the connections of meaning themselves are invisible). The child is also learning about the parent: that the parent knows about ducks, that the parent thinks the duck is worth pointing out, that ducks are not harmful and that pointing out ducks is the kind of thing parents do. In all this, who the parent is *appears* through their speech and action. Even more, in speaking the parent is *sharing* a world with the child: the world, the people (and ducks) in it are being made intelligible. The duck, the child, the parent and their connections appear in the *logos*: and they appear in a certain sort of way. The parent might have said: 'ah, *anas platyrhynchos*!' or 'that's a pest' or told a story about ducks. Bringing the duck into the *logos* presupposes and brings to light what philosophers call a 'form of life', a rough idea of the world and how to be in it through this web of language. But there is still more. The child then goes on to ask 'what's that?' about a stick, a rabbit, a tree, a thrown-away bottle. But the child might also say: 'that's a duck!' about a stick (or a rabbit). Once the word duck has appeared in the *logos*, the child can be wrong about spotting a duck. The *logos* allows both the appearing of the duck and at the same time creates the possibility of error. And this is all just about a duck, a relatively straightforward creature. In conversation, we also make manifest much more complex things: what is just and unjust (as Aristotle says, above) or even our ideas about *what and who we are*. Heidegger argued that *logos* is the "fundamental determination of the being of the human being as such" because speaking reveals ourselves and our shared world.[16]

Logos first means speech but second comes to mean giving reasons or explanations. Plato and Aristotle were discovering and inventing this reasoning process. They called it *dialectic*, roughly meaning: reasoning between people in speech. This process starts with speech (say, with the appearing of the duck in conversation) and then through argument and analysis aims to understand the object under discussion better and more truthfully. This is a process of 'taking apart and putting together' (Socrates says that he is "a lover of these processes of division and bringing together, as aids to speech and thought" *Phaedrus* 266b). For Plato and Aristotle, this process aims to make things comprehensible and consistent (which is why they so often start with what appears *inconsistent*). You can see what they mean in the names of academic subjects with the suffix -ology. In zoology, animals are 'brought to light', discussed, compared and investigated. Zoologists seek to bring together and so understand the duck, its species, habits, role in the environment and so on, and take it apart, offering finer and finer distinctions (this species and that sub-species, and so on). This process has its own risks: not just simple mistakes but errors made by, say, the very desire to be consistent. (Aristotle notes that, for example, if your principle

15

of categorisation is where creatures live, land or sea, seagulls would be a kind of fish: obviously ridiculous.) Uncovering inconsistencies and the dialectical process is hard when the subject is a duck: it's much harder for abstract and human things like art, character or justice.

These two introductory senses of *logos*, as speech and as giving reasons, also allow us to say something very introductory about the *logos* and what we call literature. The *logos* is not feelings and thoughts: it is feelings and thoughts made manifest, put into a form that can be shared. So in the first sense of *logos*, as speech, a poem makes something outside the *logos* appear in the *logos* through the careful and meaningful crafting of words together. A poem *shows* something, and (like the parent pointing out the duck) in so doing, shows us the world, the speaker and the audience (this is only an introductory description!). However, the second sense of *logos*, as explanation, causes problems between the poet and the philosopher. This second sense asks for reasons or for justifications; it seeks to place the poem in a larger dialectic process of taking apart and bringing together, and even, perhaps to fit the poem into an −ology, based on a consistent principle. We can be shaped or moved by things we cannot fully understand: a poem may make us weep but we are unsure why. More, we can believe or feel things but not (or not yet) be able to put them into words. Part of our thinking about literature explores and tries to explain why a particular text moves us, and what that means. Perhaps literature is in the (thinnest) gap between *logos*-as-speech and *logos*-as-reason, between what appears and what is explainable.

And

The *logos* and the *polis* are intimately connected. For the classical Greeks, we humans are the speaking animal, or the animal with *logos* (*zoon logon echon*). *Logos* presupposes that there are people to speak with and to share the world with (even if they are physically absent). This means that *logos* entwines our communal being with each other and so with the *polis*. The *polis*, the community, is where we, in using the *logos*, 'come to light', where we show up. That we talk about things, how we talk and understand ourselves and how we all live together are part of the same fabric. As above, Aristotle says we are a political animal because we have speech (not just 'voice') and so can discuss what is useful, harmful, just and unjust. Since the *logos* is where matters are 'brought to light', the *polis* is established and run through *logos*. To take the most obvious, prosaic example: discussion of matters brought to light between people creates laws; the laws create or maintain the state; the state and people (should) protect the laws as they do their city walls. This is why Plato and Aristotle are concerned with both *logos* and *polis*.

Today, we have many different ideas about what our communities are: community can be the family, the wider social community as well as the national or legal or even human community, and perhaps we feel we belong to several different kinds of community (geographical, cultural, professional, generational, based on shared interests and so on).What we take to be the *polis* has transformed (and the discipline of political studies explores and argues over these transformations). How we understand the idea of *logos* had changed, too. But what has not changed is the idea that *polis* and *logos*, however altered, are involved with each other at the deepest level.The 'and' remains.

This chapter has given the briefest overview of the Greek and specifically Athenian context for Plato and Aristotle, focusing on the growth of the *polis* and the kinds of speech – rhetorical, religious, political, poetic – that characterised it. As we'll see over the next five chapters, a new way of speaking and thinking emerged, which Socrates called philosophy.The next chapter introduces it.

Notes

1 Jan Assman, *Cultural Memory and Early Civilisation:Writing, Remembrance and Political Imagination* (Cambridge: Cambridge University Press, 2011), pp. 234–75.

2 Eric H. Cline, *1177 B.C.:TheYear Civilization Collapsed* rev. ed. (Princeton: Princeton University Press, 2021), p. 173.

3 Jean-Pierre Vernant, *The Origins of Greek Thought* (New York: Cornell University Press, 1982), p. 47.

4 Vernant, *Origins*, p. 63.

5 These two poems by Hesiod are fairly short, a few pages only, and easily read online in modern translations. Hesiod, *The Homeric Hymns and Homerica with an English Translation* by Hugh G. Evelyn-White (Cambridge, MA: Harvard University Press; 1914) via Perseus Digital Library www.perseus.tufts.edu/hopper/.

6 Søren Kierkegaard, *Writings, II,Volume 2:The Concept of Irony, with Continual Reference to Socrates/Notes of Schelling's Berlin Lectures*, Hong, Howard V., and Edna H. Hong, editors (Princeton: Princeton University Press, 1989), p. 16.

7 Hannah Arendt, *The Origins of Totalitarianism* (London: Harvest, 1958), p. 297.

8 Edith Hall, 'The Sociology of Greek Tragedy' in *The Cambridge Companion to Greek Tragedy*, ed. P. E. Easterling (Cambridge: Cambridge University Press, 1997), 93–126, p. 110.

9 Thucydides, *History of the Peloponnesian War*, trans. Rex Warner (London: Penguin Books, 1972), pp. 34–46.

10 Thucydides, *History*, pp. 49–51.

11 Xenophon, 'Memoirs of Socrates' 1.2.12, in *Conversations of Socrates*, trans. Hugh Tredennick and Robin Waterfield (London: Penguin, 1990), p. 74.

12 Danielle S.Allen, *Why Plato Wrote* (Oxford:Wiley-Blackwell, 2013), p. 106, p. 141.

13 Anton-Hermann Chroust, *Aristotle: New Light on His life and Some of His Lost Works* (London: Routledge & Kegan Paul, 1973), p. 147.

14 Bernard Williams, *The Sense of the Past* (Princeton: Princeton University Press, 2006), p. 156.

15 Martin Heidegger, *Being and Time*, trans. Joan Stambaugh, revised Dennis Schmidt (Albany: SUNY Press, 2010), H.32, p. 30.

16 Martin Heidegger, *Basic Concepts of Aristotelian Philosophy*, trans. Robert Metcalf and Mark Tanzer (Bloomington: Indian University Press, 2009), p. 14.

Part I

'WHAT IS TRULY WRITTEN IN THE SOUL'

—— Plato

2

PLATO'S LITERARY DEVICES

"Plato is a great artist" who created "some of the most memorable images in European philosophy" wrote the novelist and Platonist Iris Murdoch.[1] The dialogues are filled with *literary devices*: stories, allegories, metaphors, characters. The dialogue form itself is a literary device. I am going to use these to introduce Plato's thought. Why?

First, focusing on literary devices brings Plato's ideas to life. The poet Percy Shelley, too, thought that Plato was "essentially a poet" because of the "truth and splendour of his imagery, and the melody of his language".[2] There's more to this, though, than just sparkling prose. The political theorist Hannah Arendt believed Plato was a great poet but "in a philosopher's disguise".[3] All "philosophical terms" she argued "are metaphors, frozen analogies" whose force "must have been vivid" for the first philosophers to use them.[4] So when Plato

> introduced the everyday words 'soul' and 'idea' into philosophical language ... he must have heard the words as they were used in ordinary pre-philosophical language ... *Psyche* is the 'breath of life' exhaled by the dying and *idea* ... is the shape or blueprint the craftsman must have in front of his mind's eye before he begins his work.[5]

'Psyche' and 'idea' have now become dead or frozen metaphors but if we can thaw a word from its solid, taken-for-granted use and make it live and flow again, our thoughts can live and flow, too. To rediscover a term as a living metaphor, *psyche* as breath, say, is to uncover it as poetry. This uncovering allows literary devices like metaphor and character to express something impossible to put into plainer prose and to make something manifest in the *logos* we share, in a way we can grasp. Jill Gordon argues that because we are fallible humans, constantly learning, we need these literary aids to help our understanding. "Philosophy certainly includes arguments" she writes "but it relies as well on images in the form of myth, analogy, metaphor and the like. Pure reason is left to the gods, philosophy is left to humans".[6]

DOI: 10.4324/9781003097914-4

Second, and following from this vividness, it's through his powerful images that Plato's ideas have influenced poets and writers. Paintings, poems, books, films and games draw more on the devices I'm going to discuss than the dryer arguments.

Third, by using his literary devices I introduce Plato's work in a more holistic, thematic way, rather than boiling the dialogues down to a set of doctrines. The form and style of the dialogues mean they are rarely conclusive. The ideas and arguments change: for example, the 'theory of the forms', which I discuss below, is central to *The Republic* but is criticised in another dialogue, *Parmenides*. Again, in *The Symposium*, Socrates praises erotic love, but he's much more circumspect about it in *The Republic*. Plato never speaks definitively in his own voice and 'Plato's doctrines' are usually developed by people teaching, arguing about or, *ahem*, even introducing Plato's work. There's a difference between Plato's actual work and (doctrinal versions of) Platonism. For some, this is a consequence of the dialogue form itself as literature. There is a beautiful story that Plato,

> shortly before his death, had a dream of himself as a swan, darting from tree to tree and causing great trouble to the fowlers, who were unable to catch him. When Simmias the Socratic heard this dream, he explained that all men would endeavour to grasp Plato's meaning, none, however, would succeed, but would interpret him according to his own view.[7]

All this seems like a *difficultly* in reading Plato – you can't catch the beautiful bird – but really, it's more like a *gift*: through the chase itself, the dialogues continually produce new ideas and interpretations, and throw readers back onto their own wits. This book is an introduction and I am not trying to catch the swan, but by watching the fowlers (philosophers, political scientists, classicists, critics, poets, novelists) running around with nets, sticks, lettuce and whatnot in their attempts, we can learn a lot about versions of Plato, ourselves and different kinds of hunting.

One very influential interpretative approach – one gang of swan hunters – follows what's called the 'developmentalist' thesis: the idea that we can trace the growth of Plato's ideas, originating with Socrates and then evolving over his career in roughly, early, middle and late phases. To be extremely reductive: in the early phase, Plato shows how Socrates revealed inconsistencies in others; in the middle, he advances his own ideas using Socrates as a mouthpiece; in the late phase, he reflects on and criticises these ideas. While this way of reading the dialogues comes from the nineteenth century, more recent work was inspired by the great Platonist scholar Gregory Vlastos, as well as many others. Crucial for this approach is a sense of when, and in what sequence, the dialogues were written. 'Developmentalists' adduce this from their style and wider contextual history.

By contrast, 'literary contextualist' scholars have argued that it's just not possible to create such a historical ordering and we should focus on the ideas presented in the specific literary context of each dialogue.[8] The dialogues were not published like modern books, each at one given date. Instead, perhaps, they were worked and reworked by Plato. So to use a historical order is

> to announce in advance the results of a certain interpretation of the dialogues, and to canonise that interpretation under the guise of a presumably objective order of composition – when in fact no such order is objectively known. And it thereby risks prejudicing an unwary reader against the fresh, individual reading that these works demand.[9]

To simply slot any dialogue into a pre-existing story of Plato's development is *almost* not to read it. Further, as R. B. Rutherford argues, locations, characters, arguments and themes are so inextricably interwoven that each dialogue is "an independent literary artefact which does not build on its predecessors or form part of a larger structure or 'course' in philosophy".[10] Each dialogue is its own event. The 'literary contextualists' argue that Plato wants to show that philosophy arises from our lives and from each unique context.[11] Another parallel literary approach is taken by Catherine Zuckert. Agreeing that each dialogue is a specific conversation with its own setting and characters, she turns to the dates at which the dialogues are supposed to have taken place, the 'dramatic date'. She goes on: read "in the order indicated by their dramatic dates, the dialogues tell a story" of Socrates's philosophical journey, like a sequence of linked novels or a self-contained fictional universe.[12] In encountering other major philosophers, the dialogues explore the intellectual challenges Socrates meets or fails to meet. In this, she argues, Plato presents Socrates as the leading but not the only philosopher with things to say, and shows that there "is no one, fully comprehensible way of understanding the whole, because the whole is made up of essentially different kinds of beings".[13]

To be honest, for a literary reader, both the more historicist 'developmentalist' approach and the 'literary contextualist' one focus on the texts themselves, either individually or as an interlinked story, make sense. We are used to reading novels by the same author in which we can follow the development of their ideas but which are also individual and particular. No one thinks all Shakespeare's plays take place in the same 'fictional universe', yet they share thematic concerns (say, the fear of civil war, the interplay of appearance and reality). Similarly, we can see central *themes* in Plato (truth, the good, how to live, the contrast between the unchanging and the changeable, the role of the philosopher, the risks of language, *polis* and *logos*) and looking at and through his literary devices gives a more holistic but less doctrinal sense of these. More, as I suggested in the introduction, while modern philosophy is divided into separate categories (ethics, metaphysics, aesthetics and so on), these divisions are just starting to arise *in*

Plato's work and looking at his literary devices helps us avoid turning automatically to these categories to understand Plato's thought.

The fourth reason to use literary devices to introduce Plato is that the images, metaphors and analogies give a much more positive sense of what Plato is *for*: the true; the good; the beautiful (that's how I've chosen the literary devices in this chapter: to present Plato's ideas about truth). Plato is often seen as being 'against' things, most especially against literature. This is in part because of Socrates's approach, the *elenchic* (sometimes spelled *elenctic) method*. This involves asking challenging questions about accepted conventions, so revealing inconsistencies, and then following up the answers with even more challenging questions. Gregory Vlastos describes the logic behind this method charmingly and lucidly.

> He puts a question to you, 'P or not-P?' You say, 'P'. – 'But doesn't P imply Q?' – 'Yes'. – 'And Q, of course, implies R?' – 'To be sure'. – 'But earlier you said, S, didn't you? Or is my memory at fault?' – 'I did say S. And why not? Anything wrong with S?' – 'Nothing in the world. Only, doesn't S imply T?' – 'I suppose it does'. – 'Do you only suppose? Aren't you sure?' – 'Yes, I am sure'. – 'But now put T and R together. Are they consistent?' – 'No'. – 'T contradicts R, doesn't it?' – 'It does'. – 'So if T is true, R must be false?' – 'It must'. – 'And since you agreed that R follows from P, then if R is false P must be false'. – 'It must'. – 'So P and S can't both be true. Which will you have?' Usually there is not much doubt about the answer. P was very plausible at first. But you feel so much more certain about S that if one of the two must go, you have no hesitation in sacrificing P. The skeleton of the argument would be:
> P~Q~R
> S~T
> T~not-R
> But not-R ~ not-Q ~ not-P.
> Therefore, T ~ not-P.
> Therefore, S ~ not-P.
> (And S is true.
> Therefore, P is false.) This is the sort of thing that happens in Socratic arguments.[14]

This is also an example of the approach taken by Vlastos and those he influenced, translating the textual argument of the dialogues into the formal logic of analytic philosophy. Vlastos asks: "Was Socrates alive to this?", to the underlying analytic logic of his own method.[15] That is: was Socrates an analytic philosopher? This, too, is a crucial point of contention between 'developmentalists' and more 'literary' readings. On the one hand, you can see the analytic 'P or not-P' approach creates a sharp, rational clarity of argument. On the other, if taken to extremes, it loses the historical and dramatic context as well as the more complex and hard-to-pin-down but deeply meaningful and revealing interaction of ideas and character. More, it makes it impossible, perhaps, to follow the dialogues into areas where such formal logic no longer works. Gordon asks (perhaps with a touch of anachronism) if "to appeal to what is best philosophically is to appeal to what is purely rational, why didn't Plato just write arguments?"[16] In fact, as we will see, not all of Plato's dialogues use the elenchic method: they have many passages that are more straightforwardly didactic, offering "positive teaching about the best form of human existence".[17] As I'll show, the myth of the cave concerns truth and how to live; Diotima's story is about truth and beauty, and the myth of the forms is about how we come to understand that truth. There are things that distract us from that truth: our emotions (which are like the strings that control a puppet, a metaphor from the *Laws*), the nature of language itself. The role of the philosopher is to sting us back to – not to truth, perhaps – but the search for truth and focusing on what the dialogues appear to be *for*, rather than against, is a more positive way to introduce them.

The Allegory of the Cave; or, the prison break
(from *The Republic* 514a–518c)

Plato's most famous literary device is an extended metaphor known as the allegory of the cave. It's not long, five or so comprehensible pages told by Socrates: you can read it all while drinking a cup of coffee, so if you don't know it already, the very best thing you can do right now is read one of the many online versions yourself. Because, as I'll show, every retelling has an axe to grind.

So, here's a retelling: it's about the truth; it's a jail-break story about prisoners chained at the bottom of a shaft and it's about you.

> You are chained in fetters, from birth, unable even to turn your head. You face a wall. You are one of many. In front of you the shapes of people and animals move about. These mysterious figures and their booming voices are all you know, and you believe them to be all there is, to be the truth. ("It's a strange image you're describing, and strange prisoners" (*The Republic* 515a) interrupts a listener. "They're like us" replies Socrates).
>
> Suddenly you are set free, you can turn around. You realise that the figures are just shadows cast on the wall by puppeteers behind you, using a fire as a light source and casting their voices as echoes. You are in a cave. It's a prison. But behind the puppeteer-masters, and up, is a very bright light. You can't make anything out, really, and the light stings your eyes. Surely the puppet figures were something real and true? It was pretty uncomfortable, but you knew where you were and your eyes didn't hurt. As you turn to go back, someone grabs you and drags you up the steep path over jagged rocks. It hurts. You shout out. You demand to be let go but suddenly it is light everywhere, too

bright, you can't see or make anything out. You are outside the mouth of the shaft.

Slowly, your eyes get used to the light, and you can make out some sharper shadows, then some reflections in water and then, slowly, things themselves, trees, and people, not dim, in two dimensions, but solid and real. And then the stars and the moon – they are easier on your eyes which are used to darkness. But then, the light of the sun, and at last the sun itself. Bright and warm and true and real. You realise that it's the source of everything, even the dim prison cave you've been trapped in. The poor people still down there! They – you – used to play guessing games about what each passing figure was, and now you know these were just puppet shadows cast by a pitiful fire (another interruption: I'd "rather suffer anything than live like that" *The Republic* 516e). You have seen the real sun and felt its warmth and you think that the other prisoners should be free to see the sun as well.

You head back down. You have to adjust back to the dark, you can hardly see. You can't tell what the passing shadow-figures are any more in the guessing game – it seems so pointless now. The other prisoners begin mocking you and your silly story of the real world and the bright light. They hate you and your talk of the upper world. They would kill you if they could.

For Plato the prison is the world we know, a world of shadows. Unreal, uncomfortable, we are trapped in it and its silly, petty games. We are shaped and controlled, fettered even, by forces over which we seem to have no control. And yet, if we are helped to escape – it's not easy, the climb up is hard – we can find the real world of truth, goodness and beauty beyond. It's a journey out of our painful, shared human time, in which things change, into the eternal realm, in which things are forever true and unchanging. Once you have seen the light of the sun, the world of shadows is revealed as just precisely that. You need to free others perhaps, but they won't be at all pleased: they might even be murderous.

To begin with, this allegory isn't as abstract as it might appear. Athens's main source of wealth was the silver mines in Laurion, south-east of the city. Bettany Hughes writes that every day 20,000 enslaved people in fetters "were sent four miles into the dark earth to gouge out silver-bearing lead ore" and at night their "cramped boxes" were guarded by towers in a prison camp.[18] The description of the cave – with the entrance as wide as the cave itself, the fetters, the guards – does make it sound more like a mine shaft than a natural cave.

The allegory of the cave is probably the most fundamental story in Western philosophy, but – recall the swan dream – even after about two and a half millennia, no one can agree what it means. You can read it as direct allegory, in which every detail is weighted with meaning: Christopher Rowe, for example, notes that the fact that some of the puppeteers are "uttering sounds, while others are silent" may represent the difference "between written and unwritten law".[19] Or you can read it as a more general metaphor, a piece of poetic writing: the sun is the good, the real, the true, the point of origin, that which we desire and that which we desire to share with others, simultaneously in one image.

As soon as it is told, Socrates offers his own interpretation. It is about education. Learning is not really about accumulating facts but turning towards and being transformed by the real world of the good and the true. This is the kind of reading emphasised by the French historian of philosophy Pierre Hadot, who sees the work of ancient philosophy as 'spiritual exercises' which lead to a conversion. The "circles, detours, endless diversions, digressions and subtleties which make the modern reader of Plato's *Dialogues* so uncomfortable" exist not to solve "a particular problem" but as a "road along which the interlocutor, the discipline and the reader form their thought" in order to discover truth.[20] For Murdoch, this is the "pilgrimage from appearance to reality" which is the "subject of every good play and novel".[21]

The philosopher Martin Heidegger sees a crucial slip within the allegory. The sun is the true, the beautiful and the good: its light makes things visible. But in returning to the cave, the philosopher does not bring back the sun or truth. Instead, they bring back the *images* of the things which were illuminated. These are then compared with the shadow images, and truth becomes understood not as blazing illumination but as a judgement of how well the shadow-images and the images of what was outside match up. It's not truth but accuracy, right-or-wrong, standards: a subtle shift from truth-as-revelation in silent contemplation to truth-as-correctness.[22] This version argues that it's impossible to put the real moment of contemplative understanding into language, and our words, our talk inside the cave, let us down.[23]

This retelling leads Arendt to see the allegory of the cave in a different way. For her, it shows the flight of the philosopher, alone, from the "dark cave of human affairs" which we share with others, in which we are "inside time" and so cannot predict the future, to "bright sky of ideas" in which eternal knowledge is certain.[24] The sun, the good, allows Socrates – and those who came after him – to have a vision of how the world should be. But because they see their vision alone, they think not of humans together, plural, but of the singular person as if that one (he, usually) was all people ("just as in zoology there is only *the* lion").[25] This means they misunderstand the very nature of the political world within the cave: frail, yes, but also shared, plural and unpredictable. Their vision of the 'outside' world leads the philosopher to think of the people and the cave as a problem to be solved or object to be crafted by the light of that vision, as a sculptor might shape stone into a statue.

Overall, the allegory of the cave is like a great poem, impossible to summarise or retell (as I said, read it yourself). Perhaps that's part of the point for Plato: the truths are there for everyone, but it's *your* journey up the steep path and over sharp rocks to the real world. Whether the allegory of the cave is a prison break to the 'blue skies' of truth or the origin of a mismatch between the world of thought and the world of politics, the escape from the cave and the return is lonely and hard. The path is jagged; the light, on the escape, and the darkness, on the return, are both blinding. Why would you do this? The answer is: love, the subject of one of the most famous dialogues, *The Symposium*.

Higher and higher on Love's ladder: from *The Symposium* (201d–212c)

Shelley wrote a rather free but beautiful translation of *The Symposium* in 1818 and declared that Love "found a worthy poet in Plato alone of all the ancients".[26] Socrates and his friends are at a drunken party (a *symposium*, today the term for a sober, professional meeting) and decide to talk about love (an appropriate topic when drink has been taken). It's the only time we see Socrates talk directly with poets, and, as we'll see, he tries to move from a lower sense of *eros*, of love, to a higher. After others have given speeches, Socrates tells of a conversation he had with Diotima of Mantinea, a wise woman who taught him the art of love, a dialogue within a dialogue known as 'Diotima's speech' (it's the most we hear from a woman in the dialogues: and it is ventriloquised through Socrates). Part of the joke is that this time, Socrates, who usually poses the hard questions, plays Diotima's stooge.

They begin: what is love? Is love a beautiful "great god" (*The Symposium* 201e)? No, says Diotima. Love is a *daimon*, an intermediary spirit between the divine eternal world and our human, mortal world, and while we think the person we love is beautiful, Love himself is not. Diotima reveals Love's back-story: the goddess Penia (Poverty) schemed to get rich by having a child with the Poros, the god of resources and resourcefulness. When Aphrodite was born, the Gods had a drunken party: Poros "got drunk on nectar" (203b), Penia "lay beside him" (203c) and Love was conceived. Love takes after his mother, "tough and shrivelled and shoeless and homeless" (203d), always needy (think of the neediness and pain of unrequited love). But he's also like his father: "a schemer after the beautiful and good ... brave, impetuous, intense, an awesome hunter, always weaving snares, resourceful in his pursuit of intelligence, a lover of wisdom ... a genius with enchantments, potions and clever pleadings" (203e). In short, Love is like a philosopher (in the model of Socrates himself) chasing after wisdom, because wisdom is "extremely beautiful" (204b).

But what's the use of love? What's the point of loving beautiful things? Diotima says that the beautiful is good and we desire good things. Socrates thinks that having good things makes us happy. But Diotima points out that while everyone desires happiness, we don't say everyone is in love: sexual love is only *one* sort of love. Earlier during the party, the playwright Aristophanes had told a story that humans once were four-armed, four-legged creatures who became divided: love was about finding 'your other half'. This isn't so, Diotima says: we desire the good and want to possess it forever.

Diotima then says something that sounds strange: this desire is linked to giving birth. "All of us are pregnant, Socrates, in body and soul" and when the time is right, we "desire to give birth" (206c). Love, it turns out, doesn't desire the beautiful as much as it desires reproduction. Reproduction "goes on forever" and "is what mortals have in place of immortality" (207a). (There's a version of the same argument in the *Laws* 721b.) Love, really, then, is love of, is the pursuit of, immortality, escaping our changeable world of time for the eternal. It seeks what is beyond our world, our cave – or as much of that as we mortals can have. "Reproduction leaves behind a new young one in place of the old" (207d). This is why Love is an intermediary *daimon*, linking the mortal, changing, shadow world and the true, eternal world.

So, Diotima tells Socrates, there are different kinds of reproduction beyond sex. We are constantly changing and developing our own selves, our "manners, customs, opinions, desires, pleasure, pains" (207e). Studying, too, is a kind of reproduction of knowledge. Some people hope to be immortal by being remembered by their descendants; some seek immortality through creative art; but the best seek to be remembered (as Pericles's 'Funeral oration' demonstrated in Chapter 1) through beautiful and virtuous deeds, like founding a *polis* or playing a grand role in the community. (If this sounds odd, think of the way institutions – shops, universities, theatres – are named for and so memorialise the names of their founders.)

But Diotima calls these steps the lesser mysteries: the greater mystery is her final account of love. She describes how love draws you up through the physical world to a truer and real world (this is known as 'Diotima's ladder', for reasons that will become obvious). Love is the force that grabs you and propels you out of the cave to see beauty. First, you fall in love with one beautiful person. The next step is that you realise that beauty in one person is similar to beauty in another, that, actually, all bodies are beautiful. Understanding this, you realise that the "beauty of people's souls is more valuable than the beauty of their bodies" (210b): and then this leads to the discovery that beauty exists in all sorts of activities and institutions, and then in all forms of knowledge and ideas. Finally, the highest step on this ladder, you come to see that beauty is eternal and immaterial: beauty in the abstract, in the ideal form. All other forms of beauty (human, institutional, intellectual) partake a little of this beauty, but they are imperfect and pass and fade. Diotima says that this is

> the mystery of Love: one goes always upwards for the sake of this Beauty, starting out from beautiful things and using them like rising stairs: from one body to two and from two to all beautiful bodies, then from beautiful bodies to beautiful customs, and from customs to learning about beautiful things, and from these lessons ... [to] ... the end ... which is learning of the very Beauty ... to know just what it is to be beautiful.
>
> (211c)

You are drawn by love up this ladder through material beauty to the beautiful itself "absolute, pure, unmixed, not polluted by human flesh or colour or any other great nonsense of mortality, but … the divine beauty itself in its one form" (211e–212a). The form of beauty is like the 'sun' from the cave: beautiful, true, real.

Then we are bought back to earth with a bang. The speech ends with applause but shrieks, shouting and pounding on the door announce more partygoers: a drunken gang led by "self-serving pirate-king playboy" Alcibiades, the most controversial political figure in classical Athens, Socrates's former admirer and would-be lover.[27]

'Diotima's ladder' has been extremely influential. It shapes the romantic cliché that 'love ennobles'. It underlies some Christianised forms of Plato's ideas, as love for God draws the soul up: that's the force that draws Dante towards heaven in *The Divine Comedy*, for example.[28] It has the same structure as the allegory of the cave: the escape from the material, changeable, mortal world, up to an unchanging world of beauty but, as it were, allows gradations, as love reaches down the 'ladder'. Education is an act of love and crucially the philosopher is the lover: needy, shoeless, homeless and resourceful in the pursuit of wisdom. The final vision, the highest step on the ladder, is of the form of the true, the good and the beautiful. But what are the forms?

Unforgetting geometry: from *Meno* (82b–85e)

The 'ideal forms' are one of the most famous and contentious ideas in the dialogues. They are demonstrated most clearly in a striking incident from *Meno*. Meno, a visiting aristocrat from Thessaly, asks Socrates whether virtue can be taught or people are naturally virtuous (a version of our contemporary question of 'nature or nurture?'). As the conversation progresses, Socrates takes one of Meno's enslaved retinue and, drawing figures in the sand, does some simple geometry with him.[29] With Socrates's prodding, the enslaved man works out facts about a square which it seems he didn't know before. Socrates says that this untaught person makes these geometrical discoveries because he is 'remembering' them from before he was born: an 'unforgetting' called *anamnesis*. In order to 'unforget' the absolute truths of geometry, held deep in his soul, the enslaved person just needs the right help to drag him up the rocky road out of the cave: that help is Socrates's questions, his new way of philosophy-speak, the *dialectic*.

In a very detailed account of the scene, Vlastos argues that this moment marks an evolution in the dialectical process itself. Socrates begins the conversation with his usual, adversarial elenchic method but this is limited to pointing out mistakes and inconsistencies. So, as the dialogue continues, Socrates *shows* the enslaved man a piece of geometry which allows him to solve the problem and express the answer in words. This demonstration "illuminates the process by which … all inquiry – and therefore all moral inquiry – must proceed".[30]

Michael Frede makes useful distinction between these two emphases in the *dialectic*: the 'elenctic dialectic' and this new teaching or 'didactic dialectic'.[31] How you 'unforget' about geometry becomes in *Meno* a model for how you 'unforget' all knowledge, including moral knowledge. Socrates compares himself to a midwife – his mother's profession – because he helps true knowledge to be reborn.

Geometry plays a very important role in Plato's work. For us, the principles of geometry are well established but for the classical Greeks these principles were *being* established. The theoretical discoveries of geometry arose from practical and legal needs: *geometry* means 'measuring the earth'. Laying out precisely who owned what land was important for both fairness and justice, and also because being a property-owning free man gave one a position as a member of the *polis*. But for Socrates, the deeper meaning of geometry was even more significant than the theorems. Sadly for maths teachers over the centuries, it's probably a myth that 'Let no one ignorant of geometry enter here' was inscribed over the doorway of Plato's Academy.[32] However, the slogan illustrates a core thought. The truths of geometry are true knowledge: universal, eternal, unalterable. They are neither propaganda nor opinion. Pythagoras's theorem (even if it wasn't actually by Pythagoras and was only ascribed to him later) is true at all times and in all places. The success of geometry suggests that all real truths, beyond mere opinion, must be of the same sort as those of geometry, and can be discovered in the same way, through the intellectual midwifery of the dialectic.

This is why Socrates praises "people who are naturally good at arithmetic" (*The Republic* 526b) in *The Republic*. Not because their minds are agile nor because they can work out military strategy and logistics (the war with Sparta overshadowing all Plato's work): geometry is not an end in itself. Instead, the study of geometry "forces the mind to turn towards the realm where the most blessed part of reality is to be found" (526e): the Sun, to use the image from the allegory of the cave. Geometry shows how to get there: to "rely purely on intellectual processes and to aim for truth in itself" (536b). For Socrates, "geometry can attract the mind towards truth. It can produce philosophical thought, in the sense that it can reverse the downward tendencies we currently have" (527b). Geometry is where the timeless, beautiful, unchanging world, the 'higher' or 'blessed realm' of truth meets the 'downward tendencies' of the messy, complex, imperfect, changeable and time-bound world we inhabit.

Even more significant is what this leads to: the *theory of the forms*. You can demonstrate truths of Pythagoras's theorem using a scruffy triangle drawn in the sand because it imperfectly resembles the perfect triangle for which the theorem holds true. Because geometry works, it seems to indicate that there is an eternal perfect world of forms which contrasts with but touches our imperfect world. Our world is an imitation of these ideal forms, just as the drawn square is an imitation of the perfect square. This is why many scholars argue that the theory of the forms has its origins in geometry. (Hannah Arendt takes a different position: keen always to stress the importance of making for Plato, she suggests that the idea of the 'forms' was suggested to him by the practical experience of constructing things. The forms are like the plans or blueprints used in building a table or a house: a blueprint can be used over and over again making it seem eternal as well as being a point of contract between our time-bound world and eternal timeless one.)[33]

If you have in mind the difference between the ideal circle which inspired the circle you drew in your school maths book, you've got the basic idea. The ideal circle is the perfect 'Platonic form' (where is it? In your head? But it's so easily shared and explained. Does that mean it's somewhere 'out there' so everyone can share it?); the pencil or pixel one is the earthbound, imperfect version. As I've suggested, for Plato's Socrates, the forms extend beyond geometrical shapes to every aspect of our life. That material table and chair are a version, a shadow, of the ideal form of a table and chair. There are also forms for other, less tangible things. For beauty, in *The Symposium* and, in *The Republic*, for the *polis*. The theory of the forms is also crucial for Socrates's attack on literature and art, as we'll see in the next chapter.

These ideas about the forms are a theory of knowledge, an *epistemology*: epistemology means, roughly, what knowledge is and how we come to know anything. As epistemology, the idea of the forms seems highly problematic (and perhaps even looks laughable today). But as with any hugely significant philosophical idea, or great work of art, it opens up a space, or makes something visible in the *logos* for our shared discussion and understanding. Even in Plato's writing, the forms are questioned and challenged. In *Parmenides*, an older philosopher (Parmenides, obviously) takes a younger Socrates to task for the theory of the forms and makes several (hardly answered) criticisms. What are they? Where are they? Do they look like anything? How many legs on the ideal table? Are there forms for mud and hair? How is greatness for one thing the same as greatness for another? How do we know, or 'participate' in them?

Yet the theory of the forms runs deep in general Western culture outside philosophy. Lots of mathematics, as you might expect, presume something like the forms. Rebecca Goldstein cites the 2020 Physics Nobel Laureate Roger Penrose: "I view the mathematic world as having an existence of its own, independent of us. It is timeless … It is the shadow of the pure mathematical world that you see in the physical world". Penrose goes on to show the importance of this concept for science in general, which "is always exploring the way the world works in relation to certain proposed models, and those models are mathematical constructions", versions of the forms.[34] This powerful legacy is, in part, because of the mathematical and scientific work Plato's thought inspired in the Renaissance and Enlightenment. But also because, perhaps, the forms seem to address very familiar longings and feelings within us, our desires for perfection and for reality. More prosaically, the forms seem, at first, to offer some rather neat answers to complex problems. For example, they answer the problem of how we know *what* something is: we know it's a truck (or a house or a bush) because it partakes of, is a version of, the ideal form of the truck (house, bush) and somehow we intuit this. Similarly, they allow us to contrast abstractions (size, difference, change) and abstract concepts (justice, equality), because different situations (say, different national systems of justice) partake (somehow) of the ideal forms. The forms explain too, how we can make value judgements: this table is better than that table, because both are imitations of the ideal form of a table and this one is closer to it. They explain why things are the way they are: because each imitates the ideal form. Most importantly, they offer an explanation of what real knowledge is: not opinion, belief or knowledge just from the senses (empirical knowledge), but knowledge gained by the mind of what a thing really is. Although they may sound very far away and ethereal, the point of the forms is to bring us back to reality.

Some scholars have suggested that the theory of the forms is no longer 'just' philosophy but reaches towards myth, magic or religion. As we saw in *Meno*, the idea of the forms seems to be inextricable from the idea that there is an immortal soul, aware of the forms before birth. Over a century ago, F. M. Cornford argued (in a 'developmentalist' sprit) that in Plato's earlier dialogues, knowledge was simply 'clear-thinking' demonstrated by the confrontational 'elenchus' question-and-answer method. But, he suggested, in these mid-period dialogues, written long after Socrates's death, Plato has been influenced by Pythagoras and his school and so presented a more mystical side of Socrates, in which the forms had a more powerful sort of reality.[35]

By contrast, other swan hunters have argued that the forms are less mystical and bring the discussion back to the development of the *polis*. Before the *polis*, only a king, a prophet or poet, each divinely inspired, could pronounce 'truth' and often only in a ritual situation.[36] Only they, using these different ways of talking (legal, religious, artistic), could create the rules, set the norms and expectations for behaviour and explain the cosmos. However, the birth of philosophy in Athens suggested that a new class of person with a new way of speaking, *philosophers*, could explore these matters. These truths are not secrets, kept only for members of a mystery cult nor powerful knowledge securely locked-away by priest-kings: they are accessible to everyone even, with the right dialectical 'midwifery' as Socrates showed, enslaved people. (In Jo Walton's charming science fiction series which begins with *The Just City* (2015), Socrates and many inspired by him are brought back to life to live out his ideas. Silent and ignored robots do the work of enslaved people. Socrates is the first person to talk to the robots.) This is a radical idea about truth which emerges in a struggle between this new dialectical philosophy and the forces of convention which are poetry, drama, politics, power and rhetoric. What is this new way of thinking like and what can it do?

The Charioteer: from *Phaedrus* (246a–257b)

Plato's literary devices, as well as his arguments, have suggested that there is a false, imperfect world and a true, perfect world: love motivates us to discover this real world where we find beauty and truth. There is a form of reasoning, dialectic, that helps us glimpse and perhaps even enter this world. The extended metaphor of the charioteer, from the dialogue *Phaedrus*, brings out the significance of this for our lives.

Phaedrus is about speech and rhetoric (I'll be returning to this dialogue in Chapter 5). Socrates and Phaedrus, sitting in a lovely shady spot by a river, discuss speeches and how lovers speak to each other. The humorous conversation (which, of course, sounds stilted to us, in translation, and the jokes are well over 2,000 years old) slowly turns more serious. Socrates suggests that the soul is immortal and can be reincarnated, and offers an extended metaphor for the soul: "the natural union of a team of winged horses and their charioteer" (*Phaedrus* 246b) in a procession between heaven and earth.

The gods lead this procession in chariots pulled by two wonderful horses, while our human soul has Jekyll and Hyde as a pair. One horse is beautiful, "upright in frame ... with a high neck and a regal nose ... a lover of honour with modesty and self-control ... he needs no whip, and is guided by verbal commands alone" (253d). The other is quite different:

> a crooked great jumble of limbs, with a short bull neck, a pug nose ... bloodshot white eyes; companion to wild boasts and indecency, he is shaggy around the ears – deaf as a post – and just barely yields to horsewhip and goad combined.
>
> (253d)

These two are our better and worse desires. One noble and pure, the other lustful, wild, disobedient. One lifts us up, the other follows its own direction and pulls the soul this way and that. "This means", says Socrates, "that chariot-driving in our case is inevitably a painful difficult business" (246b) as the charioteer struggles to control the two horses.

If we steer by heaven, keep an eye on its reality and control our two horses well using justice, self-control and knowledge, our chariots can travel upwards following the gods. But because the horses pull in different directions, it's hard to keep heading up: some are "unable to rise ... trampling and striking one another as each tries to get ahead of the others. The result is terribly noisy, very sweaty and disorderly. Many souls are crippled by the incompetence of their drivers" (248d). 'Up' is to truth and reality, and 'down' to the confusion and obscurity of earth. Socrates says we must learn to control the two different horses of our soul.

With correct heavenly nourishment, Socrates says, we will be reincarnated closer to truth. The philosopher, living a contemplative life, is at the top of the heap:

> only a philosopher's mind grows wings, since its memory always keeps it as close as possible to those realities ... he stands outside human

concerns and draws close to the divine: ordinary people think he is
disturbed and rebuke him, unaware that he is possessed by a god.

(249c)

On the next step down, Socrates says, will be a lawful king, then, third,

a statesman, a manager of a household or a financier; the fourth will be
a trainer who loves exercise or a doctor who cures the body; the fifth
will lead the life of a prophet or priest of the mysteries. To the sixth the
life of a poet or some other representational artist is properly assigned;
to the seventh the life of manual labourer or farmer; to the eighth the
career of a sophist or demagogue, and to the ninth a tyrant.

(248d–e)

We can note how far down this list the poet is: only just above liars who lack
truth and self-control, and tyrants, who follow only their own bodily whims
and desires. Correctly driven by the charioteer and aided by speech, our desires
can help us rise to truth and goodness, or they can lead us astray. Language is
vital to this process it, but language is also how we can be led astray: Plato's work
focuses on this through another metaphor.

'Speech-as-living-thought': dialogue as device

In Plato's works, speech is very close to thinking: "what we call thought is
speech that occurs without the voice, inside the soul in conversation with
itself" (*The Sophist* 263e). But this is a particular kind of speech, not just chatter
but talk "the soul has with itself about the objects under its consideration"
(*Theaetetus* 189e). As we've just seen with the image of the charioteer, the
"nature of speech is in fact to direct the soul" (*Phaedrus* 271d). Speech, proper
speech, is a metaphor for a special kind of thought, dialectic: speech is how the
charioteer controls the horses; speech is how we uncover or remember the
truths of geometry; speech is how we climb the ladder of love from simple lust
to divine understanding; 'speech-as-living-thought' is what aims at truth, the
real, the world outside the cave.

A lot follows from this seemingly simple metaphor. For 'speech-as-living-
thought', you have to be there, present for others and even to yourself: it's only
then that real learning happens. When the interlocutors agree, often so boringly
('oh, yes Socrates'), an important point is being made about agreement and
community: sharing and agreement is being made present in the 'speech-as-
living-thought', as the *logos*.

This implies that there are forms of speech that are *not* living-thought. For
Plato, rhetoric is not thought in this important sense. Rhetoric, understood as
the art of convincing people, public speaking in the law courts or in a political
arena, is not about truth or wisdom, not about directing the soul upwards, but

about winning ("No one in a lawcourt … cares at all about the truth of such matters. They only care about what is convincing" *Phaedrus* 272d). A stronger argument can beat a truer one by appealing to public opinion and prejudice rather than truth. (This is one reason Socrates opposed the sophists who, he argued, just taught people to sound convincing.)

Poetry, too, is not 'speech–as–living–thought'. The next chapters explore this in detail but, briefly, Socrates argues that poetry is a deceptive and damaging form of imitation. This is the idea that forms the core of most literary people's introduction to, and view of, Plato.

Writing is not 'speech–as–living–thought'. I'll return to this in Chapter 5, but in *Phaedrus* Socrates invents a myth about the origin of writing from Egypt. This myth reveals that writing is the illusion of speech which actually damages our human abilities. When we try to write down our thoughts, what is left is not thought but a residue like ash: writing cannot 'speak for itself', cannot take part in the dialectic which is the source of real knowledge.

Yet it rarely escapes the perceptive reader that Plato's dialogues are, actually, written down: the dialogues themselves seem not to be 'speech–as–living–thought'. If we are to guide our souls by 'speech–as–living–thought', what role can the dialogues play?

The 'written–ness' of the dialogues is one the most complex and long-lasting issues in Platonic scholarship. The question is inextricably linked to the choices about form and style in the dialogues (but none of the swan hunters agree precisely why or how). The dialogues are literary devices themselves and, of course, allow for all the literary devices I am discussing to happen in the first place. The dialogue form works by inquiring (formally: it's zetetic), is never or rarely conclusive (formally: it's aporetic) and allows characters to develop and move their argumentative positions (we'll see this most clearly in Chapter 6, discussing *Protagoras*).

Many reasons have been suggested, over hundreds of years, for Plato's choice of the dialogue form. *Perhaps* it's just to keep it interesting. *Perhaps* the dialogue form itself is simply a literary device to encourage you forget that you are reading and point to the nature of 'speech–as–living–thought'. *Perhaps* it is to avoid dogmatism: as Michael Frede points out, Plato cannot have Socrates challenge convention and authority, on the one hand, and then, on the other, simply assert his own authority.[37] *Perhaps* it is done to give Plato 'plausible deniability' in case, like Socrates, he was accused of some offensive belief by the Athenians. *Perhaps* it is to imitate "the manyness, the variety, the heterogeneity of being", the many aspects of truth.[38] *Perhaps* it is a way to make the reader think of themselves as a participant in the discussion, identifying with different positions and arguments and then developing their own. Jill Frank calls this last twist "disidentifying": a model of the dialectical method of philosophy.[39] *Perhaps* Plato wrote to take an active, intellectual part in Athenian politics by providing models (not literary devices exactly) to "refashion Athenian political language" as Danielle Allen argues.[40] *Perhaps*, as Ruby Blondell suggests, by using the resources of drama, recognisable people in actual places, Plato shows that philosophy arises naturally from people's real lives and situations: it is not a 'head in the clouds' abstraction but part of our everyday life.[41] Some people think that Socrates is simply Plato's mouthpiece while others find a gap between what is said, usually by Socrates, and the wider aim of a dialogue: for the purposes of this book, then, roughly, between what the dialogues say *about* literature and what they say *as* literature (and we'll see this in later chapters). In any case, in the dialogues, speech and character are woven together, which means that characters, too, are literary devices.

Characters as literary devices

Plato's philosophy is alive with characters, who are almost always based on real people: Plato's elder brothers, Adeimantus and Glaucon in *The Republic*; proper friends of Socrates, as the joking with Phaedrus suggests; opponents of Socrates like the famous sophists Protagoras and Gorgias; Alcibiades, the charismatic, ambitious and unprincipled Athenian politician. Debra Nails, in her wonderful *The People of Plato*, writes Plato "did not invent Athenians" but wrote about

> real people … with reputations, families, neighbours, political
> affiliations, people who show up elsewhere in the existing historical
> record: lampooned in comedies, called as witnesses, elected to office,
> being sold, marrying, buying property, traveling, dying. Socrates' society
> was not only a matter of institutions and ideologies, but a matter of
> actual people, individuals within a nexus of familial, social, and political
> relationships.[42]

A sense of this concreteness of the world of Plato's dialogues is important for our reading of them: who "a person was can *matter*" to our interpretations.[43] Rebecca Goldstein's *Plato in the Googleplex* demonstrates this by restaging versions of the dialogues in our present using easily recognisable versions of current figures: the internet billionaire; the sex therapist; the arrogant TV interviewer.[44] These characters and their concrete reality are part of the literary, *un*abstract quality of Plato's work.

The most important character is obvious: Socrates. Born in 470 BCE, Socrates was the son of a stonemason and a midwife. As a citizen of military age, he fought as a hoplite but eventually became known for arguing in the *agora* and in other public places of the city. In Athens, a city keen on beauty and fame, he was ugly, badly dressed and uninterested in celebrity, although he attracted a cult following fascinated by his arguments. He walked barefoot, never wrote anything down and was often lost in thought. He claimed to have a *daimon* or a divine voice that warned him off from doing evil: "whenever it speaks to me it turns me away from something I am about to do, but it never encourages me to do anything" (*Apology* 31d) (see also *Euthyphro* 3b, *Phaedrus* 242b). He was challenging to be around: one old Athenian warns another that whoever talks with him

> must necessarily, even if he began by conversing about something quite different in the first place, keep on being led about by the man's arguments until he submits to answering questions about himself concerning both his present manner of life and the life his has lived hitherto. And when he does submit to this questioning, you don't realise that Socrates will not let him go before has well and truly tested every last detail.
>
> (*Laches* 187e–188a)

There are some accounts of him by his friends and followers. The historian and soldier Xenophon wrote a speech, two dialogues and a memoir of Socrates, which includes many stories of his kindness and practical wisdom, as well as his piety.[45] He's a kind of risible mad professor in *The Clouds*, a comic play by Aristophanes. After the fall of Athens, when he was 70 in 399 BCE, he was arrested and charged with impiety and corrupting the youth. He was found guilty and condemned to death. He declined the chance to escape the city because, as Plato has him say in the *Apology*, he had lived all his life under the laws of Athens so should die by them too.

We know most about Socrates from Plato. In the dialogues, Socrates is inquisitive and ironic, stern and humorous, funny and serious. He describes himself in metaphors. As we've heard, he says he is a *midwife*: he is not pregnant with ideas himself but draws them out from others (*Theaetetus* 150e). As Hughes points out, Socrates would know from his mother that midwifery was hard, messy and painful, as he says coming to the truth is.[46] He says he is a *gadfly* (*Apology* 30e) because he stings people awake and makes them examine their lives and opinions: he often upsets people, especially the powerful, although he wasn't interested in controversy for its own sake, but for how it could turn us towards truth. At the end of the dialogue *Protagoras*, Socrates compares himself to Prometheus (361d), the titan who stole fire from the Gods. Other people call him different things: Meno says he is a 'torpedo fish' or 'electric ray' (*Meno* 80a) who shocks people with questions and paralyses them ("for both my mind and my tongue are numb and I have no answer to give you" 80b). As Arendt says, this sounds like the "very opposite of the gadfly; it paralyses where the gadfly rouses. Yet what cannot fail to look like paralysis from the outside – from the standpoint of ordinary human affairs – is *felt* as the highest state of being active and alive" because it is a moment of the most intense thought.[47] Meno also says that, because of this, in any city other than Athens, Socrates would not be safe: he would be taken to be a witch (80b). The point of these metaphors is to show what sort of character Socrates is, and so what sort of person a philosopher should be.

No one can really know how accurately he is portrayed in the dialogues, or how far the ideas are his or Plato's. However, the literary questions of character lead to fundamental questions about Plato's work. Is Socrates just a mouthpiece for Plato or is he more akin to Hamlet, Macbeth or Prince Hal who offer, in words and action, their views of the world, but not Shakespeare's? Are all the dialogues linked, like a series of novels or films in the same fictional universe, or is each separate, though by a single author? In turn, are the arguments in each universal or made for a specific time and place, to win over a particular interlocutor?

The character of Socrates has exercised a fascination over very many Western thinkers. For some, he is the figure who every philosopher wants to be: he is the "one man with whom all European philosophers identify, even if they reject all his ideas".[48] (If this is true – because they *identify* with him and don't agree with him – this is a profoundly literary sort of response.) Philosophers write things like "we can feel that Plato has given us a man, not just a doctrine; it is the moral force of this Socrates which will not leave us alone".[49] Or: "to the extent we do not admire him, we are at war with ourselves".[50] (The admiration started early: Phaedo concludes his speech on Socrates's death by saying that he was "of all those we have known the best, and also the wisest and the most upright" (*Phaedo* 118a); Xenophon says he was "the perfect example of goodness and happiness".)[51] For others, he is a martyr to reason and thought.[52] But it's possible to offer a different view: we'll look at Nietzsche's attack on Socrates in Chapter 4. Indeed, while Socrates claims to talk with anyone, we see him in the dialogues almost exclusively with the Athenian elite. The campaigning journalist I. F. Stone wrote an account of his trial which justified the actions of the Athenians arguing that Socrates was an anti-democratic elitist who did his best to avoid taking up his responsibilities as a citizen while snobbishly mocking others.[53]

Conclusion: Plato's vision of light

Any introduction to Plato is going to be a story. I chose to use his literary devices because they offer a vivid, influential, holistic and poetic approach which emphasise some of the things Socrates seems to stand for: focusing on the devices, too, allows themes rather than doctrines to appear. The allegory of the cave is a prison break from our shadowy, false world to the upper bright world of reality and truth. The climb up the rocky slope to that world is motivated by love, the desire for reality and truth. The real and the true are like the ideal shapes which we discover – unforget – in geometry. Like the correct method in geometry, there is a correct method in thinking, the dialectic: geometry both models the truth and how to get to it. The truth helps guide our behaviour: the chariot of ourselves needs to be steered correctly. Speech-as-living-thought is how we come to understand truth but is not poetry, rhetoric or writing: it is clear, honest, meaningful speech between people, or with oneself. This kind of speech is undertaken by philosophers, demonstrated by Socrates who, as a stinging gadfly, a numbing torpedo fish, a midwife, a witch, shows us how to talk and think. Plato's work offers a vision of truth, beauty and goodness in one, in the light of the sun. Unchanging and eternal, it's in stark contrast to our changeable, painful, dark world, but it helps orient ourselves towards what is right and true. All these ideas are nuanced by the very written-ness of the dialogues, which puts them back into question. These are the powerful and beautiful themes of Plato's thought. By looking at *The Republic*, his most famous work, the next chapter shows how his influential vision has strange consequences for poetry and drama.

Notes

1 Iris Murdoch, *Existentialists and Mystics* (London: Penguin, 1997), p. 462.
2 Percy Bysshe Shelley, *Selected Poems and Prose*, eds. Jack Donovan and Cian Duffy (London: Penguin, 2016), p. 656.
3 Hannah Arendt, *Reflections on Literature and Culture*, ed. Susannah Young-Ah Gottlieb (California: Stanford University Press, 2007), p. 225.
4 Hannah Arendt, *The Life of the Mind*, vol. 1. (Harvest: New York, 1978), p. 104.
5 Arendt, *The Life of the Mind*, p. 104.
6 Jill Gordon, 'In Plato's Image' from *Philosophy in Dialogue: Plato's Many Devices*, ed. Gary Alan Scott (Evanston: Northwestern University Press, 2007), pp. 212–37, p. 232. See also Jill Gordon, *Turning Toward Philosophy: Literary Device and Dramatic Structure in Plato's Dialogues* (Pennsylvania: Pennsylvania State University Press, 1999).
7 This story is probably from the "latter half of the 6th century and likely arising from the Alexandrian circle of Neoplatonism". Danielle A. Layne, '*The Anonymous Prolegomena to Platonic Philosophy*' in *Brill's Companion to the Reception of Plato in Antiquity*, eds. Harold Tarrant, François Renaud, Dirk Baltzly, and Danielle A. Layne (Boston: Brill, 2017), pp. 533–4, p. 533.
8 See, for example, Jacob Howland, 'Re-Reading Plato: The Problem of Platonic Chronology', *Phoenix* 45:3 (1991), 189–214.
9 John M. Cooper (ed) *Plato: Complete Works* (Indianapolis: Hackett Publishing, 1997), p. xiv.
10 R. B. Rutherford, *The Art of Plato* (London: Duckworth, 1995), p. 3.
11 See, for a powerful example of this position, Drew A. Hyland, *Finitude and Transcendence in the Platonic Dialogues* (Albany: SUNY Press, 1995).
12 Catherine Zuckert, *Plato's Philosophers: The Coherence of the Dialogues* (Chicago: University of Chicago Press, 2012), p. 11.
13 Zuckert, *Plato's Philosophers*, p. 46.
14 Plato, *Protagoras*, trans. Benjamin Jowett, revised Martin Ostwald, ed. and intro Gregory Vlastos (Indianapolis: Bobbs-Merrill Company, 1956), pp. xxvi–xxvii.
15 Plato, *Protagoras*, intro Vlastos, p. xxviii.
16 Gordon, 'In Plato's Image', p. 213.
17 Zuckert, *Plato's Philosophers*, p. 282.
18 Bettany Hughes, *The Hemlock Cup* (London: Vintage, 2011), p. 163, p. 292.
19 Christopher Rowe, *Plato and the Art of Philosophical Writing* (Cambridge: Cambridge University Press, 2007), p. 56.
20 Pierre Hadot, *Philosophy as a Way of Life*, ed. Arnold Davidson, trans. Michael Chase (Oxford: Blackwell, 1995), p. 92.
21 Murdoch, *Existentialists and Mystics*, p. 456.
22 Martin Heidegger, 'Plato's doctrine of Truth', trans. Thomas Sheenhan, in *Pathmarks*, ed. William McNeill (Cambridge: Cambridge University Press, 1998), pp. 155–82.

23 For a powerful and thoughtful counter-reading of this version, see Jonathan Barnes, 'Heidegger in the Cave' in *Method and Metaphysics* (Oxford: Oxford University Press, 2011), pp. 77–99.
24 Hannah Arendt, *The Human Condition* (Chicago: University of Chicago Press, 1998), p. 226. See also Miguel Abensour and Martin Breaugh, 'Against the Sovereignty of Philosophy over Politics: Arendt's Reading of Plato's Cave Allegory', *Social Research*, 74:4 (2007), 955–82.
25 Hannah Arendt, *The Promise of Politics* (New York: Schocken Books, 2005), p. 93.
26 Percy Byssehe Shelley, *Selected Poems and Prose*, ed. Jack Donovan and Cian Duffy (London: Penguin, 2016), p. 668.
27 Mark A. Ralkowski, *Plato's Trial of Athens* (London: Bloomsbury, 2019), p. 59.
28 Murdoch, *Existentialists and Mystics*, p. 416: she's drawing on a powerful reading of Canto XXVII of the *Purgatorio* in F. M. Cornford, 'The Doctrine of Eros in Plato's *Symposium*' in *The Unwritten Philosophy and other Essays* (Cambridge: Cambridge University Press, 1950), pp. 68–80.
29 It's often assumed that Socrates's interlocutor is a 'slave boy', but Bernard Williams points out that 'boy' was used as a term for all enslaved males in classical Athens, "as elsewhere", he adds. *Shame and Necessity* (Princeton; Princeton University Press, 2008), p. 108.
30 Gregory Vlastos, *Socrates: Ironist and Moral Philosopher* (Cambridge: Cambridge University Press, 1991), p. 120.
31 Michael Frede, 'Plato's Arguments and the Dialogue Form' in *Methods of Interpreting Plato and His Dialogues: Oxford Studies in Ancient Philosophy: Supplementary Volume*, eds. James C. Klagge and Nicholas D. Smith, 1992, pp. 201–9, p. 210.
32 It's first mentioned by Joannes Philoponus, a philosopher and commentator on Plato from Alexandria in the sixth century AD.
33 Arendt, *The Human Condition*, p. 142.
34 Cited, Rebecca Goldstein, *Plato at the Googleplex* (London: Atlantic Books, 2014), p. 46.
35 F. M. Cornford, *From Religion to Philosophy: A Study in the Origins of Western Speculation* (London: Edward Arnold, 1912), pp. 248–9.
36 Marcel Detienne, *The Masters of Truth in Archaic Greece*, trans. Janet Lloyd (New York: Zone Books, 1999), p. 16.
37 Frede, 'Plato's arguments …', p. 217.
38 Leo Strauss, *The City and Man* (Chicago: University of Chicago Press, 1964), p. 61.
39 Jill Frank, *Poetic Justice: Rereading Plato's* Republic (Chicago: Chicago University Press, 2018), p. 16.
40 Danielle S. Allen, *Why Plato Wrote* (Oxford: Wiley-Blackwell, 2013), p. 19.
41 See: Ruby Blondell, *The Play of Character in Plato's Dialogues* (Cambridge: Cambridge University Press, 2002).
42 Debra Nails, *The People of Plato* (Indianapolis: Hackett Publishing Company, 2002), p. xxxvii.
43 Nails, *The People of Plato*, p. xxxviii.
44 Goldstein, *Plato at the Googleplex*. There is a large genre of Platonic dialogues rewritten for the contemporary world. My favourite is Luciano De Crescenzo, *The Dialogues*, trans. Avril Bardoni (London: Picador, 1985).
45 Xenophon, *Conversations of Socrates*, trans. Hugh Tredennick and Robin Waterfield (London: Penguin, 1990).
46 Bettany Hughes, *The Hemlock Cup*, pp. 250–1.
47 Arendt, *The Life of the Mind*, vol. 1, p. 173.
48 Leszek Kołakowski, *Metaphysical Horror* (London: Penguin, 2001), p. 1.
49 James Haden, 'On Socrates, with Reference to Gregory Vlastos', *The Review of Metaphysics* 33:2 (1979), pp. 371–89, p. 371.

50 Alexander Nehamas, *Virtues of Authenticity* (Princeton: Princeton University Press, 1999), p. 316.
51 Xenophon, 'Memoirs of Socrates' 4.8.11 in *Conversations of Socrates*, p. 216.
52 See, for a recent example, the loving but speculative biography-cum-film treatment, Armand D'Angour, *Socrates in Love* (London: Bloomsbury Publishing, 2019).
53 I. F. Stone, *The Trial of Socrates* (New York: Anchor Books, 1989).

3

WATCHING *THE REPUBLIC*

On first sight, for literary-minded people, *The Republic* is shocking. Socrates exiles the poets, thinks literature a silly game or, worse, a disease: personally damaging, politically dangerous and philosophically problematic. Poetry and tragedy are forms of imitation, *mimesis*, far removed from the true, the beautiful and the good. Through the power of identification, they make us imitators, too. In *The Republic*, literature stops you being yourself. By contrast, the dialectic of philosophy, by showing you the truth, frees you and makes you more yourself.

This chapter summarises *The Republic* and so puts the attacks on poetry and drama, which are concentrated in **books 2, 3** and **10**, back into the whole structure of the dialogue. I do this because literary discussions often take ideas out of context which makes them seem meaningless and arbitrary. We may want to disagree with the arguments but we need to see the wider context more fully. Parts of something only make sense in relation to the whole, while the whole is given its meaning by the parts: the principle of *hermeneutic circularity*. 'To be or not to be' would look odd, standing alone. In the next chapter, and thinking of *polis* and *logos*, I look at some well-known responses to the dialogue, both political and literary.

This fuller summary has an additional benefit. Often, though justifiably because of its complexity and length, *The Republic* is discussed as if it was simply a collection of arguments and ideas. It's full of these, but it's also a single, coherent work with an overall shape and introducing it as a whole, more as we might discuss a novel, will draw this out: a rise and fall, from the birth of a society, through its peak to decline and death. The summit is the escape to the real, eternal world, in the middle of the allegory of the cave, which offers a vision of the true, the real and the good. Rutherford's excellent *The Art of Plato* also discusses the range of linked metaphors which form this narrative. *The Republic* is full of journeys, real, imagined, in argument (435d, 504b–c); full, too, of images of ascent (452c, 568c, 584d); images of the human as animal, or becoming an animal: the mob is as a great beast (493b–c), a tyrant becomes a wolf (565d–e) the guardians are like watch dogs (375–6) and we humans have beasts inside us (588b).[1]

To achieve this in one chapter, I am going to approach *The Republic* as if it were a movie mixing quicker, wider, establishing panoramas with slower, more

DOI: 10.4324/9781003097914-5

detailed close-ups of the discussions of poetry and drama. (People often say they'll wait for the film of a successful book but there's been no summer block-buster or online streaming version of *The Republic* for nearly 2,400 years: while we wait, this will have to do.)

Opening panorama: down at the Piraeus at night

Socrates begins telling a story. We are down at the Piraeus, the port of Athens, sometime during the war between Athens and Sparta (scholars argue over pre-cisely when and what that might mean: as Debra Nails explains, if it's set in 421 BCE, the war is going well, which suggests readings that play up the humour and irony; but if it's set in 411 BCE, then it's much gloomier, encouraging pessim-istic interpretations about corruption and decay).[2] The day is a celebration of Bendis, a Thracian goddess foreign to Athens. Ruby Blondell gives an extensive and fascinating description of the men involved ("besides the usual invisible slaves"): rich, poor, old, young, Athenians and foreigners resident in Athens, democrat and oligarch, those later to be persecutors and those who will be their victims.[3] A cross-section of the elite of the city and, for Blondell, the argument of the dialogue flows out of each character's interaction with Socrates.

In **book 1** (some think this book is an addition, or a different dialogue welded to the other nine books; most disagree), the characters gather at the house of Cephalus, with the promise of seeing a night-time horseback race lit with torches. Quite naturally, conversation emerges, first between Socrates and Cephalus: what has he learned from his old age? What's the best thing about being rich? Cephalus thinks the best thing is that you can pay your debts and not have to lie and cheat (like a version of creepy old Mr Deasy from *Ulysses*: "I paid my way ... I owe nothing").[4] But is paying your way and not cheating what justice is? Cephalus's son, Polemarchus, inherits the argument: he agrees with the poet Simonides that justice is looking after your friends. But Socrates suggests that this is confused ("just like a poet" 332b) and, using the elenchic method, persuades Polemarchus that he, too, is muddled. Meanwhile another guest, a rhetorician called Thrasymachus (who has "tried many times to take over the discussion" 336a) bursts out angrily, like a "wild beast" (336b), tearing into Socrates, demanding he's upfront about his own opinions rather than just provoking others. Thrasymachus thinks it's obvious that might makes right and if being unjust is profitable for you, you should be. These three and their arguments set the tone and the topic: what is justice?

Socrates eventually answers Thrasymachus: "a just person is happy, and an unjust one wretched ... It profits no one to be wretched but to be happy ... And so, Thrasymachus, injustice is never more profitable than justice" (354a) (if this is convincing is a matter for debate). But Plato's older brothers Glaucon and Adeimantus want to know more, and in more detail: they pick up the question at the start of **book 2**. Glaucon, the bolder of the two, tells the story of the ring of Gyges which makes the bearer invisible. Even a virtuous person, free from the constraints of society and shame through invisibility, would steal, rob, rape and break other laws, "like a god among humans" (360c). As the discussion unfolds, it becomes clear that justice and ethics are not only a private matter but are inextricably interwoven with community: ethics and justice appear most clearly in the context of the *polis* (368e). So, in order to understand what the ideal form of justice and the good might be, *The Republic* builds in words, tells a story of, the ideal *polis* starting with its most basic components.

Socrates sketches a kind of rural utopia, with the people baking bread and making their own clothes, eating simple foods – Glaucon interrupts: wouldn't a "city of pigs" (372d) have the same diet? The conversation soon discovers that a fuller, sustainable society in which the people can thrive will need not only farmers and people to provide resources and necessities (shoemakers, for example) but also a whole array of others too: pastry cooks, rhapsodes, nannies and so on. For Socrates and his ideal community, it's important that people specialise in the trades they have mastered and don't do other jobs. To flourish, the community will have to expand and so will need to defend itself from its neighbours. It will need people trained in warfare: warriors or guardians. These guardians, like guard dogs, must be healthy, brave and skilled in war but more, they need to get angry with strangers "before anything bad happens" and welcome friends (376a). In order to know how to do this, Socrates argues that they need to love learning and knowledge, to be philosophical so that they can judge between "a friend or an enemy" (376b), so the discussion then turns to their education.

First close-up: untrue stories

It's at this point that the argument against poetry and drama begins. It's in two parts. The first concerns the impact on the young, and so on the *polis*, of *false stories*. Socrates and Glaucon agree that the guardians need to be healthy, brave and love knowledge and for this, education is crucial. But Socrates has a worry: "Aren't there two kinds of story, one true and the other false?" (376e). Because stories we tell our children right at the start of their lives are so important, they need to be true and "not told by just anyone" (377b). Socrates suggests that it will be necessary to "supervise the storytellers" (377b) to ensure they only tell appropriate stories.

Socrates starts working out what to censor at the top with tales about the gods, and by quoting both Hesiod and Homer extensively (and so showing that while he's shocking, he's not uncultured). Stories that misrepresent the gods, such as the one in which Chronos avenges his mother on his father Ouranos by castrating him, a tale about disloyalty and patricide, should be banned. Indeed all stories about disharmony among the family of the gods should be banned (or made 'secret knowledge' only for initiates of cults) because, in the ideal city, citizens will be taught not to hate each other and that such hate is impious. It's not just untrue stories that are inappropriate: some true ones are dangerous too. This is why Socrates outlines the rules or patterns for all stories ("epic, lyric or tragedy" 379a) in the ideal city. First, since the divine is good and so can't cause harm, any stories about the gods causing harm, such as the story of the evils for humanity stored in Pandora's box, can't be true and should be banned. Second, the divine has an unchangeable shape and does not lie, so stories about shape-changing divinities, or gods who deceive in words and actions must be untrue and should be banned. Hearing only positive and true stories about the gods will teach the guardians to be respectful of the gods, their own kin and the state.

At the start of **book 3**, Socrates expands these ideas and provides further rules for poets. He is concerned that stories about death might prevent the guardians being courageous or moral. Guardians should not hear stories about Hades, the Greek afterlife, which makes it sound horrible, frightening or demeaning: in which, for example

> As when bats in an awful cave
> Fly around screeching if one of them falls
> From the cluster on the ceiling, all clinging to one another
> So their souls went screeching.

(387a)

These kinds of stories will be a bad influence on the guardians by making them frightened of death and would give any soldier pause for thought before action. Similarly, stories of great men mourning or lost in grief might make them hesitate before combat, contemplating death and the enormity of grief. So these will be banned too because the guardians are supposed to regard weeping and wailing, being overcome with emotion, as silly and despicable: not at all how a great person should behave. Similarly, texts that show people being overcome with "violent laugher" should be banned because such laughter presages a "violent change of mood" (389d).

Socrates argues that while the rulers might have to lie to the people for the good of the *polis*, stories that are false should be banned. So, as the guardians and people will need the virtue of moderation, stories that represent ill-discipline should be banned: no disobedience to rulers and commanders or to the principles of self-discipline. Art which portrays gluttony, boozing and lust should be banned. More − Socrates is warming to his theme − any poems in which heroes or gods do immoral things should be banned.

So far, Socrates has presented rules for the stories concerning gods and heroes. But Socrates and his interlocutors pause when they get to stories about normal people. It seems likely, he says, that they won't approve of stories that suggest that unjust people can be happy, and moral ones unhappy, that the good end badly and the bad end well, and that a person can get away with behaving immorally (392a–b), but Socrates and the guests at Cephalus's house can't conclude this until they know what justice is, the very point of the whole dialogue.

Second close-up: unreal voices

Socrates says that they have finished discussing the content and now need to discuss the 'style' of telling, so they will have covered both "what should be said and how it should be said" (392c). This introduces explicitly something which has been bubbling under the discussion and is the most important idea about art and literature in *The Republic*: imitation, *mimesis*.

Socrates is concerned about how writers use different 'voices' in their work. To demonstrate, he gives an example from Homer, in which first the narrator and then the priest Chryses (393a) speak. Speaking in Chryses's voice, Homer uses dramatic characterisation or representation, a form of *mimesis* (393c). To make his point crystal clear, Socrates retells the same passage in very boring plain prose as straightforward narration. He is making obvious a distinction between different kinds of poetry and story-telling: some involve *mimesis* (tragedy and comedy: plays are obviously all *mimesis* in this sense, lacking a narrator), some don't seem to (when it's just narrated by the poet, say, or boringly by Socrates) and some mixes both modes (epic poetry, for example, Homer-doing-Chryses). This moment has often been taken as Socrates's analysis of two modes: *mimesis* (sometimes described as 'showing') as a contrast to *diegesis* (as 'telling'), but this is not really what is happening here.[5] Rather, the sense of *mimesis* being used is very wide. (Halliwell notes especially how *mimesis* "receives fluctuating and constantly revised treatment from Plato".)[6] *Mimesis* here includes the poet's use of dramatic character; the performance of a character by a poet, rhapsode or actor; and the wider sense of taking on a role, in the sense that literary art involves identification.[7] More, there is a complication: despite what Socrates intends with his dull retelling, there is no 'neutral' way of writing, no simple 'telling'. Socrates's version is leaden, less flowery and so on, but it's still an imitation: he's still representing Homer's speech ("Socrates imitating Homer narrating is every bit as much a poet as is Homer imitating Chryses pleading").[8] Nehamas argues that for Socrates, *mimesis* is "transparent", that we can "see directly through its representation" to its object.[9] Halliwell refines this by saying "Plato's critique targets the actual inclination of audiences to *treat* mimetic representations as cases of what they represent": the audience assumes *mimesis* is transparent.[10] But, in any case, *mimesis* is a difficulty for Socrates.

It is *mimesis* as a kind of ventriloquism which makes Socrates anxious. Just as the craftspeople of the city need to specialise in one trade, so the guardians need to specialise in being "craftsmen of the city's freedom" (395c): this means that they should not imitate anyone except people who are "courageous, self-controlled, pious and free" (395c). The risk of imitation is not to efficiency (the ostensible reason why craftspeople specialise) but because, as Socrates says, "enjoying the imitation, they come to enjoy the reality … imitations practiced from youth become part of nature and settle into habits of gesture, voice and thought" (395d). *Mimesis* can damage character and stop you being yourself. (Havelock suggests that this argument stems from the way the Greeks memorised and performed poetry, a psychological and physiological act of "personal commitment, of total engagement and emotional identification" for the classical Greeks but Socrates seems to be aiming at more than this.)[11]

Socrates then provides a long list of all the things the guardians must not imitate: young women; boastful or querulous old women; "slaves doing slavish things" (395e); cowards; drunks; libellers; madmen; craftsmen; people involved with ships; "neighing horses, bellowing bulls, roaring rivers, the crashing sea, thunder" (396b). Adeimantus suggests these sound like sort of noises a mad person might make. A guardian or moderate and decent person will only use the very plain narrative style Socrates exemplified a little earlier, occasionally imitating only good words and actions: this is acceptable. By contrast, a less good person will happily use many more imitations, "even the cries of dogs, sheep and birds" (397a). Although this mixed style is "by far the most pleasing to children, their tutors, and the vast majority of people" (397d), this is unacceptable, indecent and not welcome. Socrates argues that the mimetic style clashes with the constitution of the city which enforces specialisation and which wants people to be led by philosophy, explicitly or implicitly, to be only (philosophy's version of) themselves.

Very famously, this leads Socrates to say:

> if a man, who through clever training can become anything and imitate anything, should arrive in our city, wanting to give a performance of his poems, we should bow down before him as someone holy, wonderful, and pleasing, but we should tell him that there is no one like him in our city and that it isn't lawful for there to be. We should pour myrrh on his head, crown him with wreathes, and send him away to another city.
>
> (397e–398a)

Socrates will respect and honour poets but will not have them in his city: he will accept only a "more austere and less pleasure-giving poet and storyteller" (398a) who imitates only respectable people and follows the rules laid down for stories. In Susan Spitzer's translation of Alain Badiou's 'hypertranslation' of *The Republic*, she rather wonderfully calls a mimetic poet "a wizard of life" and the austere poet is described as offering a "more sober, less obviously appealing kind of poetry, which is closer to prose, or even to mathematics". The maths is Badiou's (hyper)-addition, but you can hear the sense he means in it: a more rational form of speech which makes us identify with and imitate only rationality (and recalls the importance of geometry).[12]

Socrates bunches all the literary art forms together here because of their style and content, because they use imitation and because of their impact on audience and performers. But what holds these arguments together, at this stage in *The Republic*, is Socrates's concern for what we can understand to be one of the great powers of literature, the power to create identification and the impact of this on education and self-formation. Socrates's argument is "directed against the power of poetry to enter the mind, to take hold of its beliefs and emotions, and to mold the personalities of those exposed to it".[13] It is aimed at the literary author's ability to make the "audience almost pathologically and certainly sympathetically identify".[14] Literary texts are imitative and we too can be imitative, through our identification with them. Texts are representation, and Socrates fears they make us *re-present* ourselves: instead, we should be *presenting* ourselves, 'speech-as-living-thought', present to ourselves and to others.

Identification with characters in literary texts is often thought of as being naïve, but it is a powerful part of the experience of drama and poetry, of literature, cinema and computer games, the source of "some of our most powerful, enduring and deeply felt pleasures" as well as "considerable emotional turmoil, capable of unsettling or unmooring the precarious groundings of our everyday identities", as Socrates and Plato (and, as we'll see later, Aristotle) are keenly aware.[15] Sometimes the representation of identification is amusing. Don Quixote's adventures begin because he has read too many romances and fancies himself a knight-errant. Sometimes they are tragic: Emma Bovary has read too much romantic fiction and yearns for her adventure in love. Ironically, many involved with the study of literature have sided with Socrates and been profoundly uneasy with expressions of identification or 'relatability'. But in her recent work, the American literary critic Rita Felski has defended this crucial literary experience. She writes that without "the sediments of the novels I've read, the films and TV shows I've watched, I would be another person entirely. Fictional beings serve as alter egos, ideal types, negative *exampla*, moral guides, objects of desire, imaginary friends".[16] This is precisely what Socrates disapproves of: she should be only herself, and this only through the dialectic. As we'll see in the second half of this book, this is one crucial area in which Plato's Socrates and Aristotle differ profoundly. Felski goes on to classify, rather than forbid, this everyday but powerful experience. Identification happens through alignment (whose eyes are we seeing through?); allegiance (do we share their values?); recognition (are we like them in some way? Nobody reading this sentence is an orphan in Victorian London, but we can all relate to Oliver Twist feeling lost and lonely); empathy (do we share their feelings?).[17] Identification is obviously central in our political lives, too, as we identify ourselves (or are identified by others) as members of this or that community. We also learn to negotiate overlapping demands for identification, and judge when these demands may be helpful or destructive.

Socrates is all too aware of this power of literature. In his ideal city, he seeks to avoid the guardians or others identifying with contents, behaviours, or through form, enactments of that which will harm them. Instead, perhaps, he wants to harness this power for *his* kind of discourse, for the dialectic to make us more ourselves by following his vision of rationality as the path to the true, the good and the beautiful. As we saw in the previous chapter, the very nature of the dialogues encourages identification, either with Socrates or with other characters, and this can be extraordinarily powerful (the "one man with whom all European philosophers identify ... is Socrates").[18] Jill Frank's idea of 'disidentification' adds a twist to this. Noting that *The Republic* is supposed to be read, its "heightened levels of self-consciousness of presentation" lead the reader to reflect on the "relation between truth and representation" in the same way postmodern fiction makes the reader aware that a novel is (only) a novel.[19] She suggests that these qualities of the text itself should make us wary of what Socrates is saying.

Socrates will go on to argue that music, too, in different modes, beats, rhythms and metres, indeed even "weaving ... embroidery, architecture" (401a) and other crafts can be disharmonious and inelegant and so can damage the young people of the *polis*. All these other craftspeople need supervision. The young people must live where "fine works will strike their eyes and ears like a breeze that brings health from a good place, leading them unwittingly, from childhood on, to resemblance, friendship and harmony with the beauty of reason" (401c–d).

Second panorama shot: up towards the sun, at night

Socrates, Glaucon and Adeimantus go on talking through the night. They discuss the guardians' lives and duties, and then move on to wider questions of morality and virtues. In the ideal city, the guardians are wise, their helpers brave and the other citizens, who are committed to their particular trades, self-disciplined: each of these partakes of 'goodness' and this leads, for Socrates, to the moral and harmonious city. Socrates introduces a "useful falsehood" (242b) – also known as the 'noble lie' – that everyone in the city are children of the earth and in each of them is some metal: gold for the rulers, silver for the guardians and iron and bronze for the farmers and craftspeople. This myth attempts to make natural a class division.

They continue in **book 4** by exploring the virtues in the city: wisdom (the 'golden' rulers), courage (the guardians) and self-control (everyone knows their place). These three virtues exhibited in the state, Socrates says, resemble ourselves ("a man is just in the same way as a city" 441d): wisdom which guides us; spirit, a kind of ambition spurred by honour and courage; self-control for our more material desires and our passions. This is what Bernard Williams calls Plato's 'ethical psychology'.[20] Socrates is offering a map of the human psyche, as well as of the *polis*, but one that is simultaneously physiological and ethical: our rational wisdom aims at the good, whereas our higher and lower passions stem from our bodily cravings. This ethical psychology has been astonishingly influential. This is why Socrates also warns that changes in music and poetry (424b–c) eventually change the laws: they empower the lower parts of our minds which then work to overpower the higher, both personally and politically. Adeimantus warns that by themselves, poetry and music are "harmless" but

> when lawlessness has established itself there, it flows over little by little
> into characters and ways of life. Then, greatly increased, it steps out

into private contracts, and from private contracts, Socrates, it makes its insolent way into law and government until in the end it overthrows everything, public and private.

(424d)

If lawless, unregulated art is allowed to shape the person, the person will go on to shape the *polis* in this lawless image. There's a longer version of this story in the *Laws*, warning about the rise of 'theatrocracy' (it's like the summary of a film warning about rock'n'roll in the 1950s, or punk, or rap, or hip hop, or grime, or drill…). In the 'olden days' (as the implication is), the styles of music were clearly defined and listened to in silence which was enforced "by a stick" (*Laws* 700d). But poets arose who "started to set a fashion of breaking the rules and offending good taste", talented but "ignorant of the correct and legitimate standards laid down by the Muse" (700d). Gripped "by a frenzied and excessive lust for pleasure" (700d), they mixed-up all the various genres and types of music. This gave "the ordinary man a taste for breaking the laws of music" (700e) as the theatre-goers assumed they could pass judgement on these new musics. The audience became noisy and in place of an aristocracy in music, "a sort of 'vicious theatrocracy' arose" (701a). This contempt for law in music turned into a refusal to be ruled, the rejection of parental authority and guidance, and finally a rejection of the divine.

Book 5 begins with Polemarchus getting Adeimantus to press Socrates on more detail about the city: it is here where Socrates seems to be most extreme. Running absolutely against Athenian custom, he proposes that women as well as men should be guardians. Then he proposes that the family be abolished, that children are to be raised as common to everyone (*The Republic* 457d) and that a system of preferential breeding be introduced to produce the finest human stock (459d). This is "so that our herd of guardians remains as free from dissension as possible" (459e) and so that the city is most like a person, in which a harm to one, like cutting a finger, is felt by all (463d): a 'body politic', more so because, since parentage would be unknown, anyone could be kin to anyone. (For many this is too much. Even Alain Badiou, a contemporary philosopher very inspired by Plato, makes his 'hypertranslated' Socrates himself break off the discourse to complain that *The Republic* misrepresents him. Instead of abolishing the family and running the *polis* like a breeding stable, Badiou suggests "drastically limiting inheritances", presumably influenced by the economist Thomas Piketty, and keeping lovemaking private.)[21] In any case, Polemarchus and Adeimantus wonder how this extreme city will come about.

Socrates tells them that none of this will happen until "philosophers rule as kings" (473c), or until leaders become philosophers: overall, political power and philosophy have to come together. This appears paradoxical, Socrates admits, since philosophy has been seen to be about the individual, not the *polis*. But Socrates makes his case for 'philosopher–kings'. The best ruler is the

51

most moral, and who loves or understands morality more than a philosopher? Philosophers love beauty, knowledge and truth and seek the good: they are clear-sighted, uninterested in material gain, self-disciplined, open-minded and courageous at challenging people's ideas and opinions. (Put like this, who could *not* want a philosopher as a ruler?) Socrates articulates this through the idea of the forms: philosophers come to understand the profounder reality of existence in and as the forms. Perhaps Socrates is not serious about the philosopher-kings, but rather suggests it as a sort of principle, or measure, of political leadership: certainly the conversation in **book 6** turns to the problem of a philosopher-king and its extreme unlikeliness. Socrates lays out the training for a philosopher and shows how philosophy is misunderstood. This conversation leads to the core of *The Republic*, the vision of goodness.

Although political and personal harmony come from goodness, Socrates is unable to explain clearly what goodness is, and so proposes analogies with vision. The sun creates light by which our eyes can see things in the world; similarly, the form of the good "gives truth to the things known and the power to know to the knower" (508e). Just as our eyes see by the light that sun provides, so our souls see by the light of goodness. That is, the good gives the power of knowledge. It's true we can see a little in the dark or with candles, but we see much less well: we only have moral vision by the light of goodness. Finally, the sun gives life to the things on earth but is not the same as those plants, trees and so on; similarly, goodness creates the forms but is not the forms. So, while the forms, and ourselves, are *beings*, the good is *beyond being* – a very hard concept to grasp.

Socrates says that our relationship to goodness and truth can be thought of as a line. At the lowest end of the line is the visible world in which we live. The least true kind of knowledge is based on guesswork, on the reflections or representations of things we can see (this means it's based on pictures, on second-hand accounts of what happened yesterday in the *agora*, on works of art that are only representations: imagination). The next step up is our knowledge of things that we can actually see: events, objects. The next step up from that is not visible but is still comprehensible, intelligible: the world of thought, of geometry and numbers. We still draw imperfect triangles and shapes to help us understand these perfect geometrical shapes in our mind. But the final part of the line is the ideas which exist by the light of truth itself, which we try to obtain through reason without using shapes or images to guide us. For Socrates, as we move up the line (as it were, towards the sun), our knowledge becomes more and more secure and truthful.

Book 7 takes this higher with the allegory of the cave, which I discussed in the previous chapter: Socrates's most famous and mysterious account of the good and the true, and the fate of philosophers (514a–518b). These accounts are the peak of *The Republic*. They centre on the images of climbing and height, with the sun as an analogue for the good at the summit. They change how the rest of the dialogue is understood: the second half is a descent which, in some ways, revisits what has been discussed in the first half but is illuminated by the light of the sun, or the vision of the good. Philosophers argue over whether Socrates *needs* the ideas about the aim of philosophy itself, summed up in the allegory of the cave, to make his argument about justice or whether he can get there by a 'shorter route'.[22] But because *The Republic* is an artwork as well as an argument, this ascent and descent is crucial to the narrative and an integral part of the text: sometimes the point of a journey isn't just the arrival, it's the climb, as Miley Cyrus reminds us.

Socrates, Glaucon and Adeimantus now discuss the education of the philosopher-kings: mathematics and geometry are central, as is education in argument and in the virtues. Indeed, there is the clearest account of the power of the dialectic here, as the way to find truth: "when the eye of the soul is really buried in a sort of barbaric bog, dialectic gently pulls it out and leads it upward" (533d). The person who understands both things and the dialectic can give an "account of the being of each thing" (534b). More, if that person can "distinguish in an account the form of the good from everything else, can survive all refutation, as if in a battle, striving to judge things not in accordance with opinion but in accordance with being, and can come through all this with his account still intact" (534b–c) then they know the good. But if they only know an "some image of it, you'll say it's through opinion, not knowledge, for he is dreaming and asleep throughout his present life, and before he wakes up here, he will arrive in Hades and go to sleep forever" (534c). Only the dialectic offers a path to knowledge and so only those skilled in it should rule. As Glaucon says "you've produced ruling men that are completely fine" to which Socrates replies "And ruling women, too" (540c) because both will share everything.

As **book 8** begins, the conversation takes a darker turn, a descent, as they begin to discuss how societies decay. Socrates outlines the forms of government which are less ideal than one ruled by philosopher-kings and how each decays into the next: timocracy (548), rule by the property-owning class for whom the passions run too strongly; this falls to oligarchy (550), rule by the rich, who are dominated by their material desires; this falls to a democracy (555), in which the citizens lack self-discipline; and this finally becomes a tyranny (562), where a state is ruled by the whims of a dictator. Each of these, as you can see, corresponds to one part of Socrates's version of the human psyche, his 'ethical psychology', and becomes increasingly disharmonious and further from the good. In passing, Socrates ironically notes that poets and tragedians are often tyrants' hangers-on, writing praises of them for money and honours: they praise democracies too, for money, but do not work with the higher (for Socrates) forms of government. Poets are connected to the lower forms of political life.

Book 9 begins by focusing on the character of the tyrant, and contrasting different kinds of life, just and unjust, perhaps to stress how different a tyrant is from a philosopher-king. The final sections of this book fully answer not only Thrasymachus's argument (that right is might, that injustice is alright if you are in charge) but also lays out the answer to the whole dialogue. Socrates suggests an odd and complex image that draws on all he has said: imagine a many-headed monster (like the hydra), a lion and a human all joined together and hidden, as it were, within a human. The hydra-monster is the lower material desires, the lion is the ambitious spirit and the human is the reason within. The person who praises injustice has let the lion and the hydra become over mighty and enabled them to snap at and fight each other. The just person has domesticated the hydra and made the lion's nature their ally, and so ensured that the "human being within this human being has the most control" (589b). In practice, they will strive to attain "moderation, justice and reason" (591b), look after their health and be sensible with money and with honours. More significantly, they won't be involved in politics, unless it is in this ideal state. It is here that Socrates declares that the ideal *polis* exists "in theory" (592a) or "in heaven" (592b): *The Republic* is a state, but only a state of mind.

Third close-up, first shot: two steps away from the true …

Socrates has used stories and analogies to point towards truth and goodness and now, in **book 10**, the dialogue turns back to poetry. This conversation builds on the earlier discussion and, indeed, explains it to some degree by revealing the profounder reasons why, in the discussion of education, poetry had been banned. Tragic and imitative poetry should be banned because it will "distort the thought of anyone who hears it" (595b), unless they have the drug to counteract this. He makes two arguments.

In the first, Socrates returns to discussion of *mimesis* but more clearly now his audience understand the ideal forms. Carpenters are skilled at making beds which embody (in some way) the form of the ideal, perfect bed, the blueprint. Painters, however, make representations of beds. So, says Socrates there are "three kinds of beds" (597b): the ideal bed; the carpenter's actual bed; the painter's image of a bed. This is: the true that underlies presence; a presentation (a step away); a re-presentation (a second step). (Janaway asks, rightly, if we should be surprised that a "humble craftsman" can now glimpse the forms, when earlier "much was made of the fact that only philosophers have access to the forms").[23] A tragedian is like the painter, says Socrates, creating something two steps from truth.

But there's more. A carpenter is skilled at making beds because (in the ideal state) they focus on one *techne*, carpentry. However, the painter makes imitations of anything, of things they don't understand. (When a painter paints a complex machine, they don't know what all the cogs and rods do: only that they are there.) A child or a fool would believe the painter to be magician who understands everything. Being two steps from the ideal and 'not knowing' about what is represented are linked, and they come together when Socrates turns from painting to his real enemy here, poetry.

It's claimed, Socrates says, that Homer and the poets know "all crafts, all human affairs concerned with virtue and vice" (598e). But are people simply taken in or are poets, in fact, knowledgeable about everything? And if poets did know all these things, would they not *do* them and become famous, rather than just write about them? (Would they not "be more eager to be the subject of a eulogy than the author of one?" (599b) as Socrates puts it). As his example, Socrates addresses Homer, the very greatest of the poets, on the most important issues: "warfare, generalship, city government and people's education" (599c). If he is not a kind of imitator of an imitator, what has he achieved?

Do his descriptions of medicines cure people? Are there communities that are ruled by 'Homeric' laws, as (for example) Athens was ruled by laws formed by Solon? Are there inventions Homer made, like Thales of Miletus, who is supposed to have invented the potter's wheel, or Anacharsis of Scythia, who designed a type of anchor? Did he pass down a special moral way of life? The implied answer to all these questions is, of course, the same: no. (We'll see a similar argument in Chapter 6 in the dialogue *Ion*.) Homer and all poets represent images of goodness but, in fact, have no contact with the true or the good. Socrates goes on:

> shall we conclude that all poetic imitators, beginning with Homer, imitate images of virtue and all the other things they write about and have no grasp of truth? ... a poetic imitator uses words and phrases to paint colored images of each of the crafts. He himself knows nothing about them, but he imitates them in such a way that others, as ignorant as he, who judge by words, will think he speaks extremely well about cobblery or generalship or anything else provided – so great is the natural charm of these things – that he speaks with meter, rhyme and harmony.
>
> (600e–601a)

He concludes: a flute player knows how to use a flute, and so can instruct a flute-maker how to make one best. A painter just paints a flute, with no idea at all about its use, just as a poet represents something with no knowledge of it, a "kind of game" (602b). Socrates has expanded his understanding of *mimesis*: first it applied to dramatic characterisation in poetry or acting, and to imitating behaviours (mostly bad but occasionally acceptable) from poetry and drama, now it applies to all art and all poetry.

Third close-up, second shot: ... and simply no good for you

Socrates now begins his second argument against literature. Painters use images to trick the eye, but measurement and calculation help us sort these things out truthfully: this is part of our higher, rational self. This means that imitation is untruthful and conspires, as it were, with the irrational parts of ourselves.

Socrates argues that we are often full of conflicts and confusions, and the task of reason is to resolve these as far as possible: to know and master ourselves. So when a terrible misfortune strikes (Socrates chooses the death of a son: an event that reverses the natural order of things), while one cannot be utterly calm, one should be as in control as possible, to master oneself, like a soldier in battle. Children cry when they fall over: adults shouldn't. Our emotional side has many different facets, whereas reason and self-control has only one: there are lots of ways to be overcome by emotion, but only one way to be self-controlled. Poets focus on the emotional part of people because that is easier to represent and more popular (605a). It makes more interesting theatre too (a play with lots of reasonable characters debating and agreeing might be good philosophy but boring drama).[24] So poets and playwrights appeal to the emotions, which mislead us: the poet "arouses, nourishes and strengthens" the lower, emotional part of the soul, and "destroys the rational one" (605c). This is just like occupying a city (another coincidence of the personal and the political, and a memory of war): an enemy kills the better citizens and empowers the worst ones, and so makes it easier to rule. Poetry, the invader, creates bad government for a person and a *polis*.

But this isn't the worst thing, declares Socrates. The worst thing is that even the best people (605c) can be corrupted by imitation, swept away by a beautiful or striking speech. And when this happens, we applaud it: "we enjoy it, give ourselves up to following it, sympathize with the hero, take his suffering seriously" (605d). In real life, we try to master our emotions, so is it right, he asks, to praise this in an imitation? Our baser selves are encouraged by poetry, and our higher rational selves are persuaded to lower their guard. This is true of grief, of laughter, and all the other emotions: poetic imitation "nurtures and waters them and established them as rulers in us when they ought to wither and be ruled, for that way we'll become better and happier" (606d).

So, Socrates says to Glaucon, people who praise Homer and say that his works are models for how to live are being as good as they can, and Homer is great, but only hymns to the gods and eulogies about good men are to be admitted to the ideal city (only these follow the rules he had outlined earlier). There is, says Socrates, "an ancient quarrel between philosophy and poetry" (607b). Philosophy, because it aims at justice, is more important than poetry. He's aware and respectful of poetry's power, and is open to arguments about its goodness, as long as they are made in prose by lovers of poetry and not by poets (who, presumably, are self-interested and might also 'cheat' by using poetry to sway the argument rather than the dialectic). But if these arguments are not convincing, then the poetry lover should do what you do in a bad romance: leave the toxic object of your love. The people in the ideal city need to keep reminding themselves by an "incantation" (608a) that poetry is harmful, not serious, untrue and that you must be careful around it: neither "honour, money, rule, or even poetry" must tempt one to be bad (608b).

56

Closing panorama shot

The Republic ends with a discussion on the rewards for being just, and, oddly perhaps for a dialogue about reason, ends with another myth. This is the story of Er, a man who returned from the dead and reported on the afterlife, describing the rewards for the good and punishments of the wicked: a contrast to the depiction of the poet's accounts of Hades earlier on. The whole narrative, like the myth of the cave, has climbed from darkness and ignorance, to an understanding of the good at the peak, and then returned, through the decline of states and the illusions of art, finally, to an account of death, the underworld and reincarnation.

THE END, run credits.

The next chapter, bearing in mind *polis* and *logos*, looks at some important responses to *The Republic*.

Notes

1 R. B. Rutherford, *The Art of Plato* (London: Duckworth, 1995), pp. 217–21.
2 Debra Nails, 'The Dramatic Date of Plato's *Republic*', *The Classical Journal* 93:4 (1998), pp. 383–96.
3 Ruby Blondell, *The Play of Character in Plato's Dialogues* (Cambridge: Cambridge University Press, 2002), p. 167.
4 James Joyce, *Ulysses* (London: Penguin, 1986), p. 25.
5 An excellent account of this is by Genevieve Liveley, *Narratology* (Oxford: Oxford University Press, 2019), pp. 16–17.
6 Stephen Halliwell, *The Aesthetics of Mimesis: Ancient Texts and Modern Problems* (Princeton: Princeton University Press, 2002), p. 38.
7 See: Christopher Janaway, *Images of Excellence: Plato's Critique of the Arts* (Oxford: Oxford University Press, 1995), p. 95.
8 L. A. Kosman, 'Silence and Imitation in the Platonic Dialogues' in *Methods of Interpreting Plato and His Dialogues: Oxford Studies in Ancient Philosophy: Supplementary Volume*, eds. James C. Klagge and Nicholas D. Smith, 1992, pp. 73–92, p. 78.
9 Nehamas, *Virtues of Authenticity*, p. 284.
10 Halliwell, *The Aesthetics of Mimesis*, pp. 90–91.
11 Eric A. Havelock, *Preface to Plato* (Cambridge: Harvard University Press, 1963), p. 160.
12 Alain Badiou, *Plato's Republic*, trans. Susan Spitzer (Cambridge: Polity, 2015), p. 88, p. 89.
13 Halliwell, *The Aesthetics of Mimesis*, p. 73.
14 Havelock, *Preface to Plato*, p. 45.
15 Diana Fuss, *Identification Papers* (London: Routledge, 1995), p. 2.
16 Rita Felski, *Hooked: Art and Attachment* (Chicago: Chicago University Press, 2020), p. 92.
17 See Felski, *Hooked*, ch 3; Toril Moi, Amanda Anderson and Rita Felski, *Character: Three Inquires in Literary Studies* (Chicago: Chicago University Press, 2019).
18 Leszek Kołakowski, *Metaphysical Horror*, ed. Agnieszka Kołakowska (London: Penguin, 2001), p. 1.
19 Jill Frank, *Poetic Justice: Rereading Plato's* Republic (Chicago: Chicago University Press, 2018), p. 33, p. 79.

20 Bernard Williams, *Shame and Necessity* (Princeton: Princeton University Press, 2008), p. 42ff.

21 Alain Badiou, *Plato's Republic*, trans. Susan Spitzer (Cambridge: Polity, 2015), p. 161.

22 See e.g. Dominic Scott, *Levels of Argument* (Oxford: Oxford University Press, 2015).

23 Janaway, *Images of Excellence*, p. 112.

24 Simone Weil, inspired in part by Plato, makes a comment which begins by supporting Socrates's view here, but then develops it interestingly: "Imaginary evil is romantic and varied; real evil is gloomy, monotonous, barren, boring. Imaginary good is boring; real good is always new, marvelous, intoxicating. Therefore 'imaginative literature' is either boring or immoral (or a mixture of both). It only escapes from this alternative if in some way it passes over to the side of reality through the power of art – and only genius can do that" Simone Weil, *Gravity and Grace*, trans. Emma Crawford and Mario von der Ruhr (London: Routledge, 2002), p. 70.

4

RESPONDING TO *THE REPUBLIC*

When we come out of the cinema or theatre, or after finishing a book, TV series or narrative computer game, we talk to each other. What about that bit? Wasn't it good when …? What did it mean …? Responding to an artwork, in discussion with others or even in conversation with yourself, is part of the experience of the artwork. This is true for works of philosophy too. So: how to respond to *The Republic*? What is it? A city in words or in theory (*The Republic* 369c)? A map of the human mind, or a city in the soul?[1] A blueprint for a totalitarian society (Karl Popper)? An ironic analysis of idealism revealing the real nature of the *polis* (Leo Strauss)? An attempt to establish compelling authority (Hannah Arendt)? An "attack on the existing educational apparatus of Greece" (Eric Havelock)?[2] An "effort to refashion Athenian political language" (Danielle Allen)?[3] This chapter introduces responses to *The Republic* which range from rejection to recruitment.

Bearing in mind the concepts of *polis* and *logos*, I look first at what seems so egregious to very many modern readers, the apparently authoritarian politics and 'tyranny of reason' in the dialogue. Then I turn to the way thinkers and writers have rejected or recruited Plato and the ideas about literature which the dialogue most clearly embodies and so have taken up Socrates's invitation to defend poetry.

Political responses to *The Republic*: blueprints and literary questions

The Austrian philosopher Karl Popper (1902–1994) attacked *The Republic* as a blueprint for totalitarianism, akin to George Orwell's *1984* and connected, in complex ways, to the real experiences of Nazi Germany and the USSR under Stalin. Several aspects stand out: the strict division of classes (the rulers and their guardians divided from the 'human cattle'; the identification of the state with the interests of the rulers; the regulations for breeding and education; the total command of the military; the supervision of the population and the censorship and propaganda that moulds them; even the self-sufficiency of the state ("for otherwise the rulers would either be dependent on traders or become traders

DOI: 10.4324/9781003097914-6

themselves").[4] The stability and harmony of the state are above all else in *The Republic*, and this too, writes Popper is totalitarian. He also suggests that there were arguments about freeing enslaved people in ancient Greece but Plato simply ignores them. Popper argues that Plato's approach is an "aestheticism". "Plato was an artist" he writes, and aestheticism is

> the desire to build a world which is not only a little better and more rational than ours, but which is free from all its ugliness: not a crazy quilt, an old garment badly patched, but an entirely new gown, a really beautiful new world.

For him, this attitude isn't wrong ("most of us suffer a little from such dreams of perfection") but Popper argues that it needs to be linked with reason, responsibility and a "humanitarian urge to help".[5] It also implies that *The Republic* is a vision or a blueprint that required earthly, utopian perfecting.

Hannah Arendt took a similar but more detailed and granular view, arguing that *The Republic* was the first "blueprint for the making of political bodies" and "has remained the inspiration of all later Utopias".[6] For Arendt, at the core of Plato's thought is the experience of the eternal, an act of solitary contemplation of the good, the true and the beautiful that is beyond language: the ultimate 'life of the mind' and the highest we mortals can achieve. This is what the philosopher seeks and how he or she wants to live. As a consequence, for the Platonic philosopher, the *polis*, Arendt suggests (and recalling Socrates's death), "has no aim other than to make possible the philosopher's way of life".[7] Plato (who, she notes, "thought craftsmen not even worthy of full-fledged citizenship") proposed "handling political matters and ruling political bodies in the mode of fabrication", that is, as a craftsman, building a model of a state (and shaping the humans who populate it) from a blueprint.[8] To do this, it is necessary to establish authority, and this is the aim of *The Republic*.

Plato, she argues, realised after Socrates's death that persuasion was not enough to guide people without coercion: the most effective coercion is the self-evident truths arrived at through reason.[9] But the trouble with "coercion by reason" is that only a few people can reason enough: only a few can escape the cave, for the others there is only the myth of Er, promising posthumous rewards for good behaviour. Plato turns to many models of authority to find a legitimate and powerful principle of rational coercion: helmsmen/passengers; doctor/patient; master/enslaved; head of household/the others in the domestic sphere; shepherds/sheep. In some of these, "expert knowledge commands confidence", while in others, the ruler and ruled "belong to two different categories of being, one of which is already by implication subject to the other".

Arendt suggests that Plato found the "compelling power" of reason in the forms. The philosopher escaped the cave to contemplate the "true essence of being". But on the philosopher's return to the cave, the forms, once a vision of the good beyond being, became a yardstick, a measure of accuracy. The forms "can be used as measures of human behaviour because they transcend the sphere of human affairs in the same way a yardstick transcends, is outside and beyond, all the things whose length it can measure". Back in the cave, frightened for his life, the philosopher "uses them as instruments of domination". Think of the argument Socrates makes that poetry is two steps from truth. Once you have accepted the idea of the forms in the first place, the argument that art is an imitation of an imitation is clear and logically compelling. (So much so, in fact, that it might almost make you feel a bit suspicious, as if Plato invented the idea of the forms, and his whole metaphysics, in order to explain why the way poets think is confused and destructive, and his way of thinking is better.) For Plato, the forms are like a carpenter's 'blueprint': the built bed is judged by how well it corresponds to the blueprint. In the same way, the forms become "standards for political and moral behaviour and judgement". There are experts in bed-building so there must be experts in political and moral behaviour. Nehamas writes that the

> fundamental assumption on which Plato's system depends is an image of living a life as practicing a craft, as a process that proceeds by defini-tive rules and whose product depends on how well its rules are applied. To put the point bluntly, just as we are willing to take the advice of shoemakers on the most appropriate shoes, so, he believes, we should be willing to take the advice of philosophers on what life is best for us … Today we believe in the value of freedom, even if it results in the gravest of errors. He was unwilling to sacrifice happiness, even if it mean renouncing autonomy. The issue is still open.[10]

Arendt also notes the unavoidable violence inherent in this building or craft analogy. Just as "we must kill a tree in order to have lumber", just as making an omelette involves breaking eggs, so this fundamental assumption sees people as a material to be shaped for their own sake.[11] For Arendt the forms stem from philosophical contemplation, 'seeing' with the mind. This does not 'carry over' in to the world of politics, which is about a plurality of people deliberating together and acting. Politics is about hearing, speaking and acting together, and not 'seeing'.

In contrast to Popper and Arendt, Leo Strauss (1899–1973) offers an ironic reading of *The Republic*. Strauss is a controversial figure: he is taken to be behind a neo-conservative ideology in the USA, for example.[12] He also believed that writers, especially persecuted writers, hid their true meaning in texts for only a few to find. This led him to focus on the literary form, the 'literary questions' of Plato's dialogues. However, you do not have to believe in hidden meanings or empowering elites to agree that "there is a connection between the literary question and the philosophic question".[13] Strauss argues that the 'literary question'

> is concerned with a kind of communication. Communication may be a means for living together; in its highest form, communication *is* living together. The study of the literary question is therefore an important part of the study of society. Furthermore, the quest for truth is necessarily, if not in every respect, a common quest, a quest taking place through communication. The study of the literary question is therefore an important part of the study of what philosophy is. The literary question properly understood is the question of the relation between society and philosophy.[14]

Strauss's Plato is ironic, keen to teach us our limitations, and the dialogue "one big question mark".[15] He concludes by arguing that *The Republic* is not a blueprint but is about "the nature of political things – the nature of the city". It is "the broadest and deepest analysis of political idealism" because it explores how society becomes skewed when one virtue, justice, is taken to be the most important.[16] If pure justice is our highest ambition as humans, the *polis*, Strauss argues, does not deliver it. Instead, *The Republic* shows us the limits of the city, the limits of what the *polis*, and so politics, can do.

Influenced by Strauss, Stanley Rosen's account nuances and develops this view when he argues that the text is not ironic but sincere in its "account of the procedures and institutions necessary for a just city". But, he goes on,

> each theoretically correct step toward justice is a practical step toward injustice. The unification of theory and practice, or wisdom, is impossible. But this impossibility does not suffice to prevent philosophers from attempting to accomplish it, because that is the goal of philosophy ... *The Republic* is a serious warning against the inner dialectic of philosophical rule. The cure for our illness is so strong that we run the risk of dying from its side effects. On the other hand, if we do not take our medicine, the chance of recovery is nil. The political philosopher has the duty of determining the right dosage.[17]

For Rosen, *The Republic* is not ironic but shows the difference between philosophy and politics. Uniting them is impossible but balancing them is the task of the political philosopher. (We could note, however, that if the relation between society and philosophy, between culture and ideas is the 'literary question', this same balancing duty might also be the job of *literary* writers as well as political philosophers.)

A more general awareness of the dramatic nature of the dialogues and the types of reading this demands, as well as Strauss's kind of approach, has fostered a range of more literary readings of *The Republic*, in contrast to the more strictly analytical logical interpretations. These emphasise, for example, the difference between Plato as author, Socrates as narrator and Socrates as a character, or they just stress that how the dialogues are written make us think differently about what they seem to say. Some of these more literary readings have been in counterpoint to the dominant modern ways of seeing *The Republic* as totalitarian.[18]

I mentioned Jill Frank's idea of 'disidentification' in the previous chapter. She argues that the gap between the self-conscious writing and the more simplistic account of imitation and identification creates a kind of self-reflection about *mimesis* itself which she calls 'mimetic knowledge'. This does not work through identification. Self-reflexive fiction or meta-art rejects identification (as when a novel reminds you that you are reading a novel). For Frank, reading *The Republic* is the same kind of process and this makes us think anew about the world, the text and ourselves. She writes that "knowing that a mimetic representation is all and only a 'look', and knowing too, that the partial and perspectival truth given by a look is not the same as the whole truth" means that mimetic knowledge is a kind of reflection on the gap between the text and the truth, and she finds in that gap possibilities for "becoming good".[19]

Another example of these newer readings is the work of Arlene Saxonhouse. In her 2009 article 'The Socratic Narrative', she too argues that Plato's highly self-aware literary style itself is meaningful and that the literary framing and dramatic elements of *The Republic* add significantly to the content. To whom, for example, is Socrates telling *The Republic*? She jokes, with a serious intent, might it be Socrates's wife Xanthippe? "Is *The Republic* the long answer to his wife's question: 'Where were you last night?' What would it do to our reading of the dialogue if we read it as a sheepish excuse for a long night of carousing?"[20] Her point is that there's a difference between Socrates speaking *within* the dialogue and Socrates *narrating* the overall dialogue. When it comes to the poetry that he intends to ban, Socrates offers very simple interpretations (bad poems about bad people driven by their bad desires to do bad things: this is bad) with no sense of subtext or multiplicity of meaning, characteristics that are obvious in the textually self-aware and complex dialogue itself being told. The poems are given only one meaning, just as people in the ideal city are limited to only one role. More, in banning the imitations of different voices, Socrates is *using* different voices: he's playing all the characters in the story he's telling, choosing voices while rejecting the possibility of choice in the text. Every audience member can hear the disjunction between *what* Socrates is saying and *how* he is saying it. Because of this, she argues, Plato is creating a "democratic Socrates playing a multitude of parts to present the most undemocratic regime imaginable, where no one performs multiple roles and choice (freedom) is excised from the regime".[21] In fact, in the Athenian democracy, each property-owning man had to play several roles: say, pastry chef or sailor (or philosopher) for employment, soldier in time of war, and jury, judge, voter, citizen in the *polis*, making interpretations and judgements, taking choices. Plato is demonstrating the problems of city with no choice. Seeing Plato's narrator this way gives the dialogues "a seldom acknowledged democratic orientation".[22]

I've looked at a range of relatively recent philosophical and political responses to *The Republic*: each take different lessons from it. The same is true of more literary writers.

Literary responses to *The Republic*: rejection or recruitment

The vision offered in *The Republic* is extraordinarily powerful. Many artists have sought to reject it or to use Plato's Socrates's own arguments against him or, at least, recognising his importance, to recruit him to their side. *The Republic* gives licence to this in the invitation, at the end of **book 10**, for lovers of poetry to defend poetry in prose and show it's pleasurable (which he has admitted it is: *too* pleasurable) and of benefit to individuals and the *polis*: "we'll listen to them graciously" (607d) Socrates says. Aristotle's response is the subject of the second half of this book but over the last two millennia, many others have taken up this invitation.

We might wonder if there is any point. One response to *The Republic* is just to agree with it. In his intentionally provocative *The Hatred of Literature*, William Marx applauds Plato's victory and argues that Socrates won. We are living in "the very world Plato hoped for".[23] As we've seen, in classical Athens, poetry had moral and political authority and was central to education. This was what Plato wanted to destroy, and eventually, he did. Literature has lost its significant role and, in a kind of "internal exile", is now reduced to irrelevance, claims Marx.[24] Science, one strand of human knowledge developed from Platonic dialectic, now has that authority and power. As Wittgenstein writes in *Culture and Value*, people "nowadays think, scientists exist to instruct them, poets, musicians, etc. to entertain them. That the latter have something to teach them: that never occurs to them".[25] Much of this book, and especially the discussion of Aristotle, aims to show how there is much to learn from literature, whether we realise it or not.

'The greatest enemy of art'

It is this sense of 'Socrates's victory' that led Friedrich Nietzsche to call Plato "the greatest enemy of art Europe has yet produced" and "the sincerest 'advocate of the beyond', the great slanderer of life".[26] Trained as a classical philologist, Nietzsche was a revolutionary figure for European philosophy, art and culture, in part because of his attack on (and inversion of) the ideas of *The Republic*. Although he engaged with antiquity throughout his life, I'm only going to focus on his first book, *The Birth of Tragedy* (1872), where Nietzsche makes this case most dramatically.[27] *The Birth of Tragedy* is controversial: a celebrated review accused it of wilful ignorance, offering insights gained from intuition rather than scholarship, written like a cross between a sermon and a sensationalist newspaper. This is an accurate assessment (and the crushing review, along with his poor health, led Nietzsche to give up his university post).[28] In the later 1886 edition of *The Birth of Tragedy*, Nietzsche added 'An Attempt at Self-Criticism'. This basically just doubled down on the most controversial elements because, actually, Nietzsche at heart *agreed* with the criticism: his aim was to look at classical scholarship "through the prism of the artist, but also to look at art through the prism of life".[29] Philologists and academics didn't like the book but artists loved it.

In *The Birth of Tragedy*, Nietzsche offers a highly idiosyncratic history of Greek drama and, by extension, a way of understanding all art. Tragedy is a mixture of two forces, which Nietzsche names after Greek gods, each divine figure summing up something too profound and multifaceted to explain in plain prose. One force is Apollo, the god of dreams, of prophecy, vision, the self, light (he is called 'the luminous one'): he represents order, consciousness, restraint. The other is Dionysius, who stands for music, intoxication, loss of self, wildness, drunkenness, sexual desire and enchantment, the unconscious, mysticism. Nietzsche also believed that the classical Greeks were especially sensitive to the painfulness of existence. He tells an illustrative myth: King Midas hunted Silenus, a companion of Dionysius.

> When Silenus has finally fallen into his hands, the King asks what is the best and most excellent thing for human beings. Stiff and unmoving, the daemon remains silent, until, forced by the King to speak, he finally breaks out in shrill laughter and says: 'Wretched ephemeral race, children of chance and tribulation, why do you force me to tell you the very thing which it would most profitable for you *not* to hear? The very best thing is utterly beyond your reach, not to have been born, not to *be*, to *be* nothing. However the second best thing for you is: to die soon'.
>
> (23)

This awe-ful story also underlies a moving chorus in Sophocles's play *Oedipus at Colonus*. The coming together of the Apollonian and the Dionysian in tragedy allowed the classical Greeks to transform their awareness of suffering into art, into the great works of tragedy, the same way "roses burst forth from a thicket of thorns" (23). For Nietzsche, these works were Dionysian (the Apollonian starts to fade from the argument), instinctive, reaching beyond consciousness to perform a mythic act that could not be explained: the music, the scenes and images together "reveal a deeper wisdom than the poet himself can put into words and concepts" (80). In the great tragedies, we realise that "everything that comes into being must be prepared for painful destruction; we are forced to gaze into the terrors of individual existence" (79) and we feel "the struggle, the agony, the destruction of appearances"; yet at the same time "we become one with the immeasurable, primordial delight in existence and receive an intimation, in

Dionysian ecstasy, that this delight is indestructible and eternal" (81). (We've come a *very* long way from philology.)

Nietzsche declares, however, that the playwright Euripides killed tragedy by bringing two spectators onto the stage, metaphorically speaking. The first was the audience to whom Euripides pandered, but this murderer was in league with another much more powerful enemy of tragedy: Socrates, absolutely the villain of *The Birth of Tragedy*.

Nietzsche's Socrates is a monster. Socrates's *daimon* was his instinct, which self-reflectively warned him before he did anything immoral. For Nietzsche this meant Socrates was, basically, the wrong way round as a human being. For most people, wrote Nietzsche, "instinct is precisely the creative-affirmative force" and "consciousness makes critical and warning gestures" (66). But Socrates's instinct, not his consciousness, is critical, self-reflective, reasoning, "non-mystic" (67) making him an "opponent of Dionysus" (64). Tragedy before Euripides was mystical and beyond understanding but when Socrates the monster turned his "one great Cyclopean eye" (67) to it, he saw "something quite unreasonable, with causes that apparently lacked effects and effects that lacked causes, while the whole was so varied and multifarious that it was bound to be repugnant to a reflective disposition, but also dangerous tinder for sensitive and easily aroused souls!" (68). What Socrates did not understand, he did not value. Tragedy was incomprehensible and dangerous.

Euripides created a kind of 'aesthetic Socratism'. "'Everything must be conscious in order to be beautiful', is a parallel to Socrates assertion that, 'Everything must be conscious in order to be good'" (64). The consequence of this was that Socrates's thought, his dialectic, drove music, and so incomprehensible mystery, out of tragedy and so destroyed its essence. The idea that the tragic can and should be understood curtailed art and literature and led to a kind of empty 'cheerfulness': if the mystery of literature can be 'solved', then the meaning of life, too, is a problem that can simply be solved. Socrates's view that life was to be lived by reason murdered, for Nietzsche, the mystic, tragic view of life. In the same way, Nietzsche writes, Plato's dialogues consumed the previous forms of poetry "mixing all available styles and forms together" (69) as "narrative, lyric and dramas, between prose and poetry" (69). The dialogues are like "the boat on which the older forms of poetry, together with all her children, sought refuge after their shipwreck, crowded together in a narrow space, anxiously submissive to the one helmsman, Socrates" (69). This was, he says, the "model of the novel" (69) in which poetry serves the work of philosophy. For Nietzsche, this is how Plato defeated art. As a response, artists must reject Socrates and Plato. Nietzsche is touching one of the most fundamental questions about art. His proposition is stark: if art is comprehensible, it can be reduced to simplistic equations or principles: if it is not, art opens to a different, mysterious and unsettling engagement with life.

Nietzsche's rejection perhaps risks just inverting *The Republic* and so repeating its form in that rejection. In the British literary tradition, there are three famous Platonic defences against Socrates's argument, made by creative writers who take a different, more conciliatory, approach.

Our patron: Plato as a poetic teacher of virtue

The Elizabethan courtier and soldier Sir Philip Sidney (1554–1586) was also a poet and the author of a funny, clever, urbane defence of "poor poetry, which from almost the highest estimation of learning is fallen to be the laughing-stock of children".[30] His *Defence of Poesy* (written in 1582, published posthumously 1595) is wide-ranging and was influenced by his reading of Aristotle's *Poetics* as well as Plato. Here I'm going to focus only on how it recruits Plato against Plato.[31]

First, Sidney claims Plato is already a poet. While the "body" of Plato's work, its "inside and strength were philosophy", its "skin, as it were, and beauty depended most of poetry" (5). Plato "feigneth many honest burgesses of Athens to speak", poetically describes "the circumstances of their meetings, as the well-ordering of a banquet, the delicacy of a walk, with interlacing mere tales, as Gyges' Ring and others, which who knoweth not to be flowers of poetry did never walk into Apollo's garden" (5). Plato is the "most worthy of reverence" of all philosophers because he "is the most poetical" although, Sidney writes, because of his objections to poetry he has defiled "the fountain out of which his flowing streams have proceeded" (38).

Second, Sidney argues that poets are the best for teaching virtue. The earliest philosophers, legislators and prophets were poets because only poets go beyond "the circle of a question" (8) to discover something more. Using Plato's language, he means that while other professions imitate the forms (to make saddles, for example), poets deliver the ideas as they "had imagined them" (9), with direct access to them. This is why poetry is the best "to teach and delight" (10) in religion, philosophy and virtue, as well as for the "purifying of wit … enlargement of memory, enabling of judgment and enlarging of conceit" (understanding) (12). Moral philosophers ("coming towards me with a sullen gravity" 13) teach virtue in such a complicated way that it only helps those who already understand what they mean. More, once they have "picked" knowledge "out of the sweet mysteries of poetry", they "spurn at their guides" and are "like ungrateful prentices" who not only set up their own business but "discredit their masters" (38–9), seasoned with a envy and contempt because they do not delight audiences as poets can. Similarly, historians, addled with "mouse-eaten records" (14), can only teach examples of how to behave. By contrast, the poet offers "the food for the tenderest stomachs; the poet is indeed the right popular philosopher" (18) both personal and political: the "pretty allegories" of Æsop's fables use the "tales of beasts" and "make many, more beastly than beasts, begin to hear the sound of virtue from those dumb speakers" (18); Menenius Agrippa calmed the rioting people of Rome not through a philosophical argument about the nature of the state but through the fable of the body that mutinied against itself.

Third, Sidney specifically addresses the attacks on poets from *The Republic*: that there are more "fruitful knowledges"; that poetry is "the mother of lies", and so "the nurse of abuse, infecting us with many pestilent desires, with a siren's sweetness drawing the mind to the serpent's tail of sinful fancies" and that Plato banished poets "out of his Commonwealth" (33). His responses are to each in turn. First, as he has already said, the best learning leads to virtue, "and that none can both teach and move thereto so much as poetry" (33): poetry educates best using wonder and delight. Second, poets are not liars: while intellectuals like astronomers and geometricians, or practical people like doctors affirm things to be true, the poet "nothing affirms, and therefore never lieth" (34). "What child is there that, coming to a play, and seeing 'Thebes' written in great letters upon an old door, doth believe that it is Thebes?" (34). Unlike the historian, a poet doesn't use authorities (or archives, we could add today), but only the Muse, and does not tell you what is or is not, but "what should or should not be" (34). To the third accusation, that poetry trains men to "wanton sinfulness and lustful love" (35), Sidney begins by praising love and noting that "my masters the philosophers spent a good deal of their lamp-oil in setting forth the excellency of it" (35), thinking of *The Symposium*. Why should the abuse of love make "the right use odious?" (35). Of course, he admits, poetry can abuse, but with "a sword thou mayest kill thy father, and with a sword thou may defend thy prince and country" (36). More, and bearing in mind Sidney was courier and soldier, poetry can also inspire military courage: "Alexander left his schoolmaster, living Aristotle, behind him, but took dead Homer with him" (37) because he sought to imitate Achilles. Finally he addresses the banishment: in a concise summary of *The Republic* **books 2** and **3**, Sidney argues that Plato did not want "the youth depraved" with "wrong opinions of the gods" (38). But, he says, the poets did not invent but merely reported these ideas. In fact, they piously and "superstitiously observed" their pagan gods unlike the philosophers who, Sidney asserts, "brought in atheism" (39). What Plato wanted to ban was "wrong opinions of the Deity" (40). But for Sidney, Christianity has resolved this problem, bringing poets and philosophers into alignment. Plato banishes "the abuse, not the thing" (40). Indeed, in *Ion*, Sidney points out, Plato gives "high and rightly divine commendation unto poetry" (40).

So, Sidney shows that Plato is a poet, that poetry is the best teacher of virtue because it is delightful, that poetry inspires, does not lie (because it does not claim to be factually true but morally true) and that its abuse is not an argument is against its use. He declares that Plato "shall be our patron and not our adversary" (40).

Unacknowledged legislator: Plato as a poetic visionary

Percy Bysshe Shelley (1792–1822) was the British Romantic poet most influenced by Plato. Unpublished in his lifetime but extremely influential, Shelley wrote *A Defence of Poetry* (1840) in 1821 to rebut to an article by Thomas Love Peacock called *The Four Ages of Poetry* (1820), which implied that science had made poetry outdated. Shelley Platonically defends poetry by redefining it so capaciously as to subsume philosophy and so makes Plato a poet in a 'universal' sense.

For Shelley, our minds have two faculties, reason and imagination.[32] Poetry, obviously, comes from the imagination for Shelley, and reversing Socrates, he argues imagination is the most important because, like the Aeolian harp (an instrument played by the movement of wind over its strings), our imaginations respond to the world and attune ourselves to it. To explain, Shelley tells an impressionistic history of humanity. Early humans imitated nature. Those who were especially sensitive to beauty were "poets, in the most universal sense of the word" (653). At this stage in human history, "language itself is poetry; and to be a poet is to apprehend the true and the beautiful, in a word the good" (654): like a philosopher who has left the cave, a poet "participates in the eternal, the infinite, and the one" (654). The language of these early poets was "vitally metaphorical" (653) because it established new and living relationships between things (as we'll see with Aristotle, this is what metaphors do: to say 'my love is like a storm' is to find a hidden similarity between love and storms). These metaphors, in turn, shaped thought, so, for Shelley, poets are not just artists but "institutors of laws, and the founders of civil society, and the inventors of the arts of life, and the teachers... [of] religion" (654), legislators, prophets. Poetry, inspired by a vision of the true, founded all aspects of society.

Poetry, consequently, is not simply writing in verse, but inspired and alive: Plato, though he wrote in prose, "was essentially a poet—the truth and splendour of his imagery, and the melody of his language, are the most intense that it is possible to conceive" (656). Indeed, for Shelley, all "the authors of revolutions in opinion" (656) are poets and inventors: great poets and great philosophers are the same.

In this fundamental sense, Shelley argues, poetry has a beneficial impact on individuals and on society, even if it is in a "divine and unapprehended manner, beyond and above consciousness" (657); a

> poet is a nightingale, who sits in darkness and sings to cheer its own solitude with sweet sounds; his auditors are as men entranced by the melody of an unseen musician, who feel that they are moved and softened, yet know not whence or why.
>
> (657)

Shelley explains why, with a new and characteristically nineteenth-century idea: the moral importance of sympathy. Shelley is clearly thinking of **books 2** and **3** of *The Republic* when he argues that the "sentiments of the auditors must have been refined and enlarged by a sympathy with such great and lovely impersonations, until from admiring they imitated, and from imitation they identified themselves with the objects of their admiration" (658). The idea of sympathy – roughly, having the same feeling – is how Homer led his readers to become like Achilles. Shelley expands on this. While there may be a philosophical way to 'pick' moral knowledge from poetry, poetry itself "acts in another and diviner manner" (658). Poetry "awakens and enlarges the mind" showing "a thousand unapprehended combinations of thought"; it "lifts the veil from the hidden beauty of the world, and makes familiar objects be as if they were not familiar" (658). Crucially the "great secret of morals is love" and

> an identification of ourselves with the beautiful which exists in thought, action, or person, not our own. A man, to be greatly good, must imagine intensely and comprehensively; he must put himself in the place of another and of many others; the pains and pleasure of his species must become his own. The great instrument of moral good is the imagination.
>
> (658–9)

Poetry makes the unfamiliar familiar and in so doing enlarges sympathy through identification and "strengthens the faculty which is the organ of the moral nature of man, in the same manner as exercise strengthens a limb" (659). This moral idea of sympathy allows Shelley to reverse the idea that poetry feeds our worst aspects: instead it develops our best.

Socrates and Adeimantus, as we've seen, warned that when unregulated poetry and drama get into the body of the *polis*, decay follows. Shelley argues precisely the opposite. When drama and poetry is innovative, society is strong and actually the "corruption which has been imputed to the drama as an effect, begins when the poetry employed in its constitution ends" (661). In a reversal of the closing stages of *The Republic*, he gives examples from classical Athens, ancient Rome and eighteenth-century Britain in which poetry aids the *polis*. He argues that medieval Europe was revived by chivalry, which, in turn, was inspired by poetry.

In his own age, Shelley argues against utilitarianism, the instrumentalist philosophy of 'the greatest good for the greatest number'. Shelley says there are two sorts of useful things "one durable, universal, and permanent; the other transitory and particular" (670) but he inverts the usual ('common sense') order. It is not science that is durable, but poetry, which "creates new materials of knowledge, and power, and pleasure" (673). Science deals with our transitory material needs; it follows "the footsteps of poets" and merely copies "the sketches of their creations into the book of common life" (671). Poetry creates a vision of a world: science just builds the contents (but if this "calculating faculty" (671) is allowed to dominate, it is ruinous to the state).

In the final pages, Shelley offers something like a mystical vision of the poet: poetry "makes immortal all that is best and most beautiful" (675); poetry "redeems from decay the visitations of the divinity in man. Poetry turns all things to loveliness" (675). As with the rest of his *Defence*, Shelley has taken the view held by Plato of a philosopher (Socrates as "the best, and also the wisest and the most upright" *Phaedo* 118a) and applied it to the poet, "the happiest, the best, the wisest, and the most illustrious of men" (676). In addition, as Jennifer

Wallace writes the "assertion of the exalted status of the poet was needed to counter Peacock's depressing arguments about the anachronism of poetry in the climate of scientific progress".[33] Finally and famously, Shelley writes that poets

> measure the circumference and sound the depths of human nature with a comprehensive and all-penetrating spirit, and they are themselves perhaps the most sincerely astonished at its manifestations; for it is less their spirit than the spirit of the age. Poets are the hierophants of an unapprehended inspiration; the mirrors of the gigantic shadows which futurity casts upon the present; the words which express what they understand not; the trumpets which sing to battle, and feel not what they inspire; the influence which is moved not, but moves. Poets are the unacknowledged legislators of the world.
>
> (678)

Shelley argues that the poet is the most profound kind of visionary. A poet, and a philosopher for Shelley is a kind of poet, sees the way the universe is, the beautiful, the true and the good, and so shapes society in all ages and teaches morality, not by rules but through expanding and strengthening sympathy, the shared human feeling that is, for Shelley (but not Plato), the core of ethics. Plato's poetic language reveals that he is a poet in this deeper sense. But note: Shelley has accepted something like the forms as a vision of reality and has accepted, too, that the poet does not understand them but is inspired by them. In a clear reference to the dialogue *Ion*, he asserts that poetry is "divine", not "like reasoning": a "man cannot say — I will compose poetry. The greatest poet even cannot say it; for the mind in creation is as a fading coal, which some invisible influence, like an inconstant wind, awakens to transitory brightness" (673). Poetry is inspiration not comprehension, and the legislators of the world are unacknowledged, in a sense, by their own selves (678). This is very different from the view that through the philosophical dialectic, we can come to comprehend and share the true. Perhaps influenced most by Socrates's conversation with poets, *The Symposium*, Shelley has produced a mystical poetic version of *The Republic*.

Fighting under Plato's banner: Plato as a spiritual guide

Iris Murdoch was a successful novelist, winning the Booker Prize for *The Sea, the Sea* (1978) as well one of an influential quartet of British philosophers, with Elizabeth Anscombe, Philippa Foot and Mary Midgley. Of these, she was the most explicitly Platonic and wrote that Plato was "the philosopher under whose banner I am fighting".[34] Like Shelley, Murdoch has a more mystical or spiritual view of Plato, but one that focuses more on the individual and less on sympathy, and is centred on love. For her, goodness, truth and beauty are reality.[35]

Murdoch saw *The Republic* as a "spiritual guidebook" and argued that Plato took life to be a "spiritual pilgrimage inspired by the disturbing magnetism of truth ... guided by ideas of perfection which are objects of love".[36] *Eros*, she writes, "is the continuous operation of spiritual energy, desire, intellect, love" (496) which joins us to the world, to particular people and things on which we focus our attention.[37] Plato's ethical psychology (which she sees echoed in Freud) shows how we are riven with conflicting desires between material needs, passions and our sense of reality: our egos and "obsession, prejudice, envy, anxiety, ignorance, greed, neurosis and so on and so on veil reality" (426). The defeat of these illusions "requires moral effort" (426). Beauty, she notes in Plato, is the "only spiritual thing we love by instinct" (370) and can be the "starting point for the good life" (372). Thinking of Diotima's ladder, she argues that the erotic "attractiveness of beauty turns out to be the moral pull of reality" (449).

Murdoch understands Plato's distrust of art: politically, because of its power as "persuasion or propaganda ... irrational emotion ... attractive lies ... or ... the telling of inconvenient or subversive truths" (245); because art is a trivial distraction from rational thought; because art can be a fantasy that appeals to the lowest part of us, an "emotional substitute for reality" (246). Her Plato is a puritan who rejects the joys of the world, but is also passionately, intensely aware and afraid of the power of art. Like all puritans, for example, he "hates the theatre" for its "vulgarity" and "coarse buffoonery, histrionic emotion, slanderous ridicule" (397), but these attitudes are rooted in his profoundly religious sensibility. Art "disguises and trivialises" the spiritual (443); it is noisy when thought and contemplation are quiet; it creates images which are mistaken for reality. Plato is suspicious of writing because a book cannot talk back, always says the same thing: it is not 'living thought'. Moreover, what is "really important in philosophy cannot be put into written words and scarcely indeed into words. (Language itself may be a barrier)" (405). Like sophists, writers twist or falsify knowledge to win over their audiences.

However, the profound link between the good, the true, the beautiful and the erotic means that Murdoch can make a 'Platonic' defence of art. Art can help us find our way to the good and the real because "good art is truthful" (455): "the subject of every good play and novel" (456) is the escape from illusion to real just as life is a "pilgrimage from appearance to reality" (387). Of course, clichéd art "is self-consoling fantasy" (370) but great works of art, for both their creators and their astute critics disclose the real. Despite its "trickery and magic" (455) art is

> designed to communicate and reveal. In the shock of joy in response to good art, an essential ingredient is the sense of revelation of reality, of the really real ... the world as we were never able so clearly to see it before.
>
> (454)

As in Shelley, art unveils, makes the familiar unfamiliar.

For Murdoch, art shows us not generalities but particular people and things. In an important early essay from 1961, 'Against Dryness', she writes that "literature must always represent a battle between real people and images" (295), that is between particularities and fantasies (and, because this essay is in part a response to the Eichmann trial, she means communal mythic fantasies like Nazism). Art may not be able to present the good but in its attention to particularity, it is evil's opposite, a work of moral reflection. And in the closing pages of her last philosophical work, in a beautiful, powerful passage (which again consciously parallels the steps of Diotima's ladder) she writes that the particular

> teaches us love, we understand it, we *see* it, as Plato's carpenter sees the table, or Cézanne sees Mont Ste Victoire or the girl in the bed-sitter sees her potted plant or her cat. So, the carpenter is dealing with wood, tools, measurement, Cézanne is looking at the mountain he knows so well and creating a work of art and saying to himself that he cannot paint what he sees, the girl is comforted by her plant, which is so beautiful and glossy and which she cares for and protects, and also by her cat, whom she also tends, who is a free being, a friend, a privilege to live with, they look into each other's eyes. And the physicist too, whose thoughts we do not understand, loves the beauty of his formulation. Human beings love each other, in sex, in friendship, and love and cherish other beings, humans, animals, plants, stones.

Imagination and art are in all this, and play a major role in the quest for and promotion of happiness.[38]

Art offers a more complex, particular and messy vision of the real world than philosophy with its universal and clear examples. This is why, Murdoch argues, art and literature is "the most educational thing we have, far more so than its rivals, philosophy and theology and science" (461). Through literature you learn to sort out "what is good, what is pure, what is profoundly and justly imagined from what is trivial and shallow or in some way fake, self-indulgent, pretentious, sentimental, meretriciously obscure, and so on" (450 check). Art requires "a special discerning exercise of intelligence in relation to the real" (455), open to all (not just those who know geometry). Murdoch writes that the "careful responsible skilful use of words is our highest instrument of thought and one of our highest modes of being" (462).

Murdoch's Plato is a sort of therapist, helping us strip away our self-conceit and seeing ourselves and reality as we, and it, really are. We might have questions: for example, are we learning to judge art by reality's standards or reality by art's standards? Great literature often concerns major life events: when these do befall us, when we experience, say, grief, communal fear or great love, who can say if the art has not 'pre-shaped' the reality for us?

Each of these canonical defences of poetry argues that Plato is a poet, both in his use of language and in the sense of being a visionary. Each stresses the power of inspiration and divine or spiritual knowledge in poetry. In each, literature offers a different kind of knowledge to science: the poet nothing affirms, and therefore never lies; poetry offers a deeper moral or spiritual vision of how and who we are. Literature is the best form of education: because it is the most delightful, because it extends sympathy, because it focuses on the particular and forces us to engage with the real, the good and the true. But we can also trace a historical change. Sidney is not concerned about the politics of *The Republic* (except in regard to religion), Shelley finds little to worry about and simply adopts Socrates's vision, whereas Murdoch makes a point of highlighting the political. Similarly, their views of the nature of the good shift. For Sidney, the teaching of the good is for all; for Shelley it is interpersonal, the enlargement of sympathy; for Murdoch the good is more personal, our own pilgrimage through life.

Conclusion

This chapter has looked at a range of responses to *The Republic*, first with the political and then with the literary in mind. Some thinkers have simply rejected the arguments of the dialogue, while others have worked *through* them. In both of these kinds of responses, the political, the ethical and the literary are interwoven. The next chapters explore the ideas of rejection or recruitment, and the weave of the literary and the political, *logos* and *polis*, by turning to dialogues that are (or should be) important for our understanding of literature.

Notes

1 This analogy may or may not work: see for one important discussion, 'The Analogy of City and Soul in Plato's *Republic*' in Bernard Williams, *The Sense of the Past* (Princeton: Princeton University Press, 2006).
2 Eric A. Havelock, *Preface to Plato* (Cambridge: Harvard University Press, 1963), p. 13.
3 Danielle S. Allen, *Why Plato Wrote* (Oxford: Wiley-Blackwell, 2013), p. 19.
4 Karl Popper, *The Open Society and Its Enemies* (London: Routledge, 2011), pp. 83–84.
5 Popper, *The Open Society*, p. 154.
6 Hannah Arendt, *The Human Condition* (Chicago: University of Chicago Press, 1998), p. 227.
7 Arendt, *The Human Condition*, p. 14.
8 Arendt, *The Human Condition*, p. 230.
9 Hannah Arendt, *Between Past and Future: Eight Exercises in Political Thought* (London: Penguin, 2006), pp. 108–15; all citations from these pages.
10 Alexander Nehamas, *Virtues of Authenticity* (Princeton: Princeton University Press, 1999), p. 327.
11 Hannah Arendt, 'The Eggs Speak Up' in *Essays in Understanding* (New York: Schocken Books, 1994), pp. 270–84.
12 See, for a defence, Catherine Zuckert and Michael Zuchert, *The Truth about Leo Strauss: Political Philosophy and American Democracy* (Chicago: University of Chicago Press, 2006).
13 Leo Strauss, *The City and Man* (Chicago: University of Chicago Press, 1964), p. 52.

14 Strauss, *The City and Man*, p. 52.
15 Strauss, *The City and Man*, p. 55.
16 Strauss, *The City and Man*, p. 127.
17 Stanley Rosen, *Plato's Republic: A Study* (New Haven: Yale University Press, 2005), p. 355.
18 Liam Klein and Daniel Schillinger's very clear review essay surveys this field, 'Entangling Plato: A Guide through the *Political Theory* Archive', *Political Theory* (2021), pp. 1–15 https://doi.org/10.1177/0090591721998073. This approach underlies, for example, Rebecca Lemoine's *Plato's Caves: The Liberating Sting of Cultural Diversity* (Oxford: Oxford University Press, 2020), which reads Plato as supporting forms of cultural diversity.
19 Jill Frank, *Poetic Justice: Rereading Plato's Republic* (Chicago: Chicago University Press, 2018), p. 79.
20 Arlene Saxonhouse, 'The Socratic Narrative: A Democratic Reading of Plato's Dialogues', *Political Theory* 37:6 (2009), pp. 728–53, p. 731.
21 Saxonhouse, 'The Socratic Narrative', p. 745.
22 Saxonhouse, 'The Socratic Narrative', p. 730.
23 William Marx, *The Hatred of Literature*, trans. Nicholas Elliott (Cambridge: Harvard University Press, 2018), p. 42.
24 Marx, *The Hatred of Literature*, p. 43.
25 Ludwig Wittgenstein, *Culture and Value*, ed. G. H. von Wright, trans. Peter Winch (Oxford: Blackwell, 1998), p. 42e.
26 Friedrich Nietzsche, *On the Genealogy of Morals*, trans. Carol Diethe (Cambridge: Cambridge University Press, 1989), p. 116.
27 For a wider account, see Michael Silk, 'Nietzsche's Socrateases' in *Socrates in the Nineteenth and Twentieth Centuries*, ed. M. B. Trapp (London: Routledge, 2016), pp. 37–57.
28 The reviewer was Ulrich von Wilamowitz-Moellendorff, then a young scholar who became one of the great German philologists. See James Turner, *Philology: The Forgotten Origins of the Modern Humanities* (Princeton: Princeton University Press), chapter 11.
29 Friedrich Nietzsche, *The Birth of Tragedy and Other Writings*, ed. Raymond Geuss and Ronald Speirs, trans. Ronald Speirs (Cambridge: Cambridge University Press, 1999), p. 5. Further references in the text.
30 Philip Sidney, *Sidney's 'The Defence of Poesy' and Selected Renaissance Literary Criticism*, ed. Gavin Alexander (London: Penguin, 2004), p. 4; further references in the text.
31 For Sidney's reading of Aristotle, see Micha Lazarus, 'Sidney's Greek Poetics', *Studies in Philology*, 112:3 (2015), pp. 504–36.
32 Percy Bysshe Shelley, *Selected Poems and Prose*, ed. Jack Donovan and Cian Duffy (London: Penguin, 2016), p. 652; further page numbers in the text.
33 Jennifer Wallace, 'Shelley, Plato and the Political Imagination' in *Platonism and the English Imagination*, eds. Anna Baldwin, Sarah Hutton (Cambridge: Cambridge University Press, 1994), pp. 229–41, p. 234.
34 Iris Murdoch, *Existentialists and Mystics* (London: Penguin, 1997), p. 364.
35 See the final chapter (explicitly) and whole (implicitly) of Sophie Grace Chappell, *Knowing What to Do: Imagination, Virtue and Platonism in Ethics* (Oxford: Oxford University Press, 2014).
36 Iris Murdoch, *Metaphysics as a Guide to Morals* (London: Allen Lane, 1992), p. 388, p. 14.
37 Murdoch, *Existentialists and Mystics*, p. 496.
38 Murdoch, *Metaphysics as a Guide to Morals*, p. 497.

5

LIVING AND DEAD WORDS

Phaedrus

Phaedrus, from which the image of the charioteer in Chapter 2 comes, is one of the most literary of all the dialogues. It has lot to say about speech, language, rhetoric, writing, teaching and about love. The philosopher Martha Nussbaum calls it "philosophical poetry" and sees in it a "change in Plato's position about literature and *eros*.[1] It's also the dialogue in which the idea of 'speech-as-living-thought' comes most to the fore. Here, I offer a summary of the dialogue, bringing out these aspects, then turn to one very influential discussion of the closing section by the French philosopher Jacques Derrida (1930–2004). His famous reading pulls out contradictions in 'speech-as-living-thought' through what has become a landmark of the sort of interpretation called deconstruction. This tells us about Plato, Socrates and Plato's legacy, and concerns what Derrida names *logocentrism*.

Outside the city

Unusually, *Phaedrus* takes place in the countryside outside of Athens, and, in contrast to the night-time dining room of *The Republic* or, as we'll see in the next chapter, the huge and combative crowd of *Protagoras*, the cast is only Socrates and his friend Phaedrus. Socrates, too, is in a different mood: not combative or teaching, but friendly, funny, teasing, a bit flirtatious. Part of the topic of the dialogue is how lovers talk to each other. Perhaps as a result, the dialogue is clearer to read and, at first sight, more straightforward.

Socrates meets up with Phaedrus, who is going for a restorative country walk after a morning spent listening to Lysias, a famous orator, give a speech on seduction. Socrates tags along to hear about it because he's a fan of beautiful speeches. Could Phaedrus repeat the speech from memory, does he know it by heart? He'll try, Phaedrus replies, but Socrates spots him clumsily hiding a written copy in his cloak (almost, but not quite, is that a scroll in your cloak or are you just pleased to see me?). Laughing together, they find a beautiful spot to sit and read it. Phaedrus gives the speech – a series of disjointed points to convince you, young man, that you should choose to be my lover precisely because *I don't* want to be yours – and Socrates mocks both its form and content. (Other

    DOI: 10.4324/9781003097914-7

readings are possible: Nussbaum argues this same speech asks for a thoughtful love without passionate madness: the Socrates of *The Republic* ought to approve, but that he now mocks it suggests to her that something odd is happening.)[2] Playfully challenged back by Phaedrus, Socrates makes a technically better counter-speech, as if in Phaedrus's voice, warning about love. (Again, Nussbaum finds in this speech Socrates expressing something positive about erotic love, adding it to how we think about reason: her Socrates is changing here.)

But Socrates is not finished. He thinks both these speeches – Lysias's and the one he's given as Phaedrus – are untrue and offensive, and so he gives a third speech about love and how to point one's soul in the right direction. (This includes the story of the charioteer and his two horses from Chapter 2.) The point is to show that love of wisdom is the highest sort of love, and that the young man should "devote himself to love through philosophical discussion" (*Phaedrus* 257b) instead of through sex. Socrates compares this speech to a 'pal-inode', a genre of poetry that retracts the views of a previous poem.

After these three particular speeches, the two men turn to the more abstract question of what makes oratory and writing good or bad. Although the topic appears at first to be about formal rhetoric – carefully constructed speeches used by politicians and in trials – Socrates is clearly thinking about language in general:

> isn't the rhetorical art, taken as a whole, a way of directing the soul by means of speech, not only in the law courts and on other public occasions, but also in private? Isn't it one and the same art whether its subject is great or small, and no more to be held in esteem – if it is followed correctly – when its questions are serious than when they are trivial?
>
> (261b)

Again, for Socrates, speech – *logos* broadly understood – is a way of steering the soul towards the good and the true, and so the same principles should apply to every instance. Arguing without knowledge and virtue, 'just for the sake of it' or 'simply to win', looks questionable if "one single art" (or skill, one *techne* – "if, of course, it is an art", suggests Socrates slyly) "governs all speaking" (261e). All forms of speaking should aim at knowledge and virtue, and since philosophy does this best, philosophical speaking should be the model for all speaking (just as the young man should dedicate himself to love through philosophy). If this were the case, there might after all be something good in rhetoric. This is a much more positive view from the one expressed in *Protagoras* as we'll see in the next chapter, and in other dialogues (*Gorgias*, for example, which is an attack on rhetoric).

In the light of this idea, Socrates and Phaedrus discuss famous teachers of rhetoric. Underlying this discussion is Socrates's recognisable question: how can you teach someone to speak well about something – virtue, the soul – without knowing about it? It would lead to "praising a miserable donkey as if it were a horse" (260c) because "the art of a speaker who doesn't know truth and chases opinions instead is likely to be a ridiculous thing" (262c). With that in mind, they go back to analyse the first speech by Lysias to demonstrate in detail two things: explicitly, that it's a clumsy speech in terms of its skill as well as its argument, and implicitly that Socrates knows in detail all the arts and demands of formal rhetoric. "Every speech" he says, for example, "must be put together like a living creature, with a body of its own; it must be neither without a head nor without legs; and it must have a middle and extremities that are fitting both to one another and to the whole work" (264e): it's a lesson in how to write and speak – like the advice given to students in how to structure essays – as well as a subtle reminder that speech is, must be, alive, which foreshadows the end of the dialogue. By contrast, they find (predictably) the cloth cut by many rhetoric teachers "a little threadbare" (268a): you may know how to make a speech but, unless you know about medicine, your speech about medicine will be foolish. Interestingly, Socrates imagines a foolish rhetoric expert approaching the tragic playwrights Sophocles and Euripides boasting that he could compose tragic passages and so could teach tragedy. The great dramatists would reply, Socrates suggests, that this was the "preliminary of tragedy, but not the art of tragedy itself" (269a), but he does not say of what this art might consist. Overall, to become a really persuasive speaker, like Pericles, you need to know the subject you're talking on and the true nature of your audience: "evidently" says Phaedrus "rather a major undertaking" (272b). But, Socrates points out, it's taken for granted that rhetoric doesn't need to care about the truth but only needs to sound convincing and he denounces this in an imagined speech to Tisias, one of the rhetoric teachers they have discussed.

Nussbaum's view is that this dialogue represents a change of position for Plato, a "new understanding of philosophy that reinterprets the distinction between philosophy and poetry".[3] Philosophy can be like poetry. Both are inspired by the divine and can be inspiring, too, using "mythic narrative and metaphor in the centre of teaching".[4] So there can be, then, philosophical poetry, and for her, the dialogue argues and performs this, the work of an "inspired philosopher-poet", full of literary devices, wonderful words and phrases, a beautifully balanced play.[5] She's right that their conversation is lovely to read.

Socrates and Phaedrus conclude by discussing writing, traditionally seen as a brief 'rounding off' of the dialogue. But over the last 50 years, academics, especially in literary studies (which focuses on writing, after all), have become very interested in this moment. Socrates tells a myth – Phaedrus knowingly suggests he's just made it up – about the origins of writing. In Egypt, the god Theuth discovered numbers, calculation, geometry, astronomy, dice and board games, and also writing. He took all these to Thamus, king of the gods, to judge if they were useful. Theuth claimed writing would "make the Egyptians wiser and will improve their memory; I have discovered a potion for memory and wisdom" (274e). But the king is outraged: "as you are the father of writing, your affection for it has made you describe its effects as the opposite of what they really are" (275a). Actually, the king of the gods declares, writing will

> introduce forgetfulness into the soul of those who learn it: they will not practice their memory because they will put their trust in writing, which is external and depends on signs that belong to others, instead of trying to remember from the inside, completely on their own. You have not discovered a potion for *remembering*, but for *reminding*.
>
> (275a)

On the surface, writing means you don't have to remember things because a shopping list does your remembering for you. More profoundly, in Chapter 2, I discussed Socrates's idea that knowledge was 'unforgotten': Socrates is suggesting here that writing means you don't have to do this deeper and more challenging 'unforgetting' either. The king goes on: writing will mean that

> you provide your students with the appearance of wisdom, not with its reality. Your invention will enable them to hear many things without being properly taught and they will imagine that they have come to know much while for the most part they will know nothing. And they will be difficult to get along with, since they will merely appear to be wise instead of really being so.
>
> (275a–b)

Writing means that you can learn to sound thoughtful or to say clever things without actually thinking. Everyone knows that you can learn to repeat something from a book or website, cram it for a test, without really learning it: hollow cut-and-paste knowledge. Again, real wisdom comes from unforgetting and so turning towards the good, beautiful and true. We don't have to accept Socrates's idea of 'unforgetting', *anamnesis* and an eternal soul to know there is a difference, in everyday life, between just repeating what you read and properly understanding something. (Although we can note quizzically the god king's concern that writing makes people difficult to get along with: the 'harmony' of the kingdom is the sort of thing that worries autocratic and possibly tyrannical god-kings.)

Socrates goes on to say that writing cannot answer for itself: if you ask a book a question, it just sits there. You can only read the same thing again and again. He means: you can only read the same thing again and again. A person, present, there, can explain but a book cannot engage in dialectic: it is the philosophic conversation that leads to real knowledge.

All this has two consequences. First, writing can roam around everywhere, reaching indiscriminately "those who have no business with it, and it doesn't know to whom it should speak and to whom it should not" (275d–e). Second, and linked, this means that when "it is faulted and attacked unfairly, it always needs its father's support; alone, it can neither defend itself nor come to its own support" (275e). Text by itself can be misread, and its author/father needs to come and correct these mistakes. But the written text also has a "legitimate brother ... by nature better and more capable" (276a), which is, Socrates says, a discourse that is "written down, with knowledge, in the soul of the listener; it can defend itself, and it knows for whom it should speak and for whom it should remain silent" (276a). Phaedrus adds, in case we have missed the point, "[y]ou mean the living, breathing discourses of the man who knows, of which the written one can fairly be called an image" (276a).

This is the 'speech-as-living-thought' idea. But note there are three 'members of the family': the author/father; the silent external, written on material, illegitimate text/son; and the internal written on the soul, legitimate text/son. Writing is misleading and even dangerous, the illusion of wisdom. Dialectic in speech is where we truly learn.

Socrates has a final point. A person who thinks that "a written discourse ... can only be a great amusement" (277e), that nothing "worth serious attention has ever been written in verse or prose" (277e), that writing is at best a reminder for "those who already know" what is "truly written in the soul" about justice, nobility and the good, that has "composed these things with a knowledge of the truth", that can defend their writing when challenged but also argues that their "writing is of little worth", then, says Socrates in Plato's written dialogue, "you must be called by a name not derived from these writings but from those things you are seriously pursuing ... wisdom's lover – a philosopher" (278c–d). By contrast, Socrates adds that "if a man has nothing more valuable that what he has composed or written, spending long hours twisting it around, pasting parts together and taking them apart" (278d), they are a poet or a speech writer or an author of laws (a politician). This dense section has sometimes been thought to be Plato's own reflection on his own authorship, implying that he doesn't take writing too seriously because he is dedicated to the living conversation of the dialectic.

This discussion of writing draws attention again to the 'written-ness' of the dialogues. If speech is a properly shaped living creature and writing a kind of Frankenstein's monster stitched together in the image of life, when we read we are responding to a corpse, or, at best a shuffling imitation of what's really alive, offering not real wisdom and virtue but shambling, shambolic falsehoods.

Some commentators argue this draws out Plato's rules for writing. Leo Strauss says that *Phaedrus* shows the "Platonic dialogue is a kind of writing that is free from the essential defects of writings", well-crafted, of course, but also able to "talk to some readers and be silent to others", hinting at hidden meanings open to the educated few.[6] Daniele Allen agrees that there is a kind of 'defect-free' writing. *Phaedrus* stresses the difference between the shadowy symbols of poetry and the rigorous intellectual model-making of the philosophers. These models are non-mimetic and convey abstract ideas to help discover truth: "metaphysically accurate" and "pragmatically efficacious".[7] But others have found much more to investigate here. The idea of 'speech-as-living-thought' and its problems, and the consequences of the 'written-ness' of the dialogues, is investigated and deconstructed in a long essay by Jacques Derrida.

The potion: 'Plato's Pharmacy'

A generation of extraordinarily significant thinkers, French or based in France, were shaped by arguments about Plato.[8] This group includes Jacques Derrida, Julia Kristeva, Jacques Lacan, Hélène Cixous, Michel Foucault and Luce Irigaray. They had been shaped by discussions of Plato by Nietzsche (as in the previous chapter), Heidegger and others. One of the most influential examples of this is Derrida's essay 'Plato's Pharmacy', inspired by the closing passages of *Phaedrus*. It is quoted, cited and anthologised very widely as an instance of deconstruction and is important for understanding *logocentrism*, one of Derrida's ideas about Plato's legacy. Derrida's work is provocative and often obscure, and can veer from what is clearly philosophy to what looks like avant-garde experimental prose. However, even Iris Murdoch (not generally a fan) recognised the force of this "brilliant essay".[9] I'm going to discuss it in some detail. It's about 'speech-as-living-thought'.

Derrida's argument hinges on the translation of the word 'potion' ("You have not discovered a *potion* for remembering, but for reminding" (275a)). We know from fairy tales and myths that potions are both beneficial and dangerous. The classical Greek word is *pharmakon* and can be translated as medicine, poison or drug: indeed, the word contains these opposite meanings mixed within it. (A pharmacy sells medicines which heal but can harm if used incorrectly.)

'Plato's Pharmacy' begins by pointing out how weaving is often a metaphor for writing and reading, and so for understanding: we follow threads or lines of argument, a text is a kind of web; it pulls words together. Derrida's point seems obvious and innocent: we read a text over time. We read the word right in front of us, remember the words before it and so weave the meaning together. Making sense of a text – indeed, *making a text* out of disparate words – involves memory and words which re-present themselves as signs: this is what writing is and does. It does not happen "in the present" like perceiving the drawing of a square in the sand.[10] It's as if Derrida was asking: what happens when we put reading and writing *into* time? (Of course reading and writing are *in* time but we frequently – and suspiciously, as he'll suggest later – forget this.)

The weaving metaphor also describes Derrida's own writing in the essay, which ties together threads of argument and allusion to make up a whole cloth. Derrida shows, for example, how the discussion of writing is not tacked onto the end of *Phaedrus* but is entwined throughout, uniting the whole web, "patiently interlacing the arguments" (67). Phaedrus cannot remember but has to read the speech by Lysias; at the centre of the dialogue is discussion of the ghost-writer or speech-writer, who writes speeches that someone else gives.

Pharmakon, too, threads through the dialogue. Socrates and Phaedrus sit in the spot where Boreas, the north wind, abducted the princess Orithyia while she played with her companion Pharmacia. The text of the speech which blew Phaedrus's mind is called a 'drug'. Finally, as we saw above, the myth of the origin of writing links *pharmakon* unambiguously with writing.

This origin myth shows us a great deal, suggests Derrida. The god king Thamus cannot write and does not need writing but is the origin, the father of the *logos*. There are two kinds of writing/child: speech, a living child "alive in that it has living father ... present, standing near it" (77); writing, a "half dead" (77) orphan "quite unable to defend itself or attend to its own needs" (77); a 'living' and a 'dead' *logos*. Moreover, the father of the *logos* is not a simple metaphor: the father appears in the language of the son, the *logos*. Indeed it is *only* in speech that the father of speech can be 'brought to light' ("it is precisely *logos* that allows us to perceive and investigate something like paternity" (80)). Derrida notes other times in Plato where this same structure occurs, where the parent is re-presented in or by the child. In *The Republic*, for example, Socrates says that the "good itself" is "too big a topic for the discussion" but he's willing to discuss instead "what is an offspring of the good and most like it" (*The Republic* 506e). In the myth of the cave, the sun is the "offspring of the good, which the good begot as analogue" or image (*The Republic* 508b). So the sun, the father, the good, is the "hidden illuminating" (82) which makes things appear in the *logos* but does not appear itself. More, since the sun/god/father cannot be looked at directly, because it is blinding, the *logos* is a shield from it, too (in *Phaedo*, Socrates says "I feared my soul would be altogether blinded if I looked at things with my eyes and tried to grasp them with each of my senses. So I thought I must take refuge in discussions and investigate the truth of things by means of words" *Phaedo* 99e).

Like Nussbaum, Derrida notes the myths and metaphors in the dialogue, and he argues this means that Plato had to make his "tale conform to structural laws" (85). Myth unavoidably brings a structure: day is opposed to night, life to death, father to son, speech to writing. These deep structures are inside the philosophy, and the analogies they lead to are, for Derrida, part of Plato's argument. Here, the analogy is between "the father and the son, on the one hand and a speaker and his words, on the other" (56). This is an example of what Derrida calls the "transference of a nonphilosopheme into a philosopheme" (72). These are invented words that draw on linguistics. The -eme suffix is backformed from the word 'phoneme', the smallest unit in language that conveys a distinction in meaning: the phoneme 'd' in 'dog' makes the word different from 'cog', 'log' and so on. Derrida is describing the way that a unit of meaning – an idea, basically – from outside the language of philosophy is brought into the language of philosophy.

Thamus is the sun god of life, origin of speech, father and king. Theuth his son and herald is a "god-doctor-pharmacist-magician" (90). He is also god of death because writing and death are linked: writing happens 'in time' and because of time and our mortality. It is a "re-memoration, recollection" (91), a putting back together of what is already dead and as "the breathless sign" (92) it contrasts with both "living, knowing memory" (91) and the "living voice" (92). Thamus (sun, life, speech) and Theuth (death, writing) are opposites but at the same time, Theuth is also Thamus's representative (re-presentative) to humans. As his herald, Theuth stands in for Thamus, as writing stands in for a speaker.

Derrida calls Theuth a *supplement* (93): this is one of Derrida's key terms. At first a supplement looks like a mere addition, but actually turns out to be integral to how we understand something. An everyday example. It's assumed that there are two kinds of faces, our original, natural face and a face made artificial with makeup, a supplement. But it's only once we have the idea of the made-up face that we can have the idea of the natural face. It is the contrast between the two which has created what now appears to be the more original 'natural' face. The 'made-up' face creates and is the source of the idea of the 'natural' face. Similarly, the idea of writing is a supplement: it gives us the idea of speech behind it, and in that speech, the living presence of someone.

By now in the essay Derrida admits he is no longer just commenting on Plato and makes his well-trailed intellectual move. He suggest that Plato thinks about writing via oppositions: good/evil, true/false, essence/appearance, alive/dead, inside/outside. But this only works if each of the opposed terms are "external" (103) to each other, separate, unmingled. This means that the opposition 'inside/outside' is the most important: it is the one which organises all the others. (Compare: all the rules of football only make sense if, first and most importantly, there are two opposed and unmingled teams: this is the founding principle.) But what if you "got to thinking that it can only be out of something like writing – or the *pharmakon* – that the strange difference between inside and outside can spring?" (103). What if the writing, as a supplement, created the idea of the writing (outside) and speech (inside)? (Just as the 'made-up' face creates the idea of the 'natural' face).

This means that Derrida thinks he has caught Plato in an inconsistency about memory. For Plato, there is 'live memory', present in and as your mind: think of the laws of geometry the enslaved person discovers or unforgets from the shapes in the sand. This 'living memory' is an "infinite self-presence" (109), where everything is there all at once. This is contrasted with 'dead memory', simply "re-memoration" (109), just recollecting what you have learned for the test, as a computer might do. But, argues Derrida, Plato also believes that "memory is finite by nature" and "recognizes this in attributing life to it" (109). If it is mortal, it cannot be infinite and is 'in time'. And if it is 'in time', it must work in the same manner as writing: bringing together, re-presenting, signs to make sense. Memory "always ... already needs signs" (109). Both speaking (sound) and writing (squiggles on a surface) turn out to rely on this bigger sense of writing as memory. There "would be no sentence if at the end of the spoken sentence I did not retain its beginning" Derrida writes, so understanding even a phrase would be impossible "without the retaining and gathering of past meaning".[11] Our remembering gathers together what is past and absent to make sense, as a text does. Memory is a type of writing. This means that even what Socrates calls speech, 'living memory' ('speech-as-living-thought') has 'dead memory', writing, inside it.

This changes what we think of as truth, for Derrida. For him, Plato thinks truth is only present in 'speech-as-living-thought': "knowledge as memory" (135) as the soul unforgets itself to be truly present. But following Derrida, truth can only appear in the "possibility of repetition through recall", that is, in *mimesis*, because imitation is a repetition (we imitate an original). Imagine: a young Athenian friend of Socrates could say, describing a genuine cave-escaping realisation, "oh! the Sun is like the True". But another young Athenian, carefully coached by a sophist, exclaims to impress his audience "oh! the Sun is like the True". He has no idea what this means, except it makes him sound wise. For Derrida's Plato, the first is "a repetition of truth" which reveals and makes present the true; the other is "a repetition of death and oblivion which veils and skews" because it only "re-presents a presentation, repeats a repetition" (135). But both rely on writing, on 'dead memory'. If you asked both young Athenians what they intended to mean, again, they could both just say something else ("ah! The sun is the good!"): turning to intention just repeats and does not escape the problem. The repetition ("oh! the Sun is like the True") could be both true or false, but that it's only in this repetition that either is possible. The *logos* makes it possible to manifest truth but in the same process (I was *going* to write: in the same breath) makes imitation possible too. Like the fairy tale potion, the *logos* is both beneficial and dangerous, the source of truth and falsity.

A way around this is to suggest that Plato believes that the highest truth of the good, the beautiful and the true was simply beyond language: *alogos*, an individual's pure speechless contemplation. But this may not tally with Socrates searching for truth using words.

Derrida has made a complex interlinked argument. First, because we are 'in time' and mortal, we use memory to make sense of texts, written or spoken. Because they are put together in memory, these are like writing (pulling together strands) and not like 'living speech' (all there at once). Second, this means what are taken to be 'transcendent' truths, 'beyond' in Plato, can only appear in what is not beyond (the mythological father Thamus appears only in the son Theuth; the truth appears in a text which has the possibility to be true or false). Third, in responding to this worry and by trying to enforce the 'truth' of what appears in the *logos*, 'speech-as-living-thought', Plato goes too far and pushes out 'writing-as-dead-memory'. However, a possible inconsistency in his own work shows that 'speech-as-living-thought' needs (dead) writing, memory, inside it to work. If this sounds circular, remember that Derrida is trying to show what happens when you tell a story about why you should not tell stories, or when you write: *do not believe this writing*.

Logocentrism

Derrida's discussion is important because of Plato's astonishingly powerful legacy: Derrida says (writes!) that Plato "sets up the whole of western metaphysics" (76) and develops "a pattern that will dominate all of Western philosophy". The 'speech-as-living-thought' idea becomes what he calls the 'metaphysics of presence'. That is, the idea that you can pass through writing (which is a re-presentation) to and through speech, which is the actual presence of 'living thought', which makes something outside language appear present in language. This is the idea Derrida calls *logocentrism*.[12]

Sometimes people just ignore or forget that the *logos* re-presents, and so think it 'transparently' shows the truth, as if we can simply 'bypass' representation as we see through a glass window. For Derrida, representation is not simply glass: the "glass must be read as a text".[13] This is not a very radical or unique claim: it's one many people have made over centuries. What makes logocentrism different is its concern for how the glass itself works when we forget it is glass, for how writing works almost 'by itself'. Derrida means that if we are keen to focus on the presence we imagine behind the *logos* (forgetting that the *logos* is the source of that idea of presence), we ignore some of the effects of the *logos* as writing itself. The *logos* is like a material or intellectual technology and, like any machine, has a tendency to create unintended consequences of its own. Derrida invents a name for the study of writing as writing in this way: *grammatology*.[14] Grammatology is what helps us understand logocentrism at work. You will recall that the *logos* has a range of meanings. Speech is one, bringing things to light; intelligibility, making sense of things is another; giving reasons or explanations is a third.

If things are not written about or represented, brought to light, logocentrism leads us to think they are not valuable or important (or not even there, not even present). Just because, for example, people are not represented or their stories are not written does not mean they are not or were not present. Logocentrism leads to ignoring what is outside of or other to what is already represented: it fails to see otherness, in both people and their presentation.

Making sense of things, intelligibility, is fundamental to our species. We keep hoping that we have found one idea or model which consistently unifies and explains everything: the 'key to all mythologies', the answer to everything. As we can see in Plato, we can make everything intelligible using a principle or idea that is 'transcendent' or 'beyond'. We think the principle *appears through* the *logos*, as the sun shines through a glass window, but Derrida suggests, it may appear *as* the *logos*. That is, philosophers and others imagine they have found a unifying idea 'beyond', outside the cave, but they actually found it in the *logos*. Derrida calls this a 'transcendental signifier'. This idea then works as a guiding principle which is used to make everything fit into a consistent and neat system. Derrida calls this a 'totalization'. What does not fit is excluded or marginalised.

Often, the more thinkers try to fit everything in, the more extreme their systems become. The more we can't explain something that doesn't fit, the keener we are to either make it fit, no matter how outrageous the explanation or the risk of inconsistency to our system; or we wish it away or brush it under the carpet. This too is a result of logocentrism. This is why Derrida and others reacting to logocentrism are often very interested in what seems marginal or what seems not to fit (the discussion of writing, seemingly tacked onto the end of *Phaedrus*, say). This is why, too, Derrida and others are interested in the way the boundary between 'what is philosophy' ('philosophemes') and 'what is not philosophy' ('nonphilosophemes') is policed. In the context of this book, of course, the arguments between the 'literary contextualist' and 'analytic developmentalist' readings of the dialogues are an example of this policing: issues of character, setting and tone may – or may not – be what you consider meaningful as philosophy.

Finally, because logocentricism often focuses on giving reasons, on the organising idea that is 'outside' the *logos*, it means that writing can often be interpreted by the light of that idea, whereas the actual text may not bear this out. For example, as we saw with Derrida's reading of *Phaedrus*, the analogies and metaphors which shape the text are not part of the explicit argument but are there and shape meaning, and that meaning can go counter to the apparent 'outside' idea. As Michael Naas writes,

> When Plato opposes writing to what he calls 'writing in the soul',
> what he *meant*, what he means us to *hear* or *understand*, was no doubt
> that 'writing in the soul' is another way of speaking of 'live speech'. But
> what he wrote was precisely 'writing in the soul', thus using the very
> term he just criticised to characterise what he wishes to privilege.[15]

To focus on logocentrism means reading very carefully and paying attention to the words on the page, what they actually say, as opposed to what you think or are told they say. This means, too, that reading in this way pays close attention to where a text is ambiguous or indeterminate. Lawyers, for example, know that language can be slippery so legal language strives for greater and greater precision to make manifest its meaning: by contrast, poets often uncover (and sometimes strive for) ambiguities and complexities, to make manifest, exploit, play with or soar on the workings of language itself. Writing, just as Socrates warned, goes anywhere, roams around everywhere, talks to anyone and often says what its father doesn't want it to. Its meaning is disseminated. And it can make people "difficult to get along with" (275a).

Logocentrism cannot simply be 'abolished'. It is profoundly part of the structure of Western thought: and thinking about logocentrism is thinking in that tradition. Derrida argues that it means we have to read with our minds sharpened to these issues. He wrote that the "passage beyond philosophy does not consist in turning the page of philosophy" as if we could escape these (and

Plato's) fundamental ideas: rather it is in "continuing to read philosophy in a certain way", with an eye to how inescapable logocentrism appears.[16] One minor consequence of this is in Derrida's own writing itself. Although there are recurring themes in his work, rather than invent a philosophic system (which itself would embody the logocentrism to which he is drawing attention), Derrida always analyses specific texts. In each case he revises and changes his key terms and ideas, to avoid them becoming a simple doctrine and to respond most attentively to that particular text. This often makes his work hard to read (and to introduce: when I described supplement above as a key term, I was really letting Derrida's work down). It is his version, perhaps, of the idea that Plato wrote in dialogues to avoid creating dogma.

'Plato's Pharmacy', for all its influence outside philosophy departments, is not without problems (apart from being hard to read). The essay takes as its target one particular version of Plato which is most connected to the idea of the forms and the transcendental world, and so it seems to downplay the irony, change and lack of conclusions across the dialogues. Perhaps, then, it attacks a stereotyped 'Platonism'. The essay also works as much by allusions (the structures of myth) and correspondences (memory corresponds to writing, writing to text) as by logical argument. But, as Derrida might point out, to exclude allusion and correspondences as a kind of argument is to presuppose and police how philosophy works (the relationship between 'nonphilosophemes and philosophemes' again). Is this just a result of (over) interpretation? Derrida points out that in an act of interpreting, we are either just going over what is there (in which case, why do it?) or we are adding to the fabric of the passage, in which case this is no longer 'just' interpretation. The act of interpretation does not have clear borders.

Conclusion

Nussbaum's reading of *Phaedrus* is important *for* literature: a dialogue as philosophical poetry which allows metaphors, images and stories to become meaningful as philosophy. It's important *as* literature, too, demonstrating, for Nussbaum, a Platonic account of what it is to be human which allows a greater importance for emotion. Derrida's detailed reading of this beautiful dialogue is important *for* literature, too, because it explores some key ideas about writing itself. It's also important, in a way, *as* literature, because it is a kind of very powerful literary reading: alive to ambiguity, keen not to delimit what the dialogue means by limiting the interpretation through by a series of unspoken rules (about what 'counts' as philosophy, for example). The concept of logocentrism is developed through this reading (and in other work by Derrida) by thinking about what 'speech-as-living-thought' implies. While seemingly very abstract, logocentrism clearly has consequences for how the *logos* and the *polis* shape and influence each other. First, it makes us aware of how people or issues are not represented in the *logos*, and so seem invisible to the *polis*. Second, it draws our attention to how systems of thought use a single central principle to make everything fit, when (bluntly) not everything does fit. Third, it makes us focus on the difference between what texts mean and what we might assume they mean if we don't pay close enough attention. For Derrida, this is all part of Plato's legacy.

Notes

1 Martha Nussbaum, *The Fragility of Goodness* (Cambridge: Cambridge University Press, 1986), p. 227.
2 Nussbaum's discussion is *The Fragility of Goodness*, p. 203 ff.
3 Nussbaum, *The Fragility of Goodness*, p. 227.
4 Nussbaum, *The Fragility of Goodness*, p. 227.
5 Nussbaum, *The Fragility of Goodness*, p. 227.
6 Strauss, Leo, *The City and Man* (Chicago: University of Chicago Press, 1964), p. 52, p. 53.
7 Danielle S. Allen, *Why Plato Wrote* (Oxford: Wiley-Blackwell, 2013), p. 47.
8 See Paul Allen Miller, *Diotima at the Barricades* (Oxford: Oxford University Press, 2016), pp. vii–viii.
9 Murdoch, *Existentialists and Mystics*, p. 413.
10 Jacques Derrida, 'Plato's Pharmacy' in *Dissemination*, trans. Barbara Johnson (Chicago: University of Chicago Press, 1972), pp. 63–171, p. 63. Further references in the text.
11 Jacques Derrida, *Heidegger: The Question of Being and History*, trans. Geoffrey Bennington (Chicago: Chicago University Press, 2016), p. 83.
12 Jacques Derrida, *Of Grammatology*, trans. Gayatri Chakravorty Spivak (London: Johns Hopkins University Press, 1976), p. 3.
13 Jacques Derrida, *Dissemination*, trans. Barbara Johnson (London: The Athlone Press, 1981), p. 233.
14 Derrida, *Of Grammatology*, p. 4, p. 74.
15 Michael Naas, *Derrida from now on* (New York: Fordham University Press, 2008), pp. 44–5.
16 Jacques Derrida, *Writing and Difference*, trans. Alan Bass (London: Routledge and Kegan Paul, 1978), p. 288.

6

A HERMENEUTIC DIALECTIC?

Ion, Protagoras

This final chapter on Plato's work turns to the dialogues *Ion* and *Protagoras* and, using recent scholarship, draws out further the difference between what the dialogues say *about* literature and how they work *as* literature. Recall the suggestion that the dialectic might be usefully seen in two aspects: an 'elenctic dialectic', constantly challenging inconsistencies but not advancing a position, and a 'didactic dialectic', a form of positive teaching.[1] Perhaps these two texts display or encourage something like a 'hermeneutic' or 'interpretive dialectic'. Indeed, as I'll show later, Grace Ledbetter makes a strong case for a 'Socratic theory of poetry' in these two dialogues.

Ion expands an argument about *mimesis* from *The Republic* (or predates it, as developmentalists argue this is an early dialogue). Because it seems to put these arguments forcefully, and because it is short, *Ion* is often a 'bit of Plato' that literature students read and that's one reason I discuss it. Conversely, *Protagoras* is rarely read by literary people. This is a pity: not only is it, in part, about literature, its teaching and interpretation, but it's also very exciting to read. If the *Symposium* is about Socrates charming and so out-doing poets, *Protagoras* is Socrates going head-to-head with the leading sophist of his day.[2]

Ion: or, yes, sure, you *could* be a great general ...

Ion is one of Plato's shortest dialogues. Socrates's target is poetry and what poetry knows. His stooge is Ion from Ephesus, an especially good, if rather arrogant, rhapsode: rhapsodes were professional reciters and interpreters of poetry, usually of Homer, and were highly regarded in classical Greece. Ion's just won first prize in a competition and so he has reason to feel pleased with himself when he arrives in Athens. But then he meets Socrates ...

After their greetings and congratulations, Socrates gets Ion to admit that it's only really Homer who interests him. Experts in other subjects (arithmetic, medicine) can talk about their area of expertise and differentiate between authorities and bluffers in these fields. But expert rhapsodes, apparently, can't even talk about poetry in general: only the poet in whom they specialise. Why?

DOI: 10.4324/9781003097914-8

In Ion's case, Socrates suggests, it is because he is inspired by the Muses and he offers a (rather lovely) metaphor. A magnetic rock attracts iron rings, and those rings, in turn, magnetize other iron rings, forming a chain. Analogously, a poet is inspired by the gods "and goes out of his mind and his intellect is no longer in him" (534b). Those in contact with the poet, the rhapsode reciting Homer's poetry, are the next link in the chain, inspired by the magnetism of the gods. The audience, also inspired, are next (535e) and all the other theatre people are connected too ("choral dancers and dance teachers and assistant teachers hanging off to the sides of the rings" (536a)). Socrates's sly implication is that everyone involved – from the poet to the assistant dancing teacher and certainly the audience – does not actually *know* anything but are simply inspired. There is no craft, no *techne*, in being a poet, a rhapsode or even, maybe, an assistant dancing teacher. The beautiful poems, Socrates says, "are not human, not even from human beings, but are divine and from the gods" (354e): so poets are "nothing but representatives of the god, possessed by whoever possesses them" (354e), meaning, Ion agrees, stupidly flattered, that rhapsodes are "representatives of representatives" (535a). Sure enough, it turns out that Ion, like some caricature of an actor, is swept away by the poetry he recites, crying at the sad moments, hair on end at the frightening ones: not, Socrates points out, in his right mind. But this explains why Ion only responds to Homer, not poetry in general, because it is Homer's Muse who has possessed him.

Then Socrates get closer to the nub of the matter. Homer's epics discuss particular areas of knowledge such as charioteering, fishing, medicine (and he quotes them at length to show his admiration for Homer): surely an expert in that activity is best equipped to judge if Homer is correct? Obviously. Ok, then, says Socrates, what passages in Homer can an expert rhapsode judge best? "My answer, Socrates, is, 'All of them'" (539e). But poor old Ion has already admitted that doctors can judge best if Homer's verse is right about medicine, charioteers about chariots and so on, and because of this, Socrates makes him look a fool. Is Ion implying that he, *Ion the Rhapsode*, knows better than a sailor about sailing, a doctor about healing or a cowherd about mad cows? Ion's answers get short and sulky.

Iris Murdoch suggests a better answer for Ion here: that his expertise is "a general knowledge of human life" and a "technical knowledge of poetry".[3] This insight is crucial to the dialogue. In his careful reading, Stephen Halliwell argues that Socrates is offering two alternatives about poetry: either it's a form of knowledge which instructs and overlaps with all other forms of knowledge (Socrates persuasively shows it is not) or it is a form of divine inspiration. However, we might be very happy to admit a 'technical knowledge' side to writing or performing (knowing about rhyme or how to control point-of-view; knowing various stage skills, breathing, voice projection). But could there be a *techne*, a skill for the 'general knowledge of human life' which poetry (and Murdoch's Ion) claims? (Halliwell: "how could there be *techne* of discourse about everything?").[4] More, if poetry is divinely inspired how could there be a codified technique, a set of knowledge-based procedures, for successfully producing the intense charge of imaginative absorption and emotional responsiveness which Socrates and Ion agree is a hallmark of poetic ecstasy. How, in short could there be a *techne* of poetic ecstasy?[5]

Shelley thinks the same: no one can say they "will compose poetry" because the creative mind is a "fading coal, which some invisible influence … awakens to transitory brightness".[6] Is there a space between 'knowledge-less inspiration' and pretending to know everything?

Socrates, knowing that Homer's epics are full of military speeches, tricks the now petulant Ion one last time: does a rhapsode know what a general should say to the troops? "Well" says Ion, suddenly feeling a lot less stung and numbed, "I certainly would know what a general would say" (540b). Does this mean, asks Socrates, teasingly agog, that Ion would be not only the best rhapsode but also the best general? Ion agrees: his knowledge of generalship which he learned from Homer would make him the best general in Greece.

> Then why in heaven's name, Ion, when you're both the best general and the best rhapsode in Greece, do you go around the country giving rhapsodies but not commanding troops? Do you think Greece really needs a rhapsode who is crowned with golden crown? And does not need a general?
>
> (541b–c)[7]

Socrates makes Ion look a mug and puts poetry in its place, lower than the art of war in a time of war and a long way from knowledge. Socrates rounds up the discussion, as if it were a seminar, by going over the conversation: Ion can't even explain what he knows about, or what Homer knows about. Instead, like the minor sea god Proteus who can change his form into anything (or someone wriggling out of a commitment), Ion has shapeshifted through all sorts of professions and ended up a general. But Socrates is good with a backhanded compliment, too: being possessed by a divine gift via Homer, the magnetism which makes the rings attracted to each other, means that Ion is not skilled in a profession but "lovelier" (542b) because he is someone divine.

What do we learn from this little drama? Socrates asks questions – the elenchic dialectic – which keep going until they reveal to the reader that Ion knows nothing really and his assumptions about himself pop like a balloon when he ridiculously claims that he's a great general (unlike the reader, Ion might not quite get this point). But we get to see, too, that Socrates thinks that poetry knows nothing. In contrast with being a doctor or even a cowherd, poetry offers no *techne*, no really knowing your way around: his target is really Homer, the great font of knowledge for the Greeks. In Ion's pathetic performance in the argument, we see that poetry hasn't even taught him how to think, argue or use rhetoric. Ion doesn't just admit his ignorance, he performs it. Again, Plato's dialogue shows this as much as tells it: he's as protean as Ion.

An actor may have a lot to tell us about how to perform Shakespeare: how to speak the verse clearly and movingly, how to recall the speeches and where to stand. Are we convinced that, as a consequence, they have a better overall sense than the audience of what a play means? Most particularly, an actor may not know how or why or if a play might make us better people: the issue of import- ance to Socrates. This is a criticism of the sort of esteem actors are held in – as if they are sages and not highly proficient craftspeople – not a criticism of the plays themselves. (Sometimes, when the press interview a Hollywood star on some political topic, I think of this dialogue. Acting is a highly demanding pro- fession, but this does not mean that actors know more about, say, international relations or legal reform than other people. So why, I wonder, do the journalists ask them about those things?) Similarly, a novel about (say) nineteenth-century naval warfare only has to *sound* convincing on that topic. You do not use a novel about Chicago to guide yourself around the city, although you may visit the places mentioned in the novel. *Ion* gets to the idea that literature sounds good but knows nothing. Those who love literature – poets, interpreters and us, their audience – do not learn anything but (Socrates is polite) are inspired by the gods. This is holy, but it also takes us away from our fellow human beings in the *polis*, and from shared reason. Worse, the enacting of poetry does not make one solid, but rather protean, shape shifting, neither one thing nor another. It does not make us good, for Socrates. But note, again: Plato shows this in the dialogue through Ion's character. This relationship between poetry and virtue is central to a much longer, and much more important dialogue, *Protagoras*.

Protagoras: or, the boxers

Protagoras is one of the most significant and exciting dialogues to read both *as* literature and *for* literature. Despite the fact that it is barely mentioned by lit- erary critics and theorists, it's been a touchstone for two generations of work on Plato.[8]

Set in 433 BCE, just before the beginning of the Peloponnesian War but, like all Plato's dialogues, in its shadow, this is, perhaps, the most famous encounter between Socrates and a sophist. Indeed, Protagoras was one of the most celebrated sophists, supposedly the first to charge (a lot!) for his teaching. The subject of the debate is ostensibly whether virtue can be taught (Protagoras's claim) or not (Socrates's position). Because of this and the (predictably) equivocal answers, *Meno* (discussed in Chapter 2) is sometimes seen as its sequel since it follows up this question by explaining how we might know about virtue.

From a literary point of view, the dialogue is also about the role of and use of literature: it's a reflection on stories and poems and how this reflection functions – *if* this functions – as an argument, and if so, how convincingly. Can literature convey knowledge or teach virtue? The form of the dialogue is especially important, too. Unlike *Ion*, the dialogue enacts several different styles of argument and the characters even argue about how to argue. The dialogue performs these different styles, demonstrating their strengths and weaknesses, how they stem from people's dispositions, and shows their impact on the speakers themselves and their audience.

Apart from the beginning framing sequences, the dialogue is told in flashback. An unnamed friend jokes that Socrates has been hunting the beautiful Alcibiades. Socrates replies that he was distracted by someone more beautiful, because that person was wise (recall the image of Diotima's ladder). He's as keen to tell the story as the friend is to hear it, and off they go.

Socrates was awoken before dawn by his friend Hippocrates who is very excited. The great sophist Protagoras, famous throughout Greece, is in Athens, and Hippocrates wants to go at once to learn from him, for a hefty fee. Socrates counsels caution: if you paid a doctor or sculptor to teach you, you'd know what you were getting. But what is Protagoras going to teach? Making one a clever speaker, certainly, but about what? If Protagoras is selling food for the soul, you ought to be careful about what that food is before you eat it. Duly cautioned, they go off to Callias's house, where Protagoras is staying, and they find a huge cast made up of Athens's cleverest and most sophisticated men. Then Socrates and Protagoras face off, like boxers, as Socrates will say later. It's a bout that Socrates dearly wishes to win. Round one!

Protagoras begins with a brief lecture on the origins of sophists, their past unpopularity and the consequent need to hide their art, "masking it sometimes as poetry", like Homer and Hesiod, or as "mystery religions and prophecy" (316d). So straightaway, Protagoras is claiming that literature can carry learning and knowledge. Socrates finds an opening, jabs a leading question: what will Hippocrates learn from Protagoras? Like a kind of dodgy website selling something unspecified, Protagoras claims that "every day, day after day, you will get better and better" (318b). But, pressed, in the end he claims to teach "sound deliberation" (319a) or sound judgement (*euboulia*) which is really "the art of citizenship … to make men good citizens" (319a). The implication is that this skill (knowing how to deliberate) is a virtue, and so, like any skill, virtue can be taught.

Socrates is thoughtful. He says that while the Assembly in Athens recognises experts in particular things like building or making ships, when it comes to citizenship or political judgement everyone's opinion is considered valid. What's more, good parents have bad children. How then, can virtue, which lies behind being a good citizen, be teachable? Children don't seem to learn it, or else everyone has it already.

Protagoras responds at length with a story, a founding myth, to explain: it's known as his Great Speech (320c–328d). When the gods made all the creatures, Prometheus and Epimetheus (their names mean 'Forethought' and 'Afterthought') were put in charge of giving out their attributes: horns, wings, fur, hooves and so on. Foolish Epimetheus forgot to give us humans anything. Rather than just let us begin with nothing, Prometheus stole fire from the god Hephaestus and "wisdom in the practical arts" (321d) from Athena. So fire and skills gave us a chance to survive. But there were no cities and when we did band together, we just bickered and fell out with each other because we lacked the skill of politics, the craft of living together. So Zeus sent Hermes, his messenger, "to bring justice and a sense of shame to humans, so that there would be order within cities and bonds of friendship to unite them" (322c). Hermes asks if these – justice and shame – should be distributed unevenly as other skills were (after all, not everyone is a doctor). Zeus says no, everyone needs these skills, otherwise cities will collapse. Everyone is able to comment on political matters, because everyone has a share in justice and the other civic virtues, says Protagoras. As to the question of why good people have bad children: everyone teaches virtue as best they can, and the worst in the city, even if they fail to meet Socrates's standards, are better than those without laws.

It's hard not to agree with the progressive and campaigning journalist I. F. Stone when he says that this story, which gives each man a share of justice, is "the founding fable of democracy" as well as demonstrating the "ideology of Periclean Athens" (while pointing out that it applied only to free men, of course).[9] I also want to note what it is that Protagoras has done. He has told a story and then interpreted it. It is a piece of literary criticism or theory, drawing ideas from a story and revealing what they mean: a (mostly) democratic act of 'interpretative' or 'hermeneutic dialectic'.

It's not a surprise that Socrates doesn't respond to this myth, perhaps, as Stone suggests, because he doesn't want to attack democracy so openly, or perhaps because this form of argument, story-and-exposition, is not one of which he approves. Instead, while he pretends to be impressed, he has an ingenious question up his sleeve, just "one little thing" (329b). Are all the different virtues – justice, temperance, piety and so on – one thing, one virtue, or several? And off they go: just as Protagoras has his long speech, now Socrates gets his turn, a dense question-and-answer in which he forces Protagoras to admit that there are different aspects of virtue: while Protagoras maintains something can only one have opposite, folly seems to have two opposites, wisdom and temperance. Shown that his position on these (seemingly minor matters) is confused, Protagoras (there's no other word for it) sulks and suddenly breaks Socrates's question-and-answer sequence with a longer answer. Some things can be both good or bad depending on the circumstances: olive oil, for example, is bad for plants and animals but good for humans. This gets a round of applause but Socrates upbraids him by saying that, if he were deaf, Protagoras would speak louder, but, as he's forgetful, Protagoras had better speak shorter.

Then these two men argue about the rules of arguing: Protagoras will not argue in the question-and-answer way, he needs his longer, rhetorical speeches, narratives and their exposition. By contrast, Socrates will only play if they do his kind of "dialectical discussion" (355b). An impasse. Socrates makes as if to flounce out, but his friends restrain him. The leaders in the watching crowd debate what to do: in a conversation which echoes a legal discussion, they conclude that both speakers should find a compromise between Socrates's dialectical brevity and Protagoras's long-windedness. First they'll have Protagoras's method, then Socrates's.

Seconds out, round two.

Protagoras, after all, an educator, begins his turn by saying that the greatest part of a man's education is "to be in command of poetry", to understand the "words of poets, to know when a poem is correctly composed and when not, and to know how to analyse a poem and to respond to questions about it" (339a). This is precisely the sense that poetry, centrally Homer, was the guide to how to behave, how to think and judge well: understanding a poem meant understanding how to be. Following the theme of their argument, the possibility of teaching virtue, he turns to a poem by the lyric poet Simonides (c 556–468). (Simonides's poetry, and the question of "what exactly does he mean?" (313e) also played a role in *The Republic*, setting off the whole conversation.)

The poem is now lost, except the fragments in this dialogue. However, it was well known – Socrates has it by heart – and dealt with popular poetic themes of the time, "such as the impossibility of perfection, the unbridgeable gulf between gods and men, the ineluctable vicissitudes of human life and the necessity for moderation in all things".[10] Protagoras has chosen it because it pertains to the subject, the possibility of teaching of virtue, as it begins by citing one of the famous Seven Sages, Pittacus: "For a man to become good truly is hard" (339b).

Beginning with a tiny detail, Protagoras interrogates Socrates and appears to catch him out, reversing the normal run of things. Socrates confesses to his unnamed friend that "I felt as if I had been hit by a good boxer. Everything went black and I was reeling from Protagoras's oratory and the other's clamour" (339e). But note, however, even this is damning with praise: of course, there is no glory in beating a feeble opponent so he's praising himself too. Socrates's melodramatic account also makes the point that oratory does not help you 'know yourself': it simply knocks you out, makes you unconscious. But he recovers and playing Protagoras's game gives a long and detailed literary critical analysis.

Socrates starts with a history of wisdom in Sparta. Many commentators think this is mostly a joke: Spartans were not famous for wisdom but for fighting. But the conclusion, that the tight-lipped Spartans are good at the pithy argumentative knock-out because they are wise, both illustrates what Socrates thinks Simonides was aiming for in his poem, and implies that he'll do the same. Socrates takes on the voice, as it were, of Simonides: "we have to approach this maxim of Pittacus by imagining him speaking and Simonides replying" (343e). His aim is to show that the poem is a repudiation of that first line: notice that he has already turned the poem into the sort of philosophical argument with which he feels confident, that is, a *refutation* of a conventional idea.[11] Socrates argues that the poem makes some philosophical claims (a reader may be dubious, as I'll show); suggests there are different mortal and divine forms of goodness (344b–345c); and says that the poem shows that it is

95

impossible to *be* good, only to *become* good (345d–347a), because in life one is often forced to compromise. Simonides is happy with an average person who does no great wrong, and that "is what I think was going through Simonides' mind when he composed this ode" (347a). (He is recreating the poem in the form of 'thought-as-living-speech'.)

The scholarly consensus is that Socrates is mocking the sophists and their ways of reading poems. Indeed, Socrates's reading of the poem is hard to follow because it's (politely) a very *eccentric* reading. The account of Spartan wisdom is satire (although with a point, about fighting with weapons or in words). The more interpretive section is full of what might charitably be called 'strong readings'. Nickolas Pappas gives a very clear account of some. Socrates changes the line "For a man to become good truly is hard" to "It is hard for a man to become good, Pittacus, truly" (343d–e). Pappas explains that moving the word 'truly' in classical Greek "requires a shift in phrasing, but no change in word order", a literary trope known as hyperbaton (in English, this involves moving the conventional word order around: ordering unconventionally words more impact has!).[12] He does this again to the end of the poem, changing the place of willingly in "All who do no wrong willingly/I praise and love" (345d) to "I willingly praise/all those do no wrong". As Pappas says, the "last sentence is preposterous" because Socrates was the only person to think that people did not choose to do wrong but did so through ignorance and he ascribes this view "to Simonides, allegedly in the interest of telling us what the poet thinks".[13] In addition to these hyperbatons, Socrates shifts words to their not-quite adjacent meanings, for example, from 'resourceful' to 'wise'. He goes on with almost comically extenuated readings and ventriloquises Simonides to make him speak in a Socratic way.[14] After he finishes, Hippias, another sophist and lover of poetry – and an interlocutor of Socrates on at least one more occasion – says he is impressed. If we think that the interpretation is nonsense, then Plato is showing Hippias up for a fool: if we think that the interpretation has *some* sort of value, we are being shown how Socrates can, as it were, speak the sophists' language or at least master their style of argument. (We might also wonder, sneakily, perhaps, if Socrates just isn't very good at understanding poems: this is what Nietzsche thought.)

Now in the dialogue Socrates goes on the offensive about this form of arguing-by-interpreting-poems. They should say "goodbye to odes and poetry" (778c) because "discussing poetry strikes me as no different from the second rate drinking parties of the agora crowd" (347d). Why? First, when proper, educated men meet, Socrates says, they talk together and don't need, "extraneous voices" (347e), especially not from poets who "cannot be questioned on what they say" (347e). The text of poem can't defend or explain itself: it needs a person behind it, a poet or, as Socrates has just shown, a kind of ventriloquist for it. This is an example of presuming 'living-speech-as-thought': for speech to be properly speech, you need to be there, you need to be present. (Even if the poet was there, the poem is still a made-thing, inflexible and dead.

A poet performs their poem as if it was by someone else, after all – a past version of that poet.) Second, when a "poet is brought up in a discussion, almost everyone has a different opinion about what he means, and they wind up arguing about something they never can finally decide" (347e). Why should disagreement be a bad thing? Only because it prevents a 'final decision' and no full account can be given (although this seems rarely to bother Socrates in other contexts). Third and finally, Socrates argues, they should not use poets but "converse directly … testing the truth and our very selves" (348a). The work of the poets, and ventriloquising them, gets in the way of a more honest, true and real conversion.[15]

Socrates in his turn gets to argue with Protagoras using his dialectical method, beginning again with his question of whether virtue is many things or one. Protagoras says that they are like features on a face: linked but different. His example is that courage is a virtue but is different from piety, justice, temperance and wisdom. At least two things are going on in the final section of the dialogue.

First, through his series of his questions and answers, Socrates allows Protagoras to unfold the thought that doing the right thing, virtue, is based on correct judgement, the measurement of good or bad. This is Protagoras's core idea, which has come down as the old saying that 'man is the measure of all things'. Several speakers from a number of Plato's works disagree with this idea: it means we and our actions are simply things to be measured and it makes humans, not the transcendent world beyond, the final arbiters of truth. In the *Laws*, the main speaker explicitly says it is "god who is pre-eminently the 'measure of all things', much more so than any man" (*Laws* 716c). As the dialogue continues, there is a long and sharp exchange which ends with Socrates forcing Protagoras, very reluctantly – he "would not even nod at this" (360d) – to admit that while courage is wisdom about what is to be feared or not, this is also true of cowardice. Socrates has shown that, for Protagoras, courage and cowardice are the same (as if to say to the audience: how can you trust someone who believes *this* to teach you virtue, especially during a time when voices are prophesying war?). This isn't simply a trick, although Socrates chose courage as the clearest and most emotive example. Socrates claims to have shown teaching knowledge-as-measurement is not teaching you to be virtuous: in contrast, his view that virtues are knowledge (361b) might do this. In fact, generations of scholars, whether sympathetic to Socrates or not, are unconvinced by his arguments here. So is Socrates. He announces in the conclusion that he and Protagoras have completely swapped around their positions. Protagoras began by claiming to teach virtue, and now it seems he believes he can't, whereas Socrates began by doubting virtue could be taught, but if virtue is knowledge, surely it can be taught? The boxing contest, at the level of content at least, is a draw. Some have seen this as a sign of Plato's admiration for Protagoras.[16] Indeed, Protagoras is presented mostly with respect by the dialogue: it is Socrates who is seen to behave badly. He's childish, very competitive, rude to others, even his supporters, and the remark that good parents have bad children is made pointedly in front of two of Pericles's sons.[17] This might even give us pause about his arguments.

Second, throughout this part of the dialogue, Socrates is showing, or trying to show, the superiority of his *form* of argument. Protagoras uses well-crafted speeches and a kind of honesty to show what he does. Socrates uses the quick jabs of his questioning method to show that while Protagoras claims to teach virtue, he doesn't really know what it is. The elenchic dialectic is able to show that there are, at best, some unquestioned assumptions or at worst, some confusions, at the deepest level of Protagoras's ideas (although Socrates has advanced here no ideas of his own). But again, the draw at the end suggests that none of these forms of argument are superior, although the contrast is drawn highly effectively.

The lack of a clear winner in this match might also make us think that we are offered a choice. Francisco Gonzalez reminds us of the frames of the dialogue, and of Hippocrates: it's his money to spend, after all. But he almost disappears from the dialogue and we don't hear of his decision. But Gonzales points out that "*we the readers are all* in Hippocrates' situation": we are identified with him and can choose which view we judge to be best.[18] In terms of literature, both positions have strengths and weaknesses. We learn unsurprisingly that Socrates has little time for poetry or poets. In discussing poetry we use other's voices and not our own: poetry takes us away from ourselves and others. A definitive conclusion about poetic meaning is not challenging but impossible, although with a bit of strong-armed hammering you can make a poem say what you want. All this prevents direct, honest conversation about what matters and, really, makes it all rather unclassy. Protagoras's views on poems and stories seem more positive. Indeed, sophists who teach wisdom and poets are kin: both can be enchanting like Orpheus (315b, 316d). Stories tell truths, as in his Great Speech, and so have knowledge that can be taught to – indeed *belong* to – everyone. When Protagoras says that the "greatest part" of education is "to be in command of poetry" (339a) he maps the authority of poetry and the authority of culture onto each other. Literature has a kind of authority on how to be a good citizen and morality is taught through this authority (not by simply challenging it). Poetry and its discussion can teach *euboulia*, sound deliberation (318a), good judgement both for personal and public life and for fulfilling one's potential. We learn how to be with each other from literature, and how to model and manage our lives and societies.

The wonderful poet, classicist and translator Anne Carson offers another literary view, which allows us to evade this choice between the two boxers, should we wish. The dialogue, she writes, shows us that "listening to a philosopher analyze a poem is like watching a man attack a river with a sword" (her image comes from both the *Iliad* and *Protagoras* (340a) and is a reference that all Plato's contemporary readers would recognise. Achilles, enraged, attacks the river Scamander).[19] She goes on: this "laughable ... result is achieved when poetry and philosophy confront one another" (110). Simonides's poem, she shows, is "not a poem about good, evil, gods, men, or Pittacus so much as it is a poem about praise" (120) from a genre of 'praise poetry', "the *epinikion* or epinician ode ... a song of praise sung to honour a victor in the athletic games" (113). More, it is that most poetic thing, a self-reflective poem about praise poems. She skilfully draws out Plato's implications: on the one hand, both Simonides and Protagoras are "mediators of becoming in a transaction that cannot be trusted. You can no more credit a sophist when he says 'I know' than you can believe a praise poet when he says 'I will'" (122). While, on the other hand, she shows that Socrates's hyperbaton, his 'mixing' is "outrageous" (123). However, her key argument is that

> Plato's insistence on mixing a poem of Simonides into his philosoph-
> ical discourse makes one thing very clear to readers of the *Protagoras*.
> Whatever it is that Simonides is trying to say in this poem is not what
> the philosophers get out of it. The poem escapes them – that is, it
> remains poetry: suspended, misappropriated, and unknown with the
> philosophical prose, like a seed of fire captured in a fennel stalk. You
> can always tell the poetry from the prose in a Platonic dialogue. The
> poetry is what keeps unmixing itself from everything else.
>
> (128)

That is, the poem, what the poem is, escapes the philosophical readings of it. A poem just cannot be simply boiled down to a series of philosophical propos-itions (and even Socrates can't do it without looking silly).

The differing interpretations of *Protagoras* as well as the style of the dialogue itself seem to show us that *Protagoras* might appear to be saying one thing about literature, especially if we take Socrates's side (discussing poetry is only for 'second rate drinking parties', say). But it may be saying another thing *as* literature: offering interpretive choices, diversity of opinions and contrasting different ways of arguing, and even comparing good and bad versions of these styles. What it performs seems to contradict what Socrates argues. Lacking a final resolution suggests that our choices are more open than Socrates's dis-missal of literature implies.

Conclusion: a hermeneutic dialectic?

Grace Ledbetter makes a powerful and insightful argument which, as it were, lets the literature back into both dialogues by outlining a 'Socratic theory of poetry', which differs from the views presented in *The Republic*. She suggests that Socrates believes that there is wisdom and knowledge in divinely inspired poetry, but does not think that poets, their performers and rhapsodes can interpret with any authority. Ledbetter notes that Homer and other classical poets invoke the Muses, who are outside normal, mortal time in some kind of 'continuous now': they have a divine vision of the events that they communicate to the poet, who, in turn, relates it to the audience. As the image of the magnetic rings in *Ion* showed, Socrates believes that a poem itself contains divine knowledge that passed through the poet to the audience (and on, let's not forget, to the assistant dance teachers). But *Ion* also showed that the interpretation of a poem was complex and needed knowledge and self-knowledge (qualities the dialogue shows Ion lacks). In the *Apology*, Socrates explains how he searched for wisdom, first among politicians and then poets. The poets, however, could not explain their poems, indeed, "the bystanders might have explained the poems better than their authors could" (*Apology* 23b–c). He realised that "poets do not compose their poems with knowledge, but by some inborn talent and inspiration, like seers and prophets, who also say many fine things without any understanding of what they say" (*Apology* 23c). While this made the poets *think* they were wise, they were not. This leads Socrates to think that poets have no responsibility for a poem's content. Instead it's through the "the act of interpretation that the wisdom of poetry can appear" and that poetry can be "a genuine source of knowledge".[20] Interpretation "reveals poetry's implications and exercises the same inquisitive resources that audiences apply and develop in leading an examined life".[21] If we agreed with this, we could add another aspect to the dialectic, to supplement the 'elenctic dialectic' and 'didactic dialectic' versions: a 'hermeneutic' or 'interpretive dialectic'. It's clear that Plato's *Protagoras* thinks something like this: his way of arguing shows us how stories and poems help us find out how to live (and in this way foreshadows Aristotle). More, the inconclusive dialogue offers us different views on interpretation, as if Plato offers us the choice of which path to follow. The highly literary nature of the dialogue, too, suggests this kind of interpretation.

As a coda, Marcus Folch finds in Plato's long dialogue the *Laws* an argument for an institution for literary and dramatic interpretation, which, in turn, depends upon the philosophical content of literature. The *Laws* offers some different nuances about literature to *The Republic*. For example, rather than exiling poets, the lawmakers of *The Laws* see themselves in the same line of work as poets and tragedians: "our entire state has been constructed so as to be a 'representation' of the finest and noblest life – the very thing we maintain is most genuinely a tragedy. See we are poets like yourselves, composing the same genre, and your competitors as artists and actors in the finest drama" (*Laws* 817b). The aim of the *Laws* is to set up a 'second best' city, and in this, "choral genres, poetic traditions and technologies of cultural memory and literary commemoration" play a significant role, as they did in Plato's Athens. However, in order to prevent these modes of poetry and music decaying (as discussed in **book 4** of *The Republic*, in Chapter 3), the *Laws* institutes a 'Chorus of Dionysus', a group of authoritative experts whose "knowledge of mimetic art, keen aesthetic perceptions and habituated disposition towards pleasure make them appropriate judges of poetic, music and dance excellence".[22] Their expertise consists of three areas.

> Anyone who is going to be a sensible judge of any representation – in painting and music and every other field – should be able to assess three points: he must know, first, *what* has been represented; second how *correctly* it has been copied; and, then, third, the *moral value* of this or that representation produced by language, tunes and rhythms.
>
> (*Laws* 669a–b)

That is, they judge the original story, the modes of its presentation and – while there is scholarly debate over the precise translation – the ethical import of the work. "What is developed here", Folch argues, is "not solely standard of evaluation, but the notion of criticism as a civic institution that introduces virtue within mimetic performance".[23] We don't have to agree with the aims of the 'Chorus of Dionysius', which are essentially deeply preservative, to see that the *Laws* suggests that ethics can be sought from literary and dramatic works. This task is that of the philosopher and of the critic, too. Perhaps, demonstrated in his work *as* literature, Plato allows for the beneficial philosophical discussion of literary works.

Plato *for* and *as* literature

My introduction to Plato has not tried to offer a single interpretation of his thought but to suggest a range of forking paths. The spectrum of ideas that Plato's Socrates puts forward and the ways in which they are presented demonstrates that Plato is much more complex than a 'hater of literature' and stands for more than a simplistic authoritarianism. Various aspects of his work create ample resources for how we might think about poems, plays, stories, what they might mean and how they might help us live. While Plato's Socrates seems to suggest one thing *for* literature, the dialogues may offer another *as* literature. The path now turns from Plato to his greatest pupil, Aristotle.

Notes

1 Michael Frede, 'Plato's Arguments and the Dialogue Form' in *Methods of Interpreting Plato and His Dialogues: Oxford Studies in Ancient Philosophy: Supplementary Volume*, eds. James C. Klagge and Nicholas D. Smith, 1992, pp. 201–19, p. 210.

2 For a discussion of similarities between the two, see Catherine Zuckert, *Plato's Philosophers: The Coherence of the Dialogues* (Chicago: University of Chicago Press, 2012), p. 282ff.

3 Iris Murdoch, *Existentialists and Mystics* (London: Penguin, 1997), p. 393. See also Christopher Janaway, *Images of Excellence: Plato's Critique of the Arts* (Oxford: Oxford University Press, 1995), p. 30.

4 Stephen Halliwell, *Between Ecstasy and Truth: Interpretations of Greek Poetics from Homer to Longinus* (Oxford: Oxford University Press, 2011), p. 179.

5 Halliwell, *Between Ecstasy and Truth*, p. 179.

6 Percy Bysshe Shelley, *Selected Poems and Prose*, ed. Jack Donovan and Cian Duffy (London: Penguin, 2016), p. 673.

7 The conversation immediately following this – which names three foreign generals employed by Athens – allows scholars to date the dramatic setting of the dialogue to 413 BCE. See Debra Nails, *The People of Plato* (Indianapolis: Hackett Publishing Company, 2002), p. 326; John D. Moore, 'The Dating of Plato's *Ion*', *Greek, Roman, and Byzantine Studies* 15:4 (1974), pp. 421–39.

8 See an extremely useful and very substantial article by Jonathan Lavery, 'Plato's Protagoras and the Frontier of Genre Research: A Reconnaissance Report from the Field', *Poetics Today* 28:2 (2007), pp. 191–246. Much of the philosophical discussion focuses on the issues of hedonism, the unity of the virtues (as we'll see) and *akrasia*, which means something like 'not being in charge of yourself'.

9 I. F. Stone, *The Trial of Socrates* (New York: Anchor Books, 1989), p. 48.

10 Plato, *Protagoras*, trans. C. C. W. Taylor (Clarendon Press: Oxford, 1976), pp. 147–8.

11 See also R. B. Rutherford, *The Art of Plato* (Oxford: Duckworth, 1995), p. 136.

12 Nickolas Pappas, 'Socrates' Charitable Treatment of Poetry', *Philosophy and Literature*, 13:2 (1989), pp. 248–61, p. 250.

13 Pappas, 'Socrates' Charitable Treatment of Poetry', p. 252.

14 Gregory Vlastos, *Socrates: Ironist and Moral Philosopher* (Cambridge: Cambridge University Press, 1991), p. 136.

15 Socrates's concern is for speaking in one's own authentic voice and his belief is that poetry distracts from that. There is a beautiful image in the *Laws* about this. One character takes on the voice of the poets to defend them to the law-maker:

> There is an old proverb, legislator, which we poets never tire of telling and which all laymen confirm, to the effect that when a poet takes his seat on the tripod of the Muse, he cannot control his thoughts. He's like a fountain where the water is allowed to gush forth unchecked. His art is the art of representation, and when he represents men with different characters, he is often obliged to contradict himself and he doesn't know which of the opposing speeches contain the truth. But for the legislator, that is impossible: he must not let the law say two different things on the same subject.
>
> (*Laws* 719c–d)

16 See e.g. Michael Gagarin, 'The Purpose of Plato's Protagoras', *Transactions and Proceedings of the American Philological Association*, 100 (1969), pp. 133–64.

17 Gregory Vlastos notes that Socrates is "tiresome" and sees this as evidence of Plato's genius: "Only a fine artist could worship a man yet show him life-sized, and with no crookedness of feeling, no warts or wrinkles smoothed out of the portrait". Plato, *Protagoras*, trans. Benjamin Jowett, revised Martin Ostwald, ed. and intro Gregory Vlastos (Indianapolis: Bobbs-Merrill Company, 1956), p. xxv.

18 Francisco J. Gonzalez, "The Virtue of Dialogue, Dialogue as Virtue in Plato's Protagoras" *Philosophical Papers* 43:1 (2014), pp. 33–66, p. 64.

19 Anne Carson, 'How Not to Read a Poem: Unmixing Simonides from "Protagoras"', *Classical Philology* 87:2 (1992), pp. 110–30, p. 110; further page numbers in the text.

20 Grace M. M. Ledbetter, *Poetics Before Plato: Interpretation and Authority in Early Greek Theories of Poetry* (Princeton: Princeton University Press, 2002), pp. 10–11.

21 Ledbetter, *Poetics Before Plato*, p. 13.

22 Marcus Folch, *The City and the Stage* (Oxford: Oxford University Press, 2015), p. 113.

23 Folch, *The City and the Stage*, p. 148.

Part II

'THE LOVER OF STORIES IS ...
A LOVER OF WISDOM'

——Aristotle

7

READING ARISTOTLE, FROM BEGINNINGS TO ENDS

Who was Aristotle?

Aristotle, son of Nikomachos the physician of the line of the Asklepiads, gazed around him as the ship rowed into harbour … he had had a smooth voyage from Mytilene, sole passenger in a fast war-galley sent to fetch him.

This fictional depiction of Aristotle, arriving in Macedonia to become tutor to the young prince Alexander, is by the historical novelist Mary Renault. She continues:

A gull swooped over the ship. With the reflex of many year's training, he noted its species, the angle of its flight, its wing-spread, its droppings, the food it dived for. The line of the vessel's bow-wave had changed with its lessening speed; a mathematical ratio had formed in his head, he stored it where he would find it when he had time … He was a lean smallish man, not ill-proportioned, who yet gave at first sight the effect of being all head.[1]

Renault has (clichéd all-head brain box) Aristotle pay close attention to the world because for Aristotle, philosophy begins in wonder at what is around us and so leads us to puzzle things out. His wide interests in all of nature – the gull's biology, the physics of the boat's movement – are why he is often called the founder of science.[2]

Another fictional Aristotle, from the literary critic and novelist Margaret Doody's *Aristotle: Detective*: the philosopher is Holmes to the narrator's Watson.

I was not able to enjoy the lecture very much, despite my appearance of thoughtful attention. Aristotle seemed very remote: a public man and a philosopher thoroughly absorbed in his subject. He lectured in his usual manner, speaking quickly, his eyes alight with interest, making rapid jests by the way for the attentive to catch. His subject

DOI: 10.4324/9781003097914-10

was comedy ... I tried to make notes but soon gave up the attempt. (Fortunately this lecture was one of a set ... written down and ... kept for all posterity).[3]

This shows us about Aristotle's activity as a teacher as well as a philosopher. Like Plato, he founded his own school, the Lyceum, just outside the boundaries of Athens (he wasn't allowed to own property within the city because he was a *metic*, a resident foreigner and not a citizen). Much of his philosophical writing seems more like lecture notes, sometimes quite disjointed and hard to follow. Doody is also making a sad scholarly joke. Most of Aristotle's work, despite being acclaimed for its style in antiquity, did not survive 'for all posterity'. This lecture on comedy, probably the second volume of the *Poetics*, was lost.[4]

A final fictional scene, from Dante, a much greater writer. In the *Divine Comedy*, Dante is led by the poet Virgil through Hell. Early in the journey they are in Limbo, the outermost circle of the inferno. Here, the virtuous pagans – who cannot get to heaven but are not actually suffering in hell – await the end of all time. Dante looks up and sees Aristotle, the "master of knowledge" with "a company of philosophers/all looked to him, and they all did him honour".[5] Aristotle sits highest, the greatest of them all, with Socrates and Plato next in rank. Through the commentaries on his work and preservation of his ideas by people like the Muslim thinker Ibn Sina (called Avicenna in Europe) and the Christian theologian Thomas Aquinas, Aristotle dominated the intellectual world of the medieval period.[6]

I have begun with these fictional versions because they tell us something about his thought, his activities and his reputation. Aristotle often begins his enquiries with a question (what do gulls eat? What is poetry? What is ... stuff?) then sifts through what people have already said, thinking that there was usually something worthwhile to be learned there. These are called *endoxa*, or reputable opinions "which are accepted by everyone or by the majority or by the wise" (*Topics* 100b21).[7] Using these, he moves from what appears and what is "familiar to us" (*Nicomachean Ethics* 1095b3) to more complex, unfamiliar issues: one translation of the *Metaphysics* speaks of how we "sneak up" on what's hard to understand.[8]

Born in 384 BCE in Stagira, Northern Greece, Aristotle was, as Renault writes, the son of a doctor: images and ideas of being healthy and the body recur in his work. Health is an activity for Aristotle. At around 17, he travelled to Athens to study at Plato's Academy and stayed there for 20 years, learning, studying and presumably teaching. When Plato died in 347 BCE Aristotle left: some say he was disappointed that he didn't become Plato's successor as head of the Academy. Aristotle was invited to Atarneus in Asia Minor by its ruler, Hermias, a supporter of the Academy. He stayed for three years and married Pythias, Hermias's niece. He then headed to Lesbos where he used a landlocked lagoon at Pyrrha for research on marine animals. In 342 BCE he was summoned to Macedonia to tutor Alexander. As we've seen, Alexander's father, Phillip II, came to dominate all Greece, including Athens. After he ascended to his father's throne, Alexander went on to conquer most of the world known to the Greeks, stretching as far as northern India. (The life of Alexander the Great is one of the awe-inspiring stories: as much terror as marvel.) Allied to the dominant Macedonian faction, Aristotle meanwhile returned to Athens and set up the Lyceum. (Some scholars even suggest this political allegiance shaped some of his work.)[9] He taught there, was widowed and married again, to Herpyllis, and they had a son, Nicomachus (it's traditionally thought the *Nicomachean Ethics* was written for him, but it may have been edited by him, or this may just be a nice story). Alexander died in 323 BCE: there was a backlash against the Macedonians and Aristotle was charged with impiety. He fled to Chalcis, where he died the following year, 322 BCE.[10]

Aristotle's relationship to Plato is complex, and of course, the focus of a great deal of scholarly commentary. Some scholars argue that Aristotle began as more a Platonic thinker but then developed his own intellectual trajectory: others suggest that as a young philosopher full of vim he opposed Plato (who is supposed to have compared him to a colt kicking his mother as he is born) but came over time to return to some of Plato's core ideas. Jonathan Lear suggests that both the thinkers "believed the world was a fundamentally good place" and "accessible to man's philosophical inquiry": their arguments "occurred over this framework".[11] More tersely, Martin Heidegger argued that what "Aristotle said what Plato placed at his disposal, only it is said more radically and developed more scientifically".[12] Aristotle rejects the forms, for example, but develops *The Republic*'s 'ethical psychology' in more detail. As I've suggested already, Aristotle is unlike Plato's Socrates, who seems always keen first to challenge convention. Where Socrates stings you away from the world, or paralyses you into internal contemplation about the transcendental beyond, Aristotle is interested in activity and in material things. His surviving works are treatises, not debates, and are pedagogical, witty but less dramatic than Plato's, and in his own voice. The differences between the two philosophers over literature seem especially acute. For Aristotle, poetry and drama play a significant and beneficial role in our ethical and intellectual life. Indeed, as I quoted in the introduction, "the lover of stories is in a sense a lover of wisdom, since a story is composed of wonders" (*Metaphysics* 982b19–20).[13] Martha Nussbaum writes that "there is a natural continuum between wonder and story-telling, between story-telling and theorising: continually we seek to expand the comprehensiveness of our grasp".[14]

Beginnings: reading Aristotle

For a literary reader, Aristotle's work is much harder than Plato's. The most obvious reason is that while Plato's dialogues present conversations and characters in finished works of genius, Aristotle's texts are often a bit abrupt and lacking in narrative flow. As Christopher Shields writes in his reassuring account of this, Aristotle's "manner of presentation is not likely to engage an unschooled reader".[15] It is as if "what has been delivered to us from Aristotle across the centuries is a set of telegrams" or, perhaps, his online PowerPoint slides.[16]

Another reason Aristotle is hard is simply that there is so much of his work across almost every field of intellectual endeavour. There are works that establish a basis for logic, grouped together as *The Organon*, meaning 'the tool'; his many studies which classify and analyse animals are forerunners to modern science, as is his *Physics*, an account of the forces of the natural world. His book *Metaphysics* is also foundational. Metaphysics is, approximately, our "most general attempt to make sense of things" and for Aristotle it is "first philosophy".[17] The prefix 'meta' roughly means 'beyond', so metaphysics goes beyond physics to wonder why nature is the way it is, why things are as they are, searching for causes and principles. (There is a longstanding joke that this subject was named 'beyond physics' because that book was shelved beyond the *Physics* in Aristotle's library and no one really knew what else to call these discussions.) Aristotle wrote about ethics (up to four books survive, scholars debate matters of authenticity). The *Nicomachean Ethics* has exercised a huge influence in Western thought and its sequel, the *Politics*, is another founding text. As we'll see, his books on literature, writing and speech, the *Poetics* and *Rhetoric* are seen as rather marginal, despite their influence for studies of literature and language. Everything he wrote is characterised by his sharp vision and desire to make finer and more useful categorisations and clarifications. For a modern reader, his work seems to mix description and prescription: for us, it's sometimes unclear if he means how things *are* or how things *should* be.

But I think Aristotle is hard for the more literary-minded reader because of another even more significant issue. In Plato, the same themes – truth, language, the good, how to argue – keep recurring but in Aristotle, simply, it's difficult to see what is actually going on. This is in part the gap between antiquity and now and in part the generations of scholarship that have shaped how Aristotle is understood. Pierre Hadot, who saw classical philosophy as a form of spiritual exercise, suggests that each of Aristotle's many investigations begins from a different starting point to investigate a specific problem, but that they have an "inner unity".[18] Different commentators find their version of this 'inner unity' by following different paths: some begin with Aristotle's analytic logic, for example, or with his proto-scientific thought. Mine is a more literary path. In the early 1920s, Heidegger was working through a new way of interpreting Aristotle, which, as one of his students, Hans-Georg Gadamer said, "freed the original Aristotelian text" from "the overlay of scholastic tradition and from the miserable, distorted perspective of the critical philosophy of the period": these new interpretations hit Gadamer like a "charge of electricity" and seemed to offer "an immediate, living understanding".[19] What Heidegger offered in his lectures was a clear, holistic, perhaps more literary and hermeneutical sense of

Aristotle, investigating *how we are* in the world: less a system of doctrines and more an orientation to ourselves. (However, because of Heidegger's membership of the Nazi party, and all that this entails, it's important to be especially aware of the possible ethical and political implications of his thought.) For me, it is this hermeneutic account of Aristotle's 'inner unity' which makes him so compelling and draws together the ideas of his I am going to discuss: substance, *telos* ('purpose' or 'point'), *praxis* ('doing'), *eudaimonia* ('happiness'), the moral virtues and the intellectual virtues, deliberation, ethics and politics along with, most crucially for this book, the role of language, story and metaphor.[20] This approach gives a subtly different sense to Aristotle's *Rhetoric* and his *Poetics*.

This leads to the final reason that Aristotle is hard for the literary reader. Literary people have their attention drawn constantly to Aristotle's *Poetics*. Often this is for pedagogic reasons: it's short, famous and an obvious place to start. But this is unfortunate, as I hinted in the introduction. On first reading the *Poetics* is dull and descriptive and seems only to classify and catalogue: not too tough to make your way through, but, once read, it's hard to see what all the fuss is about. Unless it is very carefully explained at great length (like explaining a joke or offering a huge commentary on a sonnet), the reader misses out on precisely the themes and thought that make Aristotle so significant. Aristotle's ideas lie so deeply under the surface of the *Poetics* as to be almost inaccessible. The book is not a good way into Aristotle's most influential beliefs and arguments about how to live well and the role literature plays in that. (Luckily, the *Poetics* has brilliant contemporary commentators, and I will be drawing on many of them).

F. R. Leavis, perhaps the most significant British literary critic of the twentieth century, did not find the *Poetics* useful at all. In 'How to teach reading', a manifesto for what he called 'practical criticism', he declared that there is no "critical apparatus to be derived from the *Poetics*" except what the aspiring critic takes there: this "is not to dispute that Aristotle was a great man or that the *Poetics* has great historical importance; but the *Poetics* does not ... in itself provide the means of making one a better critic".[21] As if in a direct reply, the most celebrated Chicago Neo-Aristotelian critic Wayne Booth wrote an essay called 'The *Poetics* for a Practical Critic', speaking in, and so updating, Aristotle's voice. Indeed, as I'll show later, Booth's major critical works disprove Leavis's point and are a thoughtful illustration of the practical use of Aristotle for understanding literature. In a question-and-answer section in his essay, Booth puts this, pointedly, to the Aristotle of the *Poetics*:

> You neglect the most important questions, the questions that really interest readers and spectators: about the meaning of life, about ethical and political and cultural and historical issues.

To which Booth's Aristotle replies:

> Read our other works. Then, when you come back to read the *Poetics* more carefully, you'll be surprised at how many of those 'more interesting' questions are implicitly addressed, once you face the constructional questions with a determination to attend to the ethical qualities that are inescapably present in any effective plot.[22]

The 'important questions' about how to live are intrinsic to literature and not simply 'added-in' as content. The point of this half of the book is to introduce 'our other works' and their ideas, because of their importance for literature and to show how they underlie the *Poetics*.

My path begins with the most basic questions and is guided by Aristotle's central concern for activity, for *praxis*. It's a point he makes again and again in his ethics and in the *Rhetoric* and *Poetics*, too: 'doing' is our orientation to the world. My path then goes on to the idea of *telos* and teleology: this will turn out to be extremely important for understanding literature, and leads on to the virtues, which are central for Aristotle. The moral virtues help our behaviours in order to make us happy, and the intellectual virtues reveal the patterns of ourselves and our world. Both show us something about the nature and importance of deliberation, too. This leads on to my discussion of the *Rhetoric*, which is about language and how we are in the world, and then, finally, to the *Poetics*, which concerns the construction and meaning of poetry and drama.

Endings with Aristotle

In his *Metaphysics*, Aristotle turns to the most fundamental questions: what is the basis and structure of all reality? Or, what is *is*? "There is" he declares "a science which investigates being as being" (1003a17). We now call this ontology (*ontos* is one of the Greek words that means 'being') and it is the task of the philosopher (for who else, except philosophers, jokes Aristotle "will enquire whether Socrates and Socrates seated are the same thing"? (1004b1–2)). For Aristotle, the question of 'what *is*?' comes down to 'what is substance?' The originally Latin word 'substance' already sounds abstract and philosophical. It means 'what you stand on', that is: the ground. As I said earlier, Hannah Arendt argues that philosophical terms are "frozen analogies" that you need to hear in their original context.[23] Heidegger argues that the Greek word for substance, *ousia*, was in common use and meant, more or less, our possessions, things we own or have around us. (We say that someone rich is a 'person of substance', meaning: they have lots of material things.) Today we might say: *stuff*.

Heidegger explains further: *ousia* means "a being in the how of its being". His point is that the word *ousia* is not some abstract thing but "a being that is there for me in an emphatic way, in such a way that I can use it, that it is at my disposal".[24] Your stuff. We get to know about things by using them in our everyday life: we sleep (mostly) in a bed; we drive a car; we build with a hammer; the activity of measuring is to see how big something is, how long it will take to get there or what size widget we need. We don't come to know about stuff in the abstract (as 'being' or 'matter' or 'atoms') but as things around us that we use. You learn about your phone by texting on it, you experience your shoes by wearing them. So, if we want to understand 'what something is', we have to 'sneak up' on it through how we use it, how it appears to us, in our everyday activities. Heidegger says that for Aristotle, we start with our normal understanding of stuff: life has a sort of "natural intelligibility", made up from our use, our doing, our *praxis*.[25] When you drink your coffee, you rarely think of the mug (unless it's chipped, bother, or lost: where is it?) and thinking about it as matter, made from atoms, is a specialised, scientific way of looking at it: atomic structure is not your first thought about your morning coffee. Life, for Aristotle, is an engagement with the world which finds it intelligible through our activity: this is how you can uncover the 'why' of something.

Very famously – it's the first line of the *Metaphysics* – Aristotle believes that we naturally desire to know, to reach out in order to understand things. Philosophy begins in wondering *why* and then attempting to puzzle things out. People "do not think they know a thing till they have grasped the 'why' of it" Aristotle writes, in the *Physics* (194b19; see also *Metaphysics* 1013a24–36) and then outlines what answers to 'why' look like. These are known as the 'four causes' and have been explained to students for well-over two millennia (we can imagine young Athenian men or medieval monks or the Edwardian women of the early years of my university pouring over them). Understandably, they have gathered a huge 'crust' of names, explanations and interpretations. The ancient (and unhelpful names) for the causes are: material, formal, efficient, final. But, as you will see (and as Aristotle says) the four are linked. They are really just four ways of explaining the same thing.

Roughly the four 'explanations' respond to the following questions.

Material: what *material* is it made of? An answer: 'the statue is made of bronze'.

Formal: what's its *form*? What's it based on? What sort of thing is it? What does it look like? What's its blueprint? (Recalling that the *logos* means 'how something is brought to light', this explanation is about how something appears). An answer: 'it's the statue of a spider'.

Efficient: Who or what was the "primary source of the change" (*Physics* 194b30)? Aristotle says that, for example, "the man who deliberated is a cause, the father is a cause of the child" (194b30–31). Who made it happen? So with the statue, 'the sculptor Louise Bourgeois made it'.

Final: What's it for? What's the point of it? This is perhaps the most important explanation for the purposes of this book. The classical Greek word is *telos* is often translated into English as 'end' but this is slightly dated: *telos* means, roughly, aim, purpose or point. 'To begin with an end in mind' doesn't mean fantasise about when you have finished but to focus on the point of what you are doing as you begin it. The point in soccer is to score the most goals by putting the ball into the net; the deeper point of playing is to, say, keep fit and make friends by playing sport; the deepest, final answer (as we'll see) is to live a good life. Heidegger warns us about taking these translations too closely: *telos* means, really, 'for-the-sake-of-which'.[26] *Telos* also emerges in the form of knowledge known as *techne*, skill, or knowing your way around something: to do something skilfully rather than just 'as you're told', you need to know why, what the point is. *Telos* also carries a sense of completion: which we'll see is important in the *Poetics*, and for this reason *telos* is close to closure. From *telos* we get *teleology*, the sense of things having a point or a purpose.

Telos, the idea of purpose in its broadest sense, is one of the things that most powerfully divides Aristotle from us, and is both a strange idea and a familiar one. It's at the core, implicitly or explicitly, of contemporary neo-Aristotelian thinkers like Martha Nussbaum and Alasdair MacIntyre who turn to narrative and storytelling in relation to questions of ethics. It's especially important for literature.

In the case of a statue, it's clear to see how the first three explanations/causes work: the fourth might be more complex ('she did it to make money', '... to honour her mother', '... to express something she felt'). But for Aristotle, *telos* underlies everything. It suffuses the natural world ("leaves grow to provide shade for the fruit" *Physics* 199a26). It shapes the movement of stars and planets. It is a truism to say that the modern world finds teleology in this huge, all-shaping sense of purpose more difficult that Aristotle did. "Only a child" writes a modern admirer of Aristotle's science "would ask 'what are stars for?'".[27]

To ask 'does life have a purpose?' takes you straight to the profoundest existential questions both personally and culturally (which my book will not answer but illustrate). For example, the acrimonious debates in the late nineteenth and early twentieth centuries over the nature of evolution were, on the surface, about whether human beings were basically animals or something more special, but at the deepest level were about our *telos* or purpose in the cosmos. In the natural world, the theory of evolution shows that the agentless sifting process of evolution through natural selection meant life that fit its environment best ('fittest') thrived. Some found it hard to find a *telos* in this and thought that to stop believing in *telos* might mean that the universe is purposeless and meaningless. Another, smaller example: the French philosopher Jean-François Lyotard defined postmodernism as "incredulity about metanarratives".[28] Postmodernism was more than a popular cultural and intellectual trend from the 1970s to 1990s or an analysis of the state of knowledge for post-industrial Western society: it was about *telos*. Lyotard meant that people no longer believed in modes of thought that rely on teleology, the purposeful stories that shaped how we understand everything. These purposeful stories included, for him, modes of religious thought; a liberal or whig sense of progress from worse to better; Marxist accounts which explain all past and future histories, from oppression through revolution to utopia, by reference to teleological principles like the movement of history; popular scientific accounts which reduce human behaviour to a simplistic story. Some found Lyotard's account convincing; others wanted to believe in a purpose; others, too, found different ways of thinking about life's purposes. The point of these two examples is to show how profoundly ideas about *telos* are woven into both individual lives and wider social and political ideas.

Why is teleology important for literature?

As we can see from the too-brief discussion above, *telos* and narrative, and so literary narratives, are bound together in the most profound and complex ways. One of the great advances of literary critical thought of the past century or so has been in analysing and coming to understand this conflux of ideas in and about narrative (to explore this in any detail would be more than a book-length study). Narratology, the quasi-scientific analysis of the parts of narrative and their significance is one aspect of this and was inspired by Aristotle, as we'll see. Another aspect, and again influenced by the *Poetics*, has been the growth of creative writing courses and books, which teach forms of writing: "since Aristotle wrote *The Poetics*" writes screenwriting authority, Robert McKee "the 'secrets' of story have been as public as the library down the street".[29] Both narratology and the discipline and business of creative writing explore and advocate for the aspects of writing that we could call 'technical teleology', the 'what-its-for'.

One of the most familiar and obvious examples of this 'technical teleology' is the principle of 'Chekhov's gun'. In advice to young writers, the Russian author Anton Chekhov (1860–1904) proclaimed that, if the story introduces a gun on the wall, it ought to be fired (that's what it for). Significant details in narrative have a purpose, a *telos*. But in his excellent introduction to narrative, Abbott notes this combines two ideas: that the presence of the gun raises expectations and that the author must fulfil them with a bang. Abbott suggests there are all sorts of ways in which those expectations might be fulfilled: at a significant moment, the gun might be found to be unloaded; it could be discovered to be a toy or made of chocolate to be eaten after a lover's tiff.[30] What is key is the *potential*.

'Chekhov's gun' is really only a well-known example of 'for the sake of which' which underlies plot. Plot, "a constant of all written and oral narrative" is the "principle of interconnectedness and intention which we cannot do without in moving through the discrete elements – incidents, episodes, actions – of narrative".[31] This interconnectedness of plot is fundamentally teleological, because, in a narrative plot, things happen purposefully towards an end. E. M.

Forster's familiar example makes this clear: for him, a story is made up of events told in their chronological sequence, like a chronicle, but a plot emphasises the causality, the 'for-the-sake-of-which', the *why*. Forster writes

> The 'king died and then the queen died' is a story. 'The king died and then the queen died of grief' is a plot ... or again: 'The queen died, no one knew why, until it was discovered that it was through grief at the death of the king'. This is a plot with mystery in it.[32]

Explaining events, to yourself or another, means explaining *why* they happen, and a plot is a kind of explanation. Well-made plots are teleological: we long to know what happens *and* why, and when we find out, we achieve *closure*, a kind of pleasure in understanding.

This allows us to see an even wider sense of teleology which inheres in any narrative, philosophical, historical, fictional or scientific. We may disagree about the particular cause ('the queen died of grief' or 'she caught the same infectious disease' or 'she was poisoned immediately afterwards by an ambitious heir') but we do not disagree on the possibility of there being a cause. As soon as we explain or emplot, we tell a story, and so we invoke a sense of a teleology, a 'for the sake of which', made manifest in narrative. *Telos* is instantiated in narrative and narrative is a teleological form or explanation. Plots "organize reality" and so introduce "a *telos* in the disorder and creates the ordered, contrived areas of intensity that Sartre called 'adventures'".[33] *Telos* forms a certain sort of *logos*. Our language is suffused with this teleological language of purpose. For example, the language in which evolution is described is almost always teleological: a gene is 'selfish' in its attempt to survive; evolution is ascribed agency when it 'does' something.

There is a more complex reflection on the relation between *telos* and narrative, suggested by Frank Kermode's *The Sense of an Ending*. These lectures look at the role of literature in shaping the purpose of our lives, our own *telos*. Kermode argues that to make sense of our short human span, we "need fictive concords with origins and ends": these 'concord fictions' are "like the plots of novels".[34] But Kermode is not primarily interested in the *content* of these fictions, whether they are personal, literary, religious or historical. Instead, he is interested in *how* they come to be, in "making sense of the way we make sense of the world".[35] He writes:

> Let us take a very simple example, the ticking of a clock. We ask what it *says*: and we agree it says *tick-tock*. By this fiction we humanise it, make it talk our language. Of course, it is we who provide the fictional difference between the two sounds; *tick* is our word for a physical beginning, *tock* our word for an end. We say they differ. What enables them to be different is special kind of middle ... The clock's *tick-tock* I take to be model of what we call a plot, an organisation that humanises time by giving it a form.[36]

This is an advance on Forster: even a story has a plot. Literature has turned these noises in time into a form, a plot, a little 'humanised' fictional life, in which we can find a meaning.

Mere starting and stopping become more: beginning and ending. Literature offers a "fictive model of the temporal world" and novels "have beginnings, ends, and potentiality, even if the world has not".[37] But Kermode's work allows a more challenging thought than noting that literary texts inevitably have a teleological pattern. We humans often come to understand ourselves reflectively through what we see and engage with in the world (as when we draw metaphors to describe ourselves). If the narratives we use and engage with are teleological (because all narratives have a 'technical teleology'), perhaps we take that teleology, that sense of an ending, from them. Perhaps *telos* is not taken from life, or the intelligible universe, and embodied in stories, but taken from stories, from how stories work, and then embodied in life. The 'technical teleology' of how stories work may be an 'existential teleology'.

We may no longer believe in *telos* for everything, or that the universe is teleological, but narratives are: their tick-tock has a meaning. Aristotle's ideas about purpose tie internal teleology to wider concerns for making meaning in the world.

Conclusion

Beginning with what writers have said about Aristotle, I've introduced his life and suggested why he might be hard to read. However, taking a thread from Heidegger's lectures on his work, I've begun by emphasising his approach to how we use things and how this gives us their 'why'. This, in turn, leads to the 'four causes', to the importance of *telos*, and its significance for literature.

Crucially, Aristotle thinks that, just like everything else, human beings have a *telos* too. A hammer is for hammering; a cat for catching mice; a car for driving. Our *telos* as humans is for 'happiness'. In English, 'happy' sounds rather shallow and facile: the proudly intellectually *un*adventurous poet Philip Larkin is taken to be profound in his poem 'Days' where he mocks the idea of happiness. But the Greek word, in Aristotle, is much more complex and interesting: *eudaimonia*. What it means and the ways it can be achieved are the topic of the next chapter.

Notes

1 Mary Renault, *Fire from Heaven* (London: Virago, 2014), pp. 172–3, 175–6.
2 See, for an accessible account, Armand Marie Leroi, *The Lagoon: How Aristotle Invented Science* (London: Bloomsbury, 2014).
3 Margaret Doody, *Aristotle: Detective* (London: Arrow, 2002), p. 260.
4 See Umberto Eco's astonishing thriller, *The Name of the Rose*. The history of the text of the *Poetics* is discussed in Chapter 10.
5 Dante Alighieri, *Inferno*, Canto IV, l. pp. 131–3, *The Divine Comedy*, trans. C. H. Sisson (Oxford: Oxford University Press, 2993), p. 64.

6 The history and reception of Aristotle's work from classical Athens to the pre-
sent is an amazing intercontinental and intercultural story: a good introduction
is *Aristotle Transformed: The Ancient Commentators and their Influence*, ed. R. Sorabji
(London: Duckworth, 1990); *Aristotle Re-Interpreted: New Findings on Seven Hundred
Years of the Ancient Commentators*, ed. R. Sorabji (London: Bloomsbury, 2016); F. E.
Peters, *Aristotle and the Arabs: The Aristotelian Tradition in Islam* (New York: New York
University Press, 1968). There are chapters on the medieval Arabic and medieval Latin
reception of Aristotle in *The Oxford Handbook of Aristotle*, ed. Christopher Shields
(Oxford: Oxford University Press, 2012). An accessible general reader account of this
scholarly history, though without much reference to Aristotle, is Violet Moller, *The
Map of Knowledge: How Classical Ideas Were Lost and Found: A History in Seven Cities*
(London: Picador, 2020).

7 See also Jonathan Barnes, 'Aristotle and the Method of Ethics' in *Method and
Metaphysics* (Oxford: Oxford University Press, 2011), pp. 174–94.

8 Aristotle, *The Metaphysics*, trans. Hugh Lawson-Tancred (London: Penguin, 1998),
p. 176.

9 See Edith Hall, 'Aristotle's Theory of Catharsis in its Historical and Social Contexts'
in *Transformative Aesthetics*, eds. Erika Fischer-Lichte, Benjamin Wihstutz (London:
Routledge, 2017), pp. 26–47.

10 See Carlo Natali, *Aristotle: His Life and School* (Princeton: Princeton University Press,
2013); Anton-Hermann Chroust, *Aristotle: New Light on His Life and Some of His
Lost Works* (London: Routledge & Kegan Paul, 1973). Perhaps a (potted) biography
doesn't really tell you very much about a philosopher: at the start of his lecture
course on Aristotle in 1924, Martin Heidegger says, rather brutally, that "regarding
the personality of a philosopher, our only interest is that he was born at a certain time, that he worked, and that he died". Martin Heidegger, *Basic Concepts of
Aristotelian Philosophy*, trans. Robert Metcalf and Mark Tanzer (Bloomington: Indiana
University Press, 2009), p. 4. His students Hannah Arendt, Hans-Georg Gadamer
and Jacob Klein remembered this stark assertion all their lives, and it took on a nas-
tier and more evasive meaning after 1933 when Heidegger became a Nazi.

11 Jonathan Lear, *Aristotle: The Desire to Understand* (Cambridge: Cambridge University
Press, 1987), p. 266/7.

12 Martin Heidegger, *Plato's Sophist*, trans. Richard Rojcewicz and André Schuwer
(Bloomington: Indiana University Press, 2003), p. 8.

13 Jonathan Lear argues against this interpretation of wonder, principally because,
while "wonder provokes us to understand, in the *Poetics*, understanding provokes us
to experience wonder", 'Katharsis', *Essays on Aristotle's Poetics*, ed. Amélie Oksenberg
Rorty (Princeton: Princeton University Press, 1992), pp. 315–40, p. 324.

14 Martha Nussbaum, *The Fragility of Goodness* (Cambridge: Cambridge University
Press, 1986), p. 260.

15 Christopher Shields, *Aristotle*, 2nd ed. (London: Routledge, 2014), p. 25.

16 *Aristotle's Ethics*, revised, ed., trans. Jonathan Barnes and Anthony Kenny
(Princeton: Princeton University Press, 2014), p. 3. The chapter of PowerPoint-like
slides does work rather beautifully in Jennifer Egan's 2011 novel *A Visit from the
Goon Squad*.

17 A. W. Moore, *The Evolution of Modern Metaphysics: Making Sense of Things*
(Cambridge: Cambridge University Press, 2012), p. 1.

18 Hadot goes on to suggest that Aristotle's aim was not to teach an answer but
"the techniques of using the correct methods in logic, the natural sciences and
ethics" just as one interpretation of Plato's dialogues sees them as less concerned
with doctrine and more with the process and demonstration of argument itself.
Pierre Hadot, *Philosophy as a Way of Life*, ed. Arnold Davidson, trans. Michael Chase
(Oxford: Blackwell, 1995), p. 105.

19 Hans-Georg Gadamer, *Heidegger's Ways*, trans. John W. Stanley (Albany: State University of New York Press, 2004), p. 7, p. 32, p. 113.
20 On Heidegger and Aristotle, see, *intra alia*, Theodore Kisiel and John van Buren (eds) *Reading Heidegger from the Start* (Albany: State University of New York Press, 1994); Walter Brogan, *Heidegger and Aristotle* (Albany: State University of New York Press, 2005); Drew Hyland and Johan Panteleimon Manoussakis, eds., *Heidegger and the Greeks* (Bloomington: Indiana University Press, 2006); Franco Volpi in Whose Name? Heidegger and 'Practical Philosophy', *European Journal of Political Theory* 6:1 (2007), 31–51; Thomas Sheehan, *Making Sense of Heidegger* (London: Rowman & Littlefield International, 2014).
21 F. R. Leavis, *Education and the University* (London: Chatto and Windus, 1948), p. 133.
22 Wayne Booth, 'The Poetics for a Practical Critic' in *Essays on Aristotle's Poetics*, ed. Amélie Oksenberg Rorty (Princeton: Princeton University Press, 1992), pp. 387–408, p. 402.
23 Hannah Arendt, *The Life of the Mind*, vol. 1. (Harvest: New York, 1978), p. 104. For example, she points out that in the Athens of Aristotle's time, the word *katēgoria* (category) was a legal term used in court, meaning, roughly, the charges laid against someone in court, an indictment. Aristotle was the first to use it as philosophical term (something like 'predicate') "resting on the following analogy: just as an indictment ... hands something down ... to a defendant that he is charged with, hence that belongs to him, the predicate hands down the appropriate quality to the subject" (105): it lists the qualities that belong to something.
24 Martin Heidegger, *Basic Concepts of Aristotelian Philosophy*, trans. Robert Metcalf and Mark Tanzer (Bloomington: Indian University Press, 2009), p. 19.
25 Heidegger, *Basic Concepts*, p. 21.
26 Heidegger, *Basic Concepts*, p. 57.
27 Leroi, *The Lagoon*, p. 80.
28 Jean-François Lyotard, *The Postmodern Condition*, trans. Geoff Bennington (Manchester: Manchester University Press, 1986), p. xxiv.
29 Robert McKee, *Story* (London: Methuen, 1999), p. 5. See also Michael Tierno, *Aristotle's Poetics for Screen writers* (New York: Hyperion, 2002). For histories see D. G. Myers, *The Elephants Teach: Creative Writing Since 1880* (Chicago: University of Chicago Press, 2006); Mark McGurl, *The Program Era: Postwar Fiction and the Rise of Creative Writing* (Cambridge, MA: London: Harvard University Press, 2009).
30 H. Porter Abbott, *Narrative* (Cambridge: Cambridge University Press, 2002), p. 56.
31 Peter Brooks, *Reading for the Plot* (Cambridge, MA: Harvard University Press, 1984), p. 5.
32 E. M. Forster, *Aspects of the Novel*, ed. Oliver Stallybrass (London: Penguin, 2000), p. 87.
33 Guido Mazzoni, *Theory of the Novel* (Cambridge, MA: Harvard University Press, 2017), p. 50.
34 Frank Kermode, *The Sense of an Ending* (Oxford: Oxford University Press, 2000), p. 7, p. 190.
35 Kermode, *The Sense of an Ending*, p. 31.
36 Kermode, *The Sense of an Ending*, p. 45.
37 Kermode, *The Sense of an Ending*, p. 54, p. 138.

8

HOW TO LIVE

Happiness, the virtues and literature (*Nicomachean Ethics*)

Introduction: *eudaimonia*

In the last chapter, I said that Aristotle thinks that we humans have a *telos*, a 'for-the-sake-of-which'. Leaves protect and nourish a plant; a shoe is for wearing; a cat is for catching mice (or possibly for interrupting online meetings); a human being is for happiness. 'Happiness' sounds trite. Aristotle's term is *eudaimonia*. Because *eudaimonia* is the point of our existence, it's important to understand what it might mean.

There is no simple translation: 'happiness', 'well-being', 'prosperity', 'good fortune' and so on all have subtly different connotations in English. *Eu* as a prefix means 'good' (as *eu*logy, the 'good words' we say at a funeral) and a *daimon* is a sort of semi-divine spirit. An older translation has "watched over by a good genius".[1] Arendt argues that *eudaimonia* means

> neither happiness nor beatitude; it cannot be translated and perhaps cannot even be explained. It has the connotation of blessedness, but without any religious overtones, and it means literally something like the well-being of the *daimon* who accompanies each man throughout life, which is his distinct identity, but appears and is visible only to others.[2]

Part of the sense of *daimon* is akin to the idea of your persona, which is, as it were, you seen from the outside by others. (How well do we know how we appear? Significantly, in Latin, the *persona* was the mask worn by an actor playing a role, through which they would speak: you cannot see a mask as you wear it, as we cannot easily see our personas.) This captures the sense that *eudaimonia* is only in part under our control. Heidegger translates *eudaimonia* as something like *authenticity*.[3] For him, *eudaimonia* means you being there for yourself as much as possible within the possibilities the world has given you.

Perhaps a close modern word is 'fulfilment'. We use this in saying 'their life was fulfilled' or 'I found this fulfilling'. If we're asked: 'what's the point of life?', we often answer: to live a fulfilled life, to be fulfilled. This also gets the sense

                    DOI: 10.4324/9781003097914-11

that *eudaimonia* is both final and, because it's 'for-the-sake-of-which', present all the time: "I want to look back on a fulfilling life and I want each day to be fulfilling", or "I want to be my best self every day". This doesn't mean that each day is happy: revising for an exam or beginning to get fit may not be fun, but they are fulfilling because they have a purpose. 'Fulfilment' also gets the sense that we may be prevented from *eudaimonia* by something utterly outside ourselves. Finally, fulfilment is an activity (and Aristotle is a philosopher for whom life is about doing): *eudaimonia* is an activity. So we might say (roughly), 'I want to *do* something fulfilling with my life' or 'their life was fulfilled *by* ...'.

What is fulfilling? Aristotle asks this in the *Nicomachean Ethics*. Pleasure is: but does a life of drink, food, sex, drugs and music really satisfy? Russell Brand, who was a famously pleasure-seeking celebrity, reports back from his wild years: no.[4] Aristotle is more condemnatory: a life centred on these pleasures is only "a life suitable to beasts" (*Nicomachean Ethics* 1095b20). Moving away from bodily pleasures, people seek to be fulfilled by the admiration of others. 'Honour' is a rather old-fashioned term, but that's what we mean: 'respect' carries some of right sense. But as the worlds of politics and celebrity show, honour and respect come and go: so, for Aristotle, these rely too much on the whims of other people to be fulfilling. Our *eudaimonia*, our fulfilling life must belong to each of us alone (we must *do* it, not have it *done to* us or *for* us). Moreover, fulfilment must be somehow beyond the brittle chances of life, although it is interwoven with them. (*The Fragility of Goodness* is the title of Nussbaum's book on the topic: this fragility was a great concern for the classical Greeks.) It is here in the *Nicomachean Ethics* (and not in the *Poetics*) that Aristotle mentions the 'wheel of fortune' (1100b4), an idea and an image which has become so central to literature, and especially to Shakespearian drama. (Pistol talks of "Giddy Fortune's furious fickle wheel" (*Henry V*, III.iii.27) and Edmund, at the end of *King Lear*, of how the "wheel is come full circle" (V.iii.203). These and many others rely on the metaphor that fate is a spinning wheel: we find ourselves at the top and spin down through bad luck, or, conversely, we are suffering and the wheel takes us up to good luck and prosperity.) Making money isn't fulfilling as a purpose because you make money to do something else: live your life, pay for things, go to the beach, win the respect of your peers and competitors, and so on.

So *eudaimonia* isn't a simple goal.[5] But from this discussion, Aristotle takes several threads. First, *eudaimonia* must be an overall 'final' or 'complete' answer because other activities are undertaken 'for the sake of' it. Second, it is self-sufficient to a degree: he doesn't mean that we have to live an isolated life by ourselves like hermits (we are communal or "sociable by nature" (1097b11)). He means that if we think our fulfilment depends on, say, the happiness of our distant relations or friends or on the shifting praise of our peers, we've made a mistake. Finally, fulfilment doesn't just happen. We have to work at it: it's an activity.

So, how do we work at achieving fulfilment? As usual, Aristotle begins with familiar examples in our everyday world. Take people who are skilled at playing musical instruments. If you want to be a great flute player, you have to see what characteristics a great flute player displays: breath-control, learning to have nimble fingers, developing musical sense to follow or make a tune and so on. All these characteristics need practice, discipline and are learned through doing. (After all, to say that you can play the flute brilliantly *in theory* means almost nothing: you learn to play with and because of the music, just as you learn to swim in and because of the water.) If that is true for playing the flute (or driving a car, writing an essay, arranging flowers, sailing a boat, making a speech, etc.), then it's true for our whole life. Using our reason and the *logos*, we find out how to live a fulfilled life, and then learn and master the dispositions and skills for this. Aristotle calls these the virtues (or, rather, his English translations call them that). The virtues are the characteristics that fulfil your life. The *point* of the virtues – having a fulfilled life – and *doing* them are the same. Exercising the virtues is fulfilling and not simply ways to achieve a goal: *eudaimonia* isn't like a checklist of good things. It is an activity, and that activity is characterised by the virtues, the fullest and best use of our capabilities.

Aristotle has two categories of virtues: the moral virtues, to do with our behaviour, reinforced through habit, and the intellectual virtues, to do with our thinking and acting. While they overlap in a complex way, the difference between them is significant and ultimately stems from his view of the human soul. For Aristotle, the soul – ourself – is divided into two parts, the irrational and the rational: a version of Plato's 'ethical psychology' from *The Republic*. We might consider this division between our more 'animal' selves, concerned with hunger and desire, for example, and our 'thinking mind'. But Aristotle then subdivides again the 'thinking mind' into two: one part which focuses on things "whose principles cannot be otherwise" (1139a7) and one part which focuses on "variable things" (1139a9). The first is made up of those things that cannot change: a triangle always has three sides. The second is made up of those things that can change: you can make shoes in lots of different styles. (This will make more sense as he continues to explain the intellectual virtues.) I'm going to discuss the moral virtues first.

The moral virtues: how should I behave?

The Aristotelian way of thinking about goodness and fulfilment in philosophy (and in many other areas like education and sport) is called *virtue ethics* and focuses on what we might call character: how to develop as a virtuous person and so be happy, achieve *eudaimonia*. These ideas, often unrecognised, have had an enormous influence on Western culture: they are more influential on Western literature, for example, than the *Poetics*.

The slogan 'moderation in all things' is usually taken these days to apply to what we eat and drink, but for Aristotle, it applies to all our behaviours as well: the Greek idea of *sophrosyne*, moderation, which I discussed in the first chapter. It is Aristotle's principle for working out how to apply and understand

120

the moral virtues. In each range of behaviours, the moderate or middle point is the right one. "Excess and defect are characteristic of vice", whereas the virtue is the middle point, for people "are good in but one way, but bad in many" (1106b34–35). Aristotle is less keen on Plato's idea that there is a single universal good because, while the method for discovering what is virtuous is the same, what that actually consists of varies from person to person: the precise virtues of a general are not the same as those for a doctor or teacher, just as the diet that's right for big Milo the wrestler doesn't suit a weedy old philosopher.

This principle is most easily understood by example. In courage: to be overly courageous is to be reckless; to have too little courage is to be cowardly. Proper courage is between these two extremes. Or, similarly, in confidence: you can be over confident and arrogant, or too lacking in confidence, and so nervous and diffident. The right amount, assertiveness, is in the middle of these. Temperance, another old-fashioned word, means self-restraint. Some people have no self-restraint about eating, drinking or other bodily pleasures and are led by "appetite to choose these at the cost of everything else" (1119a). This is self-indulgence and childish, as Aristotle notes, since children "live at the beck and call of appetite" (1119b6). The opposite of this vice has no real name, but Aristotle suggests we call it 'insensibility', a lack of interest in the bodily pleasures. It's good to have the right level of interest in appetite, in physical pleasures: we need to eat to survive. How we deal with money and respect is important, too. Being too generous with money is prodigal and not being generous enough is miserly. To want too much money is greedy and avaricious: to need none looks careless and unworldly. Showing off too much wealth is vulgar; not showing enough off is mean. Wanting too much respect is vanity, and wanting too little is self-effacement: a justified desire for respect is right. Again, for Aristotle, seeking the midpoint should guide our behaviour.

Aristotle is very interested in how the moral virtues help us live together and are crucial for the very existence of the *polis*. He discusses justice and politics at length. Friendship is most significant "for without friends no one would choose to live" (1155a5). For us, two and a half millennia later, friendship is thought of as a private matter (although we do praise people publicly for being 'a good friend') but for Aristotle, this virtue has a political sense as well. Friendship is what makes the *polis* work as a community, a kind of 'civic-mindedness'. With people, you should be friendly, neither over-friendly, eager to please and obsequious (those who "praise everything and never oppose" (1126b14)) nor sulky, rude and stand-offish (those who "oppose everything and care not a whit about giving pain are called churlish and contentious" (1126b15–16)). Again, one should tell the truth about oneself, and neither boast nor self-deprecate; one should be convivial, but not a buffoonish class-clown (who "spares neither himself nor others if he can raise a laugh" (1128a36)), nor a crushing boor ("for he contributes nothing and finds fault at everything" (1128b3)), nor dull. One's temper, too, should have a medium position:

Hot-tempered people get angry quickly and with the wrong persons and at the wrong things and more than is right, but their anger ceases quickly – which is the best point about them ... Sulky people are hard to appease, and retain their anger long, for they repress their passion.

(1126a14–19)

The virtues are "concerned with passions and actions" (1109b30). They are not just the work of the reasoning mind (as the good is for Plato) but offer a fuller view of ourselves and our interactions with others.

There's also a very illuminating passing discussion of poets (1167b28–1168a8). Aristotle is discussing benefactors (we might say today, mentors or career champions). Benefactors cherish and love the people they have helped, even if that person is "not any use to them and never will be". Why? Because "every man loves his own handiwork better than he would be loved by it if it came alive". This happens most with poets who "have an excessive love for their own poems, doting on them as if they were their children". Why do benefactors, craftsmen and poets cherish their products? Existence is

a thing to be chosen and loved, and that we exist by virtue of activity (i.e. by living and acting), and that the handiwork is in a sense the producer in an activity; he loves his handiwork, therefore, because he loves existence.[6]

The poet loves their poems because it is the poems that gives them existence as a poet (the writing makes the writer, paradoxically). Two ideas are foregrounded here. First, an artwork is a product created by skill, not by divine inspiration. Second, this discussion reminds us that we live by activity, that our activity is our life. (And, of course, Aristotle's discussion makes us think of the myth of Pygmalion or its retelling as Pinocchio. Geppetto the puppet maker desired to be a father so wanted a son – almost, a product – whereas Pinocchio wanted to be a "real boy", presumably with free will and choice: not a product. The same story is retold in *Frankenstein*, *My Fair Lady* and others.)

The significance of the moral virtues for literature

It's almost impossible to read Aristotle's discussion of the moral virtues without thinking: how do these apply to me? How have I behaved? When have I tipped from being, say, properly convivial into being a boor? Indeed, the *Nicomachean Ethics* is in part like a guide, a 'conduct book' which seeks to tell us how to conduct ourselves, how to behave in society. Aristotle emphasises this repeatedly: for example, "the present inquiry does not aim at theoretical knowledge like the others (for we are inquiring not in order to know what excellence is, but in order to become good, since otherwise our inquiry would have been of no use)" (1103b27–30). A doctor's son, he is scathing of those who think that just reading about the virtues will help.

It is by doing just acts that the just man is produced, and by doing temperate acts the temperate man; without doing these no one would have even a prospect of becoming good. But most people do not do these, but take refuge in theory and think they are being philosophers and will become good in this way, behaving somewhat like patients who listen attentively to their doctors but do none of the things they are ordered to. As the latter will not be made well in body by such a course of treatment, so the former will not be made well in soul by such a course of philosophy.

(1105b9–17)

It is not enough to know, you have to *do* (Philip Sidney: "as Aristotle saith, it is not *gnosis* [knowing] but *praxis* [doing] must be the fruit").[7] This is why the moral virtues are like habits: you practise them, like playing an instrument, and so you become better at them.

Literature helps us see this. Gilbert Ryle, not a literary critic but a philosopher, explained how Jane Austen's work demonstrated the virtues in an Aristotelian way. While her novels display the morals of her time, and sometimes she is didactic ("in the tones of an anxious aunt"), more importantly, Ryle says, her work comes from a "deep interest in some quite general, even theoretical questions about human nature and human conduct".[8] The titles of her novels demonstrate this. *Sense and Sensibility* is about finding a balance between being too sensible and being too sensitive: the "ecstatic emotionality of her Marianne is made to stand out against the sham, the shallow, the inarticulate and the controlled feelings of Lucy Steele, Willoughby, Edward and Elinor" (288). *Persuasion* is about "persuadability, unpersuadability and over-persuadability" (although this "particular theme-notion of persuadability was, in my opinion, too boring to repay Jane Austen's selection of it" (289)) and in "*Pride and Prejudice* almost every character exhibits too much or too little pride, pride of a bad or silly sort or pride of a good sort, sham pride or genuine pride and so forth" (289). *Emma* could "have been entitled Influence and Interference" (290). These are fictional, Aristotelian explorations of human behaviours in society: *polis* and polite. Characters are not either bad or good but different from each other, placed on scales ("A is a bit more irritable and ambitious than B, but less indolent and less sentimental. C is meaner and quicker-witted than D, and D is greedier and more athletic than C" (295)). Ryle is not suggesting that Austen is a philosopher but that she has imbibed Aristotelian ideas from her milieu; probably, he speculates through the work of the philosopher Lord Shaftesbury from the generation before her. Ryle also notices something very important about Austen's "ethical vocabulary" (297): it is full of aesthetic terms: 'moral taste', 'moral and literary tastes', 'beauty of mind', 'the beauty of truth and sincerity', 'delicacy of principle'. Behaving correctly and having good artistic taste are correlated (and recall Protagoras's argument to the same effect in Chapter 6). The implications of this view are these. First, that stories help us find the midpoint between being, say, too sensible or too sensitive, too proud or too lacking in confidence: they help us understand and live the virtues. Second, that the qualities that help us judge stories aesthetically are profoundly linked with those qualities that help us make judgements about our virtues and the virtues of others, about how to live.

The virtues are not individual but work together as an integral whole to build fulfilment and the good life for each of us and our communities. Their integral nature is revealed by the idea, present in Shakespeare, of the 'tragic flaw': Macbeth is too ambitious, Othello loves not wisely but too well, Hamlet thinks too much. But a flaw is not a failing or excess in one characteristic, as it is usually assumed to be. Rather, the failure in one virtue makes a flaw, a crack, in the whole person, and a crack in a beautifully gilded glass bowl means the whole will easily shatter if pressed even softly. For Aristotle, the whole of the person is integral and linked together, as is the community: if one part of a community is flawed or damaged in some way, the whole community is at risk. One implication is that growing in the virtues needs the right conditions. We need a good environment, the right *polis* to thrive. Virtues are shared between people: indeed, the virtues of good citizenship and conviviality can only exist in sharing, and many of the virtues similarly involve other people.

Aristotle's discussion of the virtues brings to mind stories about behaviour and gives us tools to make moral judgements. More, his image of 'fortune's wheel' leads to stories which explore the fragility of human life. But there is something even more important both in his argument and implied by what it presupposes.

As I suggested earlier, Aristotle takes what people say or what is conventional and then explores this to find wisdom within it. He draws on Homer and other writers to provide his arguments. His thought suggests that we don't *invent* the virtues from first principles but instead we learn or discover them from what's gone before. We have models of courage or confidence and we can choose to follow them or not. This means that the moral virtues turn out to *rely* on literature in the widest sense, because they are activities, learned from and shared with others, and not just the result of our own reasoning mind.

Alasdair MacIntyre, one of the most significant thinkers for the revival of 'virtue ethics', shows why this is so. How would we know what courage was unless we had examples of courage, recklessness and cowardice from which to learn? Stories are how we work out what we should do and why, how we orient ourselves in the world. This is why MacIntyre expands the idea that we are the 'animal with language' to argue that we are "essentially a storytelling animal":

> I can only answer the question 'What am I to do?' if I can answer the prior question 'Of what story or stories do I find myself a part?' We enter human society, that is, with one or more imputed characters – roles into which we have been drafted – and we learn what they are in order to be able to understand how others respond to us and how our responses to them are apt to be constructed. It is through hearing

124

stories about wicked stepmothers, lost children, good but misguided kings, wolves that suckle twin boys, youngest sons who receive no inheritance but must make their own way in the world and eldest sons who waste their inheritance on riotous living and go into exile to live with the swine, that children learn or mislearn what a child is and what a parent is, what the cast of characters may be in the drama into which they have been born and what the ways of the world are. Deprive children of stories and you leave them unscripted, anxious stutterers in their actions as in their words. Hence, there is no way to give us an understanding of any society, including our own, except through the stock of stories which constitute its initial dramatic resources.[9]

The stock of stories, literature, is crucial not only for educating us in the virtues but as the *carrier* of virtues, both for individuals and for society. To understand and inhabit a virtue, we need a story to create its setting and give it meaning. What we do makes sense only if we know why we are doing it, if we know the *telos*. The *telos* and virtues are brought together in the narrative, and this, too, has social effects: *polis* and *logos*.

This binding together appears in three further characteristics for MacIntyre: it creates unity in our lives, makes our lives intelligible and helps hold us and others accountable.

MacIntyre and many others argue that modern life 'atomises' or compartmentalises us into different roles which appear to make contrasting and occasionally conflicting demands on us. Sometimes we are an employee, sometimes a boss, sometimes a student or a teacher, a sibling, a citizen. These might seem to make us different people. But thinking in terms of the virtues helps with these divisions: the whole person is united through their virtues. The courage you show dealing with an intolerable boss in private is the same virtue of courage you show speaking up at a confrontational local meeting or in dealing with pain.

MacIntyre suggests that the virtues, the *telos* that underlies them and the narrative which instantiates them work together to make us intelligible to ourselves and others. In real life, as in literature, we ask ourselves: but why did so-and-so (or I) do that? How does it fit into the story? Each of us is the protagonist in our own story and, in and as story, we come to understand, frame or reframe ourselves. With story, too, we come to understand how we and others fit together. Finally, stories for MacIntyre are how we hold ourselves accountable: "I did this because …". It's also how we hold others accountable, too. In understanding, contextual framing and accountability, *logos*, as story, and *polis*, as community, are bound together.

Finally, stories are not simply vital for their 'content' but also for their form. That a story has a beginning, a middle and an end, for example, teaches us about the nature of life; moments of recognition in fiction teach us about moments

125

of recognition in life; and the style of work of fiction tells us something about reading the world. From our actions, and from explaining our actions to ourselves and others, we come to recognize who we are. Perhaps, too, we learn to discern key moments, turning-points, in our lives.

MacIntyre's argument goes one step further. The stock of stories make up a 'tradition' and it is only in relation to a tradition that we can orient or understand ourselves. 'Tradition' is a powerful and controversial idea: some want to embrace traditions; others find traditions stultifying, overpowering and oppressive. For MacIntyre, both these extremes are mistaken. Tradition is unavoidable:

> all reasoning takes place within the context of some traditional mode of thought, transcending through criticism and invention the limitations of what had hitherto been reasoned in that tradition; this is as true of modern physics as medieval logic.[10]

In unthinkingly accepting traditions, we give them power over us and our societies, while in simply rebelling against traditions, we express and affirm them by that opposition. In pretending traditions do not exist by ignoring them, we are usually unknowingly following them or some other unquestioned idea.[11] In throwing traditions away, we lose the resources to question or uncover them or what lies behind them, although, absolutely, we do not have to accept them as they are. For MacIntyre

> when a tradition is in good order it is always partially constituted by an argument about ... its particular point and purpose. So when an institution – a university, say, or a farm or a hospital – is the bearer of a tradition or practice or practices, its common life will be partly, but in a centrally important way, constituted by a continuous argument as to what a university is and ought to be or what good farming is or what good medicine is. Traditions, when vital, embody continuities of conflict.[12]

A tradition, for MacIntye, when it is working properly, 'in good order', is less like a constricting convention and more like a conversation going on through time: it has intersecting voices, some shouting louder, some quieter. New people join the conversation with new ideas ("how about ...?") or go back to older points ("hold on, going back to what you said earlier ...?"). Tradition is where you have the conversation and how you have it.

Following up this idea, I suggest that healthy traditions, embodying sites and continuities of conflict, might have three further characteristics.

First, they are hybrid, whether they acknowledge this or not, in their foundations and in the continued existence. No tradition is 'just itself' but is made up by mixing, addition and engaging with novelty. For example, the tradition of Greek philosophy is not 'pure' but was and is constantly mixed in with other ideas, other traditions and interpretations. Martin Bernal's provocative *Black Athena* (1987) argued that Egypt, North Africa and Asia were the sources of what was taken to be Greek culture. However, in order to assert a uniquely European origin to this tradition, historians and philosophers over the last three hundred years or so minimised this 'non-European' history. Less contentiously, but equally firmly, Walter Burkert has shown that there was a great deal of what we'd now call cultural exchange in and before Plato and Aristotle's age, and demonstrated this both by textual scholarship and through new archaeological discoveries. Burkert argues that while the question 'What is Philosophy?' arises from a Greek foundation, Plato and Aristotle read their predecessors (the 'Pre-Socratics') who, in turn, were influenced by literature from the East, especially "cosmogonic myth, or stories of creation" and "wisdom literature" (recall the brief discussion of Hesiod in Chapter 1).[13] The mathematics and astronomy that Plato and Aristotle drew on had contemporary parallels, too, in Babylon.

Second, no tradition is really unified or final or completely smoothed out. Any tradition is full of questions, things that aren't quite resolved, bumps and contradictions. Those who inhabit a tradition are sometimes keen to ignore or marginalise these, but lumps, jagged edged and unanswered questions are often the places from which a tradition can renew itself. These are exactly the sort of inconsistencies, of course, that Socrates was so keen to uncover.

Finally, as we've seen, the openness of the tradition is also part of that tradition: traditions can be more open or more closed, willing to examine their contradictions or not, to change and adapt. This, in turn, is inextricably tied up with the political power of traditions. Some of the most important discussions we have today are about power and the relationships between different traditions. Here are three very brief examples of the way traditions interact, all to do with literature.

In his important book, *Decolonising the Mind*, the globally significant Kenyan writer Ngũgĩ wa Thiong'o argues that language is both "communication and a carrier of culture".[14] As everyday talk builds up over generations in stories and other forms of culture, there is a "gradual accumulation of values … right and wrong, good and bad, beautiful and ugly, courageous and cowardly, generous and mean … Culture embodies those moral ethic and aesthetic values" and becomes the way people see themselves and their world.[15] Culture is a people's identity. This matches the ideas about stories, values and virtues that MacIntyre tells. But Ngũgĩ has a different point to make. He grew up as Gĩkũyũ in British-colonised Kenya, speaking Gĩkũyũ in the fields and at home, hearing and telling Gĩkũyũ stories. He went to a colonial school, and was forced, often through humiliating punishments, to speak English. Indeed, speaking good English led to his educational success in the colonial school system. While a peer did brilliantly in his exams but failed English, Ngũgĩ did well in English and only passed the other exams: but it was Ngũgĩ who went on to a coveted elite colonial secondary educational place. Studying in English and reading English literature both undervalued his Gĩkũyũ culture and overvalued the colonisers, alienating him from his own world. In addition to demeaning images of Africans, this literary education enforced and rewarded a different cultural system, offering a different valuation of the virtues. This is the *imposition* of a tradition as a tool of power. Ngũgĩ rejected this colonial literary tradition and chose to write in Gĩkũyũ and has become a major world writer.

Another relation to the interaction of traditions is taken up by Salman Rushdie and Homi K. Bhabha. Again, faced with the interaction of both British and a range of South Asian traditions, Rushdie sought to develop and celebrate hybridity,

> intermingling, the transformation that comes of new and unexpected combinations of human beings, cultures, ideas, politics, movies, songs ... Melange, hotchpotch, a bit of this and a bit of that is how newness enters the world. It is the great possibility that mass migration gives to the world.[16]

This is a powerful sense that traditions develop through combinations and encounters. Bhabha's critical work analyses precisely this hybridity.

A third approach is used by Ato Quayson who explores how a range of African writers (including Chinua Achebe, Wole Soyinka and Tayeb Salih) have developed the form of tragedy. This involves an "interleafing" of texts and ideas.[17] This is neither a rejection nor a hybridisation of tradition but a kind of exploring side-by-side. To the understanding of ideas on tragedy developed by Aristotle, he adds a concept from Akan culture in Ghana: *musuo*, a social infraction which 'harms the souls' and so deeply impacts the victim that it may "cause the affected individual to suffer a loss of faith in society" which "may consequently also affect their capacity for making ethically informed choices".[18] From the anti-colonial activist and thinker Frantz Fanon, Quayson takes the idea that self-knowledge can be split and the tragic protagonist can both be "suffering impediments to the articulation of *eudaimonia*" and also be, at one remove, a spectator to that "unravelling".[19] These two ideas 'interleaf' with the tradition inherited from Aristotle to offer a different account of tragedy.

The moral virtues are often explicitly demonstrated in literature: so too are the consequences of our flaws and the 'wheel of fortune'. Literature as a narrative is the carrier of these virtues and ideas across time and in society. These narratives help us to become intelligible to ourselves and others, hold ourselves and others to account and to recognise the shape of our lives. For MacIntyre, the stock of stories is a tradition within which we exist and about which we may hold a range of views. Traditions are contentious and sites of conflict: hybrid, never really complete, and tied up with power. How we engage with traditions and how we negotiate the conflict of different traditions is a feature of our lives.

The intellectual virtues

I've looked at what Aristotle calls the moral virtues: how we behave with others and with ourselves. Aristotle also describes the intellectual virtues, which, in part, help direct the moral virtues to find the 'middle way' between excess and deficiency, to help us be courageous, say, and neither reckless nor cowardly. They are about how we understand, and what that understanding means.

They have an even greater significance, however. For Aristotle, "thinking constitutes reality at the highest level".[20] Because for him, the world is comprehensible, thinking and the world's intelligibility mirror each other. Parts of our souls, of ourselves, map onto what they think about since it is because of "a certain likeness and kinship with the objects that they have the knowledge they have" (1139a10–11). So the shape of the intellectual virtues, which think about the world, is also the pattern of our world. Aristotle expresses this by saying that they are "the states by virtue of which the soul possesses truth" (1139b15): the intellectual virtues are how 'truth appears'. This is a central claim on which Heidegger builds a great deal, and it's hugely influential for Arendt, too.

As I said earlier, Aristotle's model of the soul is divided into two parts, the irrational and the rational, and then subdivided again into those parts which think about things that can change (our emotions; materials we work on; the world of politics) and those that cannot change (a geometrical square always has four sides). This builds a distinction into Aristotle's thought that still exists in the world today, between the active, practical life and the 'life of the mind' or 'contemplative life'. This model of the soul structures the five intellectual virtues, as Aristotle teases out distinctions in our thinking, based on the activities and subjects about which we think.

The five intellectual virtues are **knowledge** (*episteme*), **intelligence** (*nous*), **understanding** (*sofia*), **craftsmanship or skill** (*techne*) and **wisdom** (*phronesis*). Again, as we have seen, the translations of classical Greek words vary and these virtues have all been given different names at different times. Each choice of translation offers a slightly different contemporary nuance. (If 'wisdom' is translated as 'prudence', for example, it seems to summon up stereotyped great aunt or old-fashioned bank manager.) More, what they are precisely is still the object of scholarly and philosophical debate, so here, I am only trying to give a rough, contemporary sense of their meaning. Each, too, illuminates and contrasts with the others.

The three highest intellectual virtues, that most exemplify the life of the mind, are really forms of contemplation. These play no role in practical matters, although as the very highest kind of life, they are closest to truth.

Knowledge (*episteme*) is the knowledge of things that have to be as they are: that is, unchanging things. In maths, for example, there are some universal principles which have been discovered and are always true (*pi*, the ratio of a circumference to a diameter of a circle, say) and some principles which can be deduced from these (the formula for the area of a circle). These can be demonstrated and so can be taught (think about how you learned about circles in maths, learning first principles and then their implications). Knowledge is proven and is not a matter of opinion or discussion (1142b1).

Intelligence (*nous*) is closely connected to knowledge. Knowledge is about what we know, and what stems from that: what we can deduce from first principles. But how do we come to those first principles? It's not a craft (it isn't a question of making something) nor is it wisdom (which deals with our ever-shifting world and not with unchanging things) nor is it knowledge (in Aristotle's sense) because it can't be simply taught (it's not like a mathematical fact we can learn). Intelligence is more like 'abstract thinking'. A dog can catch a ball in the air but can't work out from that catch the more abstract principles which underlie gravitation and the movement of objects. Cats know how to find warm spots but have not discovered how to make and control fire (luckily).

Understanding (*sofia*) is the highest of the intellectual virtues for Aristotle: it combines both knowing 'first principles' and knowing about what comes from them. That is, in Aristotle's terms, it combines both knowledge (what unchangeable things are) and intelligence (the 'abstract thought' that deduces first principles). Understanding is concerned with things that do not change: what is "straight is always the same", while "what is healthy or good is different for men and for fishes" (1141a22–3). Understanding is concerned with truth, not human interests or practical matters: after all, animals are practical and have "a power of forethought with regard to their own life" (1141a28–29) but this is not understanding. For Aristotle, this is the reason for the oldest joke about academics, the 'absent minded professor'. People say that the great thinkers have understanding "but not wisdom" because they are "ignorant of what is to their own advantage" and that "they know things that are remarkable, admirable, difficult, and divine, but useless" because they are not practical (1141b5–7).

Aristotle is very concerned with practical matters, as we've seen, so the two remaining intellectual virtues concern these, as we move from the 'life of the mind' to the active life. So **craftsmanship** or skill (*techne*) is not about contemplation but about producing or making things. It means 'knowing-how-to' make something: how to make a pair of shoes, a healthy meal, rewire a house, write a formal letter or essay or sonnet. It is not simply knowing-by-rote. A person skilled in carpentry knows much more than 'how to nail a plank': they know what tools to use, how to solve a wood-working problem, the significance of different types of wood and so on. Their skill is purposefully directed towards an end, which they understand and is, as it were, present in their mind as they work. Writing is craft, for Aristotle, as we will see when we look at the *Poetics*.

The person is the origin of the made object (say, shoes) but the person is not that object.[21] This (seemingly obvious) point is important because the aim of *techne* is to make a product. *Making* something is different from contemplating something: the *telos*, the point of the activity is the thing that's produced (the shoe, the sonnet). Aristotle hammers this distinction home:

a carpenter and a geometer look for right angles in different ways: the former does so in as far as it useful for his work, while the latter inquires what it is or what sort of thing it is, for he is a spectator of the truth.

Nicomachean Ethics 1097b29–33

These virtues tend, for Aristotle, to very different kinds of life.

Wisdom (*phronesis*) is the most complex and interesting of the intellectual virtues: the word 'wisdom' seems to summon up a Dumbledore figure but Aristotle means much more than this. Heidegger argues that what is vital in *phronesis* is *praxis*, that is, action, activity, *doing*.[22] The word 'wisdom' sounds a bit too passive for this in English, which is why *phronesis* is often translated as 'practical wisdom'.

Wisdom "is concerned with things human and things about which it is possible to deliberate; for we say it is above all the work of the man of practical wisdom, to deliberate well" (1141b8–10). Deliberation is a form of action, not just chatting. A wise person can "deliberate well about what is good and expedient" (1140a26). This is not about the technical details of what makes a healthy meal or how to mend a car engine because knowing these stems from a skill. This deliberation is more about living the right kind of life as a whole (which might then involve, for example, the decision to eat healthy meals or to debate whether to repair an engine or to sell it as scrap). No one deliberates about eternal things (we don't argue over whether a triangle has three sides). Part of wisdom is being good at deliberating, or, as we might say, good at weighing things up, seeing issues from different points of view, discussing choices. Perhaps we all know people with whom it's useful to talk things through (although we may not agree with them or follow their advice). The opposite is also the case. Aristotle argues that the person who has been "ruined by pleasure or pain" (1140b17) or who is 'intemperate' is not wise. Similarly, young men, writes Aristotle, become expert geometricians and mathematicians, but this does not make them wise.

Wisdom is not a craft: it doesn't *make* anything, and its point is you and your own life. It isn't knowledge because thinking your way around a situation in life, discussing it with your friends is not the same as discovering the mathematical truths about a circle. Of course, in deliberating, you will draw on examples of situations and events which have gone before or that you've read or seen, but no life or situation is quite the same. Each needs its own deliberation and part of this process is paying close attention to its particularities as well as seeing similarities with other examples.

Wisdom is useful: it is concerned with individual cases and moments, and not universal, eternal principles. It's interested in the best course of action. This is why experience helps with wisdom: it helps deliberation. Wisdom is also how we know what virtues to inhabit and when to apply them. Wisdom tells us when and how to be confident, for example, which is why people who are unwise can also be unvirtuous.

Wisdom, too, is the key virtue for politics. Good leaders are wise because they deliberate the best action for a group or community to take in each case. This means that wisdom is not the most virtuous or highest of the virtues (because "man is not the best thing in the world", (1141a21)) neither does it concern eternal things. Indeed, to use an even older phrase, you might call this virtue 'worldly wisdom', as it concerns our shifting and shifty world. (We'll see the political topics for deliberation in the next chapter.) Not all of politics is deliberation, however. The part of political life that involves 'setting things up' is, for Aristotle, more like craftsmanship. Legislation is a craft and the product is a law (indeed, Bills in Parliament or on Capitol Hill are drafted, like blueprints for buildings). People call it wisdom ('worldly wisdom') when you look out for yourself and your own but in the realm of politics, politicians are also often seen as "busybodies" (1142a2). Yet, as Aristotle says, your own good cannot exist without managing your own affairs or without a system of government (1142a9–10).

Some other dispositions come from these virtues. Judgement is akin to wisdom and is about those things over which you deliberate (but does not, like wisdom, make commands, only judges). The virtue of sympathy, like judgement, is tied into the virtue of fairness: and, in turn, these, as part of fairness, rely on intelligence, because to work out how a particular event or case is connected to a 'first principle' is the work of intelligence. Cleverness, too, is a capacity of action, and can be used for good or bad (we can admire a villain's cleverness).

Just as with the moral virtues, the intellectual virtues work together. Diet is an example (recall that Aristotle's father was a doctor). For Aristotle, you might *know* that light meats are digestible and healthy (first principle) but might not know *which* meats are light, so may not eat healthily. Conversely, a wise person has experienced that chicken is easier to digest than beef, and so chooses one over the other. In terms of action, wisdom is preferable to knowledge, though best to have both, as Aristotle says.

Crucial in Aristotle is the idea of *prohairesis*, another of the words that is very hard to translate into English: 'choice', 'moral purpose', 'intention', 'purposive choice'. Charles Chamberlain suggests that 'commitment' is the nearest English idea.[23] *Prohairesis* is the combination of knowing you need to do the right thing and then the action or habit of doing it. This links the intellectual and moral virtues. We come to understand something intellectually (that we should exercise, or not smoke, or not eat meat) and then make that part of our actual, daily life. The first step is coming to understand something requires you to be a good deliberator. When we fail (to take exercise, say), we are suffering from *akrasia*, weakness of the will or lack of self-mastery, a contrast to *prohairsis*. Our thinking leads us to commit to a course of action and our behaviour is that commitment.

Finally, Aristotle makes a point about the highest form of life, the 'life of contemplation'. It cannot exist by itself. He writes that, "all human things are incapable of continuous activity" (1175a4) and "one will also need external prosperity; for our nature is not self-sufficient for contemplation but our body also must be healthy and have food and other attention" (1178b33–34). More, your own affairs need management and that, in turn, relies on the *polis* and its government as a whole. For these reasons, you cannot live by contemplation alone: to live, you need the whole person, all of the soul. To map this onto the story of Plato's cave: you can leave the cave and stand in the Sun, in a moment of pure apprehension of the 'good beyond being', but you will have to come back down into the cave to eat, exercise, take care of business and deal with your duties in the *polis*. You can see here clearly a difference between Plato and Aristotle: recall that at the end of **book 9** of *The Republic*, the philosophers refuse to take part of the running of the *polis* (*The Republic* 592a).

Literature and the intellectual virtues

Stories, poems and plays may both demonstrate and carry the moral virtues, but this discussion of the intellectual virtues reveals another important and perhaps counter-intuitive relationship.

Recalling the match between our intellectual virtues and their objects for Aristotle, we can see that creating and discussing literary texts are not the three highest virtues of 'the life of the mind': a literary work is not an unchanging eternal thing (*knowledge* like *pi*) nor like the first principles of *nous*, nor pure understanding, *sofia*. Their intelligibility and meaning come from the 'practical life', the virtues of *techne*, craft and *phronesis*, practical wisdom. Since we humans made literary texts and they exist in time, this is hardly a surprise, but this has some important implications. Most obviously, the creation of literature is, as we'll see, mostly an act of *techne* for Aristotle. A poem or drama is a sort of product, constructed with a *telos*. I'll discuss this more in Chapters 10 and 11. It also reminds us that literary texts are 'in time' and so can change. Our experiences of poems, novels and plays change over time as we age. Our society's views of texts change and develop too.

Even more interesting is the act of responding to literary works, which I have suggested is an inextricable part of our experience of literature. This, for Aristotle, turns out to be, can only be, part of wisdom, *phronesis*. This turns Socrates's view on its head. Literature plays a vital role in thought and in virtue. We can get a hint of this in how we talk about discussing literature. We *calculate* the solution to an equation but we *deliberate* together the meaning of a poem; a physicist *discovers* an answer but a critic *persuades* of an opinion; we *recall* data and information but we *grow to understand* meaning. Discussing a literary text is an *activity*, done with others or by yourself: it is inextricable from the experience of the text itself, and is part of what literary reading is, really. These are characteristics of *phronesis*.

That discussing a text is a form of *phronesis* runs against the convention that art and culture are somehow cut off from everyday life. Angela Curran summarises the origin of this view. The eighteenth-century thinker Alexander Baumgarten "coined the term 'aesthetic' (from the Greek work *aesthesis*, sense perception) to refer to the experience of beauty and sensory pleasure available in art": in turn, this led to the idea that art offers a "distinct and special sort of experience, aesthetic experience which became the focus of philosopher's attention, and a new field of philosophic inquiry, aesthetics, was born".[24] Yet, thinkers who begin from the study of literature have sat uneasily with this model of artistic contemplation. Around a hundred years ago, I. A. Richards, one of the founders of modern literary criticism, wrote that when "we look at a picture, or read a poem, or listen to music, we are not doing something ... unlike what we were doing on the way to the Gallery or when we dressed in the morning".[25] The experience of an artwork is "more complex and ... unified" but it's fundamentally of the same kind as our everyday experience.[26] There's no huge gap between our experience of art and our everyday experiences: our experiences make a continuum. For Richards, this is true of our choice of words too: he is less interested in a word or phrase's beauty than in what it can do. A literary "discussion of the reasons for the choice of words – which too often seems a trivial exchange of whimsies – can become an introduction to the theory of all choices" he suggests, and "the better we understand what place words hold in our lives the readier we shall be to admit that to think about their choice is the most convenient mode of thinking about the principle of all our choices".[27] Aristotle's work allows a way of approaching literature which challenges the idea that the arts are "a private heaven for aesthetes".[28]

As a part of deliberation and *phronesis*, literary texts have an important role for our thinking about how to live. Wisdom and deliberation are highly significant for Martha Nussbaum who, following Aristotle, argues that literature is vital for our 'ethical theorizing' for several interconnected reasons.

First, she argues that literature "searches for patterns of possibility – of choice and circumstance, and the interaction between choice and circumstance – that turn up in human lives with such a persistence that they must be regarded as *our* possibilities".[29] Literature finds shapes of life that seem common to us and that we can, perhaps in more complex ways, share with each other.

Second, when we deliberate artworks, we can find ourselves dealing with whole, intricate characters, their rational and emotional aspects, and the multifaceted situations and events in which they find themselves. More generally, literary texts bring together the confused and muddled state of our existence better than neat philosophical examples. This makes our deliberations richer and more useful, more rooted in our experience. In addition, we also face the intricacies of the text before us in all its complexity of form and style (characters, after all, exist in text). Through this, we become aware of the gaps or slips in the text and the way it shapes how we respond: in turn, this shows us something akin to Frank's 'mimetic knowledge', revealing the complications and difficulties of deliberation, and the need for self-reflection, too.

This second reason leads to a third. By being rooted in concrete particular situations, we are encouraged in the "intense scrutiny of particulars" (Nussbaum takes the phrase from Henry James).[30] This helps us learn to pay attention to specific moments and events, not as cases or examples, but as themselves (in a way akin to Murdoch's account of loving particular objects, animals and people from Chapter 4). We deliberate and become wise in relation to particular, time-bound situations, not general and eternal universal principles, in life and in literature.

Fourth, for Nussbaum, literary texts work *heuristically* through the problems: we 'live in' a book or a story and so experience it profoundly. It is not a separate 'realm' for us, in this view, but part of our everyday life. Form and style, ways of shaping and telling, as well as content are significant. Finally, and echoing Philip Sidney and Aristotle, exploring and understanding moral problems through lit-erature is "an experience open to everybody" because literary texts use shared rather than technical language.[31] This shared experience helps to build a 'we', a community: art becomes part of our communal experience, part of how we deliberate together. This sense of publicness is explored in the next chapter.

Conclusion

This chapter began with *eudaimonia* and looked first at the moral virtues which help achieve it. These turn out to be closely involved with literature, not only because literary texts demonstrate them or their lack, but also because they are passed on through stories. We are, for Alasdair MacIntyre, 'a storytelling animal'. The stock of stories we share make up the traditions we inhabit and our engagement with these traditions can be fraught. The intellectual virtues, for Aristotle, model our world. For literature, *techne* and *phronesis* are the most significant, and these allow us to see the significance of literature in helping us to think and to live. This is a very different conclusion to that of Plato's Socrates. Aristotle thinks that stories, poems and plays are highly important for how we live and our philosophical and ethical reflections. Indeed, without literature in the broadest sense, we would be lost, unable to navigate ourselves or our soci-eties, and unable to reflect, deliberate and become wise. As we draw out the implications of this, in terms of traditions as well as reflection, we see how *polis* and *logos* for Aristotle are intrinsically and powerfully linked. The next chapter turns to the *Rhetoric* and explores the significance of this link.

Notes

1 W. D. Ross, *Aristotle*, 5th ed. (London: Methuen, 1949), p. 190. 'Genius' here means 'spirit'.
2 Hannah Arendt, *The Human Condition* (Chicago: University of Chicago Press, 1998), p. 193.
3 *Eudaimonia* is "the presence of the finished state of the living being with regard to its highest possibility of being" Martin Heidegger, *Plato's Sophist*, trans. Richard Rojcewicz and André Schuwer (Bloomington: Indiana University Press, 2003), p. 119.

4 See Russell Brand, *Revolution* (London: Century, 2014); see also Raymond Geuss, 'Russell Brand, Lady T, Pisher Bob and Preacher John', *Radical Philosophy* 190 (March/April 2015), pp. 2–7.

5 In fact, at the end of the *Nicomachean Ethics* (but not the *Eudemian Ethics*), Aristotle does have a partial answer to a goal for *eudemonia*, one we might suspect after reading Plato. He says – some commentators think rather half-heartedly – that the 'fulfilling life' is the 'contemplative life', the life of the mind.

6 Plato's Socrates offers an analogous but interestingly different view: "don't be surprised if everything naturally values its own offspring, because it is for the sake of immortality that everything shows this zeal, which is love" (*The Symposium* 208b).

7 Philip Sidney, *Sidney's 'The Defence of Poesy' and Selected Renaissance Literary Criticism*, ed. Gavin Alexander (London: Penguin, 2004), p. 22.

8 Gilbert Ryle, *Critical Essays: Collected Papers Volume 1* (London: Routledge, 2009), p. 286. Further page numbers in the text.

9 Alasdair MacIntyre, *After Virtue* (London: Duckworth, 1985), p. 216.

10 MacIntyre, *After Virtue*, p. 221.

11 As Keynes wrote: the

> ideas of economists and political philosophers, both when they are right and when they are wrong, are more powerful than is commonly understood. Indeed the world is ruled by little else. Practical men, who believe themselves to be quite exempt from any intellectual influences, are usually the slaves of some defunct economist. Madmen in authority, who hear voices in the air are distilling their frenzy from some academic scribbler of a few years back.
>
> John Maynard Keynes, *The General Theory of Employment, Interest and Money* (London: Macmillan, 1936), p. 383

12 Alasdair MacIntyre, *After Virtue* (London: Duckworth, 1985), p. 222.

13 Walter Burkert, *Babylon Memphis Persepolis; Eastern Contexts of Greek Culture* (Harvard: Harvard University Press, 2004), p. 54. With thanks to my late father for giving me this wonderful book.

14 Ngũgĩ wa Thiong'o, *Decolonising the Mind* (Nairobi: East African Educational Publishers, 1986).

15 Ngũgĩ, *Decolonising the Mind*, p. 14.

16 Salman Rushdie, *Imaginary Homelands: Essays and Criticism 1981–1991* (London: Granta Books in association with Penguin, 1991), p. 394. See also Homi Bhabha, 'How Newness Enters the World' in *The Location of Culture* (London: Routledge, 1994), pp. 212–35.

17 Ato Quayson, *Tragedy and Postcolonial Literature* (Cambridge: Cambridge University Press, 2021), p. 302.

18 Quayson, *Tragedy and Postcolonial Literature*, p. 10.

19 Quayson, *Tragedy and Postcolonial Literature*, p. 19.

20 Jonathan Lear, *Aristotle: The Desire to Understand* (Cambridge: Cambridge University Press, 1987), p. 253.

21 Although there are exceptional cases: for example, those about whom we say that they 'sculpted their body' through exercise. Here, the person is objectifying themselves, making their body a product.

22 Heidegger, *Plato's Sophist*, p. 96.

23 Charles Chamberlain, 'The Meaning of *Prohairesis* in Aristotle's Ethics', *Transactions of the American Philological Association* 114 (1984), 147–57.

24 Angela Curran, *The Routledge Philosophy Guidebook to Aristotle and the Poetics* (London: Routledge, 2016), p. 99.

25 I. A. Richards, *Principles of Literary Criticism* (London: Routledge, 2001), p. 12.

26 Richards, *Principles of Literary Criticism*, p. 12.

27 I. A. Richards, *The Philosophy of Rhetoric* (Oxford: Oxford University Press), p. 86.

28 Richards, *Principles of Literary Criticism*, p. 13.

29 Martha Nussbaum, *Love's Knowledge: Essays on Philosophy and Literature* (Oxford: Oxford University Press, 1990), p. 171.

30 Nussbaum, *Love's Knowledge*, p. 148. Nussbaum is obliquely citing Henry James, *The Art of the Novel* (New York: Scribner, 1934), p. 149.

31 Martha Nussbaum, *The Fragility of Goodness: Luck and Ethics in Greek Tragedy and Philosophy* (Cambridge: Cambridge University Press, 1986), p. 14.

9

EVERYDAY PEOPLE

The *Rhetoric*

Introduction

The journalist Sam Leith, in his funny *Words like Loaded Pistols*, defines rhetoric in the usual way, as the "art of persuasion", "a field of knowledge … susceptible to analysis and understanding in the same way as poetry", "a practical skill" that "Aristotle described as a *techne*". With intentional comedic bluntness, he concludes that rhetoric "is hustling".[1] Rhetoric was a core subject in European education for over two millennia, taught, as we've seen, by sophists like Protagoras and others. Aristotle's *Rhetoric* is almost always understood as one of the earliest of very many handbooks on the subject.

But actually, the *Rhetoric* is a very odd book to read and looks like a very peculiar handbook. Indeed, Aristotle explicitly says that the point of his *Rhetoric* is *not* to teach persuasion (*Rhetoric* 1355b10) (he is not a sophist teaching you to hustle, after all). The book is full of examples, topics, fragments of poetry, analyses of people's character, views and opinions (*endoxa*) that seem to have nothing to do with a lawyer's or politician's well-crafted speech. Even sympathetic accounts find the book problematic.[2] *Why* is it the way it is? The answer turns out to be very revealing for literature and for the history of rhetoric, as well as offering an explanation for its disappearance as a subject.

The oldest enemy, the oldest ally?

The French philosopher Paul Ricoeur offers one explanation for both the peculiarities of Aristotle's book and the death of the discipline of rhetoric. Rhetoric expired because it lost its link to philosophy and so to the wider vision and purpose that Aristotle gave it. Rhetoric became more and more just a *techne*, a craft for the debate team or a skill based on a "penchant for classifying figures of speech", what Ricoeur dismissively calls "mere botany", and so less and less relevant to our general everyday concerns. The consequence: it withered away.[3] But, as we saw in the first half of this book, "before becoming futile, rhetoric was dangerous", Ricoeur writes, "philosophy's oldest enemy and its oldest ally" (10). An enemy

DOI: 10.4324/9781003097914-12

because it is always possible for the art of 'saying it well' to lay aside all concern for 'speaking the truth'… the power to manipulate words … and to manipulate men by manipulating words.

(10)

Recall the fear in Plato's work of making the weaker argument stronger. Words are weapons, as Leith's title reminds us. By contrast, Aristotle's *Rhetoric* sought to show how rhetoric and philosophy are allies by offering an original analysis of how rhetorical arguments themselves actually work. Philosophy can never rule in the government or law court ("Philosophical discourse is itself just one discourse among others, and its claim to truth excludes it from the sphere of power"(11): think of Socrates withdrawing the philosophers from the *polis* in **book 9** of *The Republic*. But for Aristotle, Ricoeur thinks, philosophy can

delimit the legitimate uses of forceful speech … draw the line between use and abuse, and … establish philosophically the connections between the sphere of validity of rhetoric and that of philosophy. Aristotle's rhetoric constitutes the most brilliant of these attempts to institutionalize rhetoric from the point of view of philosophy.

(11)

Discovering what "distinguishes persuasion from flattery, from seduction, from threat" (11) and what it means to persuade and influence people is a philosophical task that allies both the persuader and the thinker. For Ricoeur, the *Rhetoric* is about domesticating "the dangerous power of eloquence" (11) under the "the watchful eye of philosophy" (10). Not a book teaching rhetoric, then, but one disciplining it.

How we talk to each other, what we talk about and what this all means

Martin Heidegger offers another more radical answer to the question of why the *Rhetoric* seems so odd: he argues that it has been profoundly misunderstood. It is a much more important book than people think, as he explains while offering a "unique spin on the rhetorical tradition".[4] Heidegger's understanding of the *Rhetoric* ties explicitly into the discussion of the 'whole person', *phronesis* and deliberation in Aristotle from the previous chapter, and so shows clearly the link between the *Rhetoric* and works of literature. Like Ricoeur, he sees a deeper meaning in the *Rhetoric*, but one less about taming the power of persuasion through logic and more about the fundamental ideas of how we are together: we might call this being-with-each other, or social ontology. His view also explains some of the oddities of the book.

Heidegger wrote, in the early 1920s, that the "current way of considering rhetoric is … a hindrance to the understanding of Aristotelian *Rhetoric*".[5] No one understood *what* the book was really about and he scoffed that in the famous Berlin academy edition, "they did not know what to do with it so they put it at the end! It is a sign of complete helplessness" (75). He went on:

> The tradition lost any understanding of rhetoric long ago, since it had become simply a school discipline even in the time of Hellenism and in the early Middle Ages. The original sense of rhetoric has long ago disappeared.
>
> (75)

However, he argued that because of his focus on ontology (on the question of what being is, what we are) that he *does* understand the point of the book, as he explains in his own idiosyncratic philosophical idiom (which I'll explain further below):

> rhetoric is nothing other than the discipline in which the self-interpretation of being-there is explicitly fulfilled. *Rhetoric is nothing other than the interpretation of concrete being-there, the hermeneutic of being-there itself.*
>
> (75)

Formal occasions, "in public meetings, before the court, at celebratory occasions", are examples of "customary speaking" of how "being-there speaks itself" (75/6). In his most important book, *Being and Time* (1927), he wrote that the *Rhetoric* was the "first systematic hermeneutic of the everydayness of being-with-one-another".[6]

What he means, more or less, is this. You will recall that *logos*, originally meaning speech, gave us and our world intelligibility, and came to mean reasons or explanations. One form of *logos* is *dialectic*, which began as general 'philosophical' discussion (dialogues!) but which evolved into highly technical enquiries, what we'd call science and, as we've seen, into detailed philosophy. There are also technical languages for specific skills (carpentry-talk for carpenters; medicine-talk for doctors).

In contrast to the *logos* of a highly skilled craft or of an abstruse enquiry into knowledge, we also talk with each other about all sorts of things in our everyday and non-specialised language. (You might discuss zoology in the lab, or talk shop at work, but you are an everyday person at home.) Yet this everyday language, while it may lack a scientific precision and certainty, is vitally important. It is absolutely central to all our shared activities, whether directly to do with the state (government, law) or other activities in public (job interviews, business meetings, retirement parties, weddings, funerals, graduations, any shared events). It's crucial in our more run-of-the-mill daily lives, talking with our friends, asking advice, working out what to do, deliberation.

The *Rhetoric*, while taking public speeches as its central examples, is the first study of this everyday non-technical, shared kind of talking that we do with each other. It's a book about how we speak to each other not as philosophers or logicians or zoologists or pharmacists, but as everyday people in everyday language. This is why, as we'll see, Aristotle says rhetoric does not have a special *techne* or subject area. It deals with – Heidegger-talk again – "speaking as a basic mode of the being of the being-with-one-another of human beings them-selves": how we talk to each other, what we talk about and what this means.[7] Speaking is communication, "deliberative … speaking-with-one-another" and "*logos* is the mode of being of human beings in their world such that this being is, in itself, being-with-one-another".[8] The fact of speaking in an everyday way shows we are political animals, woven in with each other.

This explains why the *Rhetoric* is so full of sayings, thoughts, opinions, *views*: as Heidegger says, our "being-with-one-another moves in definite, always modi-fiable views regarding things: it is not an insight, but a 'view', *doxa*".[9] A *doxa*, a view, here contrasts to something that has been investigated and worked out. To be in the world means we have, and are constantly offered opinions and ideas. Some things can be investigated and presented as certainties (triangles have three sides! This vaccine prevents that disease!) but other matters can only be deliberated (what should I do about …?). Or, as Heidegger puts it, what we deliberate "cannot be 'scientifically proven'" and is not worked out by "theor-etical axioms": instead it "consists of basic opinions … that life has cultivated in everydayness".[10] Rhetoric does not offer specific knowledge but "treats what one debates in life in a customary way, and the manner and mode of talking it through".[11] He's talking, as we can see from the last chapter, about deliberation and *phronesis*. The account of language in the *Rhetoric* is an account of who we are: as one commentator writes,

> we are human in so far as we can generate shared contexts, articulate our fears and desires, deliberate and judge in the appropriate terms of our day and act meaningfully in a world of common concern. Moreover in all such activities we are simultaneous agent and patient, mover and moved (to use Aristotle's terminology).[12]

This is what it means to be the speaking animal.

A beautiful metaphor from Wittgenstein illuminates this idea about speaking (or, rather about the different sorts of language we speak). He writes that

> Our language can be seen as an ancient city: a maze of little streets and squares, of old and new houses, and of houses with additions from various periods; and this surrounded by a multitude of new boroughs with straight regular streets and uniform houses.[13]

The specialised and technical languages make up some areas of the city: over here, zoology, over there, physics, here, the shop talk of a sector of business, and perhaps this little square is the in-jokes and argot of you and your friends. These languages can be very different (scientific notation refers to reality in a very different way from slang, for example, and both differ from language about dreams). But using Heidegger's suggestion, we could perhaps think of 'everyday' language as what we speak in the *agora*, the central square of the city that we all, ideally, share. (Although we must be careful to check: is what I take to be the 'central square' the same as everyone else's? Are we sure everyone can get there, and is welcome and able to speak? These are more challenging questions than they look. Further, we don't have to agree in the *agora*, but we have to talk with each other to understand why and over what we disagree.) Having a sense of the general views and opinions is "Knowing-the-way-around in everyday being-there for those who wish to be occupied within the circle of the *polis*".[14] You need to know how to talk about everyday things in an everyday way to be a person in the city.

This is why *all* (!) everyday topics of conversation seem to be covered in the *Rhetoric*: everything we talk about when we are not delving into some technical, scientific or specialist matter. Aristotle made detailed observations of birds and fish: here his observations focus instead on what we are like in our shared human life by paying attention to our everyday talking (we are the speaking animal, after all). These are collected by Aristotle from his own experience and from extensive evidence, which is principally literary. The *Rhetoric* is not about a skill, it's an understanding and orientation to our daily life (another description and prescription). Martha Nussbaum says Aristotle's philosopher is "what we might call a professional human being".[15] I take this to mean something like what my students say when they talk about 'adulting'.

This is also why the *Rhetoric* is interested, as we'll see, in emotions: as Heidegger says all people have emotions, moods. (He says in *Being and Time* that we always have moods, which sounds like we are always sulky. What he means is that we are always in some kind of emotional state: even 'being calm' is a state.) Heidegger writes that the speaker "speaks to" this mood "and from out of it" and so "needs an understanding of the possibilities of mood in order to arouse and direct it in the right way".[16]

To recap: for Heidegger, the *Rhetoric* is the "first systematic hermeneutic of the everydayness of being-with-one-another", the first interpretation of what we are like when we are together.[17] So, it's not primarily a handbook for learning how to give formal speeches (although if you are giving formal speeches, it's important to know about who and how we are, to do it impressively). It really is a guide for *how to be*; this means, in turn, how to be with others; this means, in turn, how to speak and deliberate with others; this means, in turn, knowing topics of conversation, how to compose and what your audience (other humans!) is like.[18] This view, rather than Ricoeur's, is going to shape my discussion of the *Rhetoric* below.

The *Rhetoric* follows on from the conclusion of the last chapter, which suggested the importance of deliberation and the whole person. Rhetoric is not "immediately the power of persuasion, as the sophist would have it, but rather the cultivated power of a situational insight, *phronesis*, of being able to see, hear and feel, in a temporally particular situation of action".[19] It also leads to the next chapter: understanding how people talk, understanding deliberation, how language reveals itself and us are important for the *Poetics* and for literature. Literature is in common, in the 'public square' and so not a technical language, but an intensified, patterned version of everyday talk.

Commentary

Aristotle begins Rhetoric (**book 1.1**) with the statement that rhetoric "is the counterpart of dialectic" (*Rhetoric* 1354a1). This is because neither dialectic nor rhetoric are about specific subjects (like seabirds, physics, carpentry) and we all use them both to discuss things, either "at random" or "from acquired habit" (1354a6–7). While you can learn to speak successfully, he writes, the study of how and why that works is also a skill, a *techne*. His book is an analysis of why and how persuasion works and not a handbook for doing it (again: he's not a sophist!). He is not training people in how to speak and win, but teaching people how to think about speaking. (Compare: you can learn to cook delicious food without understanding the chemistry and physiology behind flavour, without knowing why food tastes good, but you would understand much more about cooking if you did. This is what Aristotle is suggesting, a nice but very important distinction.) Other writers on rhetoric, he says, are only interested in winning arguments, and have not explained the central element to rhetorical success, what Aristotle calls the proofs of speaking: *enthymemes* (and he'll describe these more in detail later).

Aristotle goes on: the study of rhetoric is the study of persuasion; persuasion is a kind of demonstration, using enthymemes; an enthymeme is a kind of deduction, the business of dialectic; this means that the expert in deduction and dialectic (the philosopher) will understand enthymemes. He is stating that he can explain why rhetoric persuades better than a sophist or a famous public speaker, a lawyer or politician can. He concludes by contrasting the titles 'sophist', 'dialectician' and 'rhetorician'. A rhetorician might either be an expert about rhetoric or an expert user of rhetoric. A dialectician is called that because of their abilities (in dialectic), but a sophist is not named a sophist because of their abilities but because of their choices (to use false arguments to win, presumably). Aristotle seems to mean that a sophist might be as insightful as a dialectician but, because of their different interests (victory not truth), they are a different sort of person. This is illuminated a little by a passage from the *Metaphysics*, where he writes that sophistry, dialectic and philosophy all have the same sorts of things as their domain and so "dialecticians and sophists assume the same guise as the philosopher" (*Metaphysics* 1004b18–20). However, dialectic is something like the skill of argument, which uses ideas but does not necessarily understand them and is "merely critical" (1004b25): to be good at arguing is not necessarily to be good at philosophy, which is about learning to live a virtuous life. Similarly, sophistry, which looks a bit like philosophy, does not have the same purpose as philosophy. When discussing rhetoric (without attacking it, as Socrates had), it's important for him to be really clear about these different forms of language use: argument as a skill (dialectics), argument as a tool (sophistry) and argument as a way of both finding the truth and living a virtuous life (philosophy, which uses dialectics and also exceeds it).

The next chapter of the *Rhetoric* (**book 1.2**) restates that rhetoric is "the faculty of observing in any given case the available means of persuasion" (1355b26). Technical languages persuade in their technical language (you argue geometry in the language of geometry, medicine in the language of medicine) but rhetoric covers any topic. Some forms of persuasion don't come from the speaking itself but from an external source (a witness statement or material piece of evidence, for example): these must be used by the speaker. But some forms of persuasion do originate with the speaker, and Aristotle defines three ways, his well-known triad of *ethos, pathos* and *logos*.

You can persuade through your character (*ethos*) or your comportment: who you are and, more importantly, how you represent yourself in a speech. We believe good people "more fully and more readily than others" (1356a6), Aristotle says, and your speech needs to convey this impression. You can persuade through the feelings or emotions of the audience (*pathos*): your audience may come to different views if they are hostile, angry, grieving or happy. These are not just feelings but – recall Aristotle's insistence on action – feelings towards or drawn out by things in the world. One way of describing these are 'affects'. You can persuade through the speech itself, by proving "a truth or an apparent truth by means of the persuasive arguments" (1356a20), by making something clear or bringing it to light or giving reasons (*logos*).

To understand rhetoric, you need to understand character and ethics; recognise and respond to peoples' feelings; know how to reason and use syllogisms. This means that rhetoric is "an offshoot of dialectic and also of ethical studies" (1356a25). 'Ethical studies' is connected to the *polis* and so rhetoric is connected (as you might expect) to politics.

Aristotle now explains enthymemes. In the final chapter of one of his books on logic, *Prior Analytics*, he says that an enthymeme is a deduction, a syllogism "starting from probabilities or signs" (*Prior Analytics* 70a10–11). To step back: in strict dialectic there are two forms. One is the syllogism, the *deduction* in which premise A and premise B lead you, therefore, to deduce conclusion C ('Socrates is a man; men are mortal; therefore Socrates is mortal'). The other is *induction* which moves from "particulars to universals" (*Topics* 105a13–4): the skilled helmsman is best; the skilled charioteer is best; so we can induce that the skilled person is best at their role. Because rhetoric is akin to dialectics, there must be analogies: *enthymemes* are like *syllogisms* and *examples* are like *inductions*. When you talk, you offer both striking thoughts (that is: enthymemes) and examples.

Leith writes, however, that an enthymeme is only a "half-assed syllogism".[20] They are half-assed in two ways. First, in logic, the premises of syllogism (the

144

A and the B) must come from other syllogisms to be recognised as true. But in rhetoric, that's unnecessary as the hearer supplies the premise. So, for the logician, 'Dorieus won an Olympic event; an Olympics winner gets a garland; therefore Dorieus has a garland' but for the ordinary person 'Dorieus has a garland' is quite enough. This is an abridged syllogism, in which there is a hidden taken-for-granted premise. Second, in logic, all the premises and conclusions must be certain (humans are mortal!). But in rhetoric, they can also be probabilities (that is: things that usually happen, cats usually but not always catch mice) or signs. Signs work from the particular to the universal. ('Socrates is wise and just; thus all wise people are just'; but this sort of sign is easily refutable and not logically valid). Signs also work from the universal to the particular (a fever is a universally recognised sign that a person is ill). Signs can be wrong (being breathless is a sign of being ill, but it may be because you have been exercising).

Examples in rhetoric work a bit like induction. When the ruler Dionysius asks for a special unit of soldiers as a bodyguard, other examples come to mind. Both Pisistratus and Theagenes asked for the same, and they both used them to establish themselves as tyrants. So, by example, we see that asking for a bodyguard is a step towards plotting a tyrannical coup.

Here, Aristotle is drawing out exactly the distinctions between the dialectic and rhetoric. So: logic has the syllogism (also known as the deduction) and induction. Rhetoric has enthymemes and the examples. Unlike syllogisms, enthymemes can be abridged (not full), probable (not certain) or just a sign. Examples are akin to induction: you can spot similarities.

We use rhetoric to deliberate on what Aristotle calls common or shared topics, when there are no specialisations or sciences which produce straightforward answers. He means that we don't deliberate, again, how many sides a triangle has or, more demandingly, we don't deliberate (say) the ways to reintroduce wolves to a region because we know *how* to do this: but we do deliberate together on *whether* this would be a good idea or not for our shared community.

Before exploring some common topics, Aristotle defines what kinds of rhetoric there are (**book 1.3**). Speaking has three parts, the speaker, the subject and the audience: the point (the *telos*) is the impact on the audience. The subject of the speech can be about the future (say, an elected representative thinking in public about the future good of the community, or someone in private talking through what to do), the past (so an example: a juror in a court case) or the present. So there are three kinds of rhetoric corresponding to whether you are talking about the past, present or future. Deliberative rhetoric is aimed at the future, and is about encouraging, exhorting or discouraging, deterring a course of action, for or against some helpful or harmful potential action. Forensic rhetoric faces the past and attacks, prosecutes or defends, and aims at justice or injustice. Display (or epideictic) rhetoric deals with the present, is either about praise or denigration and concerns good qualities or their lack.

Aristotle now lays out the kinds of topics that people talk about. This is because they make up the common concerns in the shared world that we discuss, either formally (at a meeting) or informally (with our friends). It's also not at all what a 'guidebook for how to win arguments' would do.

Deliberative rhetoric covers (**1.4**) revenue, war and peace, defence of the realm, imports and exports, legislation: traditionally political subjects. It also covers *eudaimonia* (**1.5–1.7**) which he describes as

> prosperity combined with excellence; or as independence of life; or as the secure enjoyment of the maximum of pleasure; or as a good condition of property and body, together with the power of guarding one's property and body and making use of them.
>
> (1360b14–17)

This is not Aristotle's definition but, rather, he says, "pretty well everyone" (1360b18) would agree happiness is one or more of goodness, freedom, health, security and wealth. The things that move you towards *eudaimonia* are birth to a good family, a virtuous circle of friends, wealth you can use, creditable and extensive children, honour and health, a comfortable old age, physical virtues like strength and size, good luck and virtue. But he goes on over the next three chapters to list a large number of topics concerned with the good: some public and political, some personal and some almost characteristic of conduct or 'wisdom literature' ("what is often useful surpasses what is seldom useful" (1364a27)); "what a man wants to be is better than what a man wants to seem, for in aiming at that he is aiming more at reality" (1365b5–6). It covers a huge range of topics over which one could deliberate. Finally it returns (**1.8**) to the conventionally political in discussing the four different kinds of government: democracy, oligarchy, aristocracy and monarchy.

Display rhetoric (**1.9**) praises noble actions of justice, courage, restraint, splendour, magnanimity, liberality, prudence, wisdom. Again, Aristotle provides a huge range of topics. Forensic rhetoric covers the past and begins (**1.10**) by looking at why people do wrong (chance, nature, compulsion, habit, calculation, anger, appetite) and then at what things are pleasurable (**1.11**): memories are pleasant, for example, as is looking forward to something, and, of course, friendship – Aristotle has a long and interesting list. Next (**1.12**), he looks at why people do unjust things, their means, motives and opportunities, and then (**1.13**) categorises all crimes and punishments: against community or individuals, against the written law or against unwritten laws or conventions, either an excess of virtue or vice against fairness or an omission of the written law. He considers the seriousness of crimes and doing wrong actions (**1.14**) and, in a chapter which is historically fascinating (**1.15**), analyses the kinds of proof the court will accept: these include laws and sayings, witnesses, contracts, tortures and oaths. Importantly, for this book, Aristotle includes poets as witnesses. What Homer has to say, for example, makes up the kind of knowledge about the world that we use in deliberation and discussion.

The second book of the *Rhetoric* concerns emotions and is the first study in the ancient world of how people feel. Aristotle argues (**book 2.1**) that since the point of rhetoric is a judgement (a court case is the paradigmatic example) the disposition of the speaker is important. He's covered how we influence people through common sense and virtue and now turns to how we influence each other through goodwill and friendship, through emotions. Our ever-changing moods influence how we decide things. Aristotle takes anger as his example to 'sneak up' on moods in general: what is the state of mind of anger, who are people angry with and when? He's interested in what an emotion is, who caused it and how. Anger (**2.2**) is a response to a belittlement, and Aristotle gives a long list of types and examples. This is contrasted with calm and the placation of anger (**2.3**). A lovely chapter on friendship (**2.4**) lists the reasons for and types of friendship: a friend is someone you wish well for, for their own sake and not some motive of your own. He contrasts this with some forms of enmity. (**2.5**). Fear and confidence are explored and compared. Heidegger notes that Aristotle says that fear makes men deliberative: "fear sets us thinking what can be done" (1383a6). Aristotle goes on: when

> it is advisable that the audience should be frightened, the orator must make them feel that they really are in danger of something, pointing out that it has happened to others who were stronger than they are, and is happening, or has happened to people like themselves, at the hands of unexpected people, in an unexpected form and at an unexpected time.
>
> (1383a8–12)

This will be significant for the *Poetics* and the role of tragedy. Aristotle continues by contrasting shame and shamelessness (**2.6**). Favour (**2.7**) is doing someone a good turn. Pity (**2.8**), which will be important for the *Poetics*, too, is the pain you feel at "an apparent evil, destructive or painful, which befalls one who does not deserve it, and which we might expect to befall ourselves" (1385b13–15). Its opposite (**2.9**) is indignation, a pain over someone's undeserved good luck; we envy (**2.10**) something our peers have achieved or acquired and are jealous (**2.11**) at not having it ourselves. (Interestingly, neither forgiveness nor sympathy discussed, which may seem a lack to we moderns.)

Aristotle turns to the people's characters next, analysing both thoughtfully and I think quite amusingly what is stereotypically distinctive about young people (over-full of desire, ambition, hope, noble ideals) (**2.12**), and old people (disbelieving, opinionated, sour, small-minded, self-loving, pessimistic and morose) (**2.13**). People in their prime (**2.14**) – bodily aged 30–35, in soul, 49 – like Goldilocks's third porridge, are just right. Good birth, wealth and power also shape one's character (**2.15-17**).

The next two chapters (**2.18-19**) concern how to talk about common, that is, non-specialised subjects: issues we all share. Speakers need to use shared knowledge (think of the difference between a witness and an expert witness, who brings specialised, technical knowledge to a court).

Aristotle turns back (**2.20**) to the sorts of proofs rhetorical discussions use, enthymemes and examples. Examples can be taken from history or invented, like Aesop's fables or be pointed comparisons (if jurors are chosen by a lottery to represent the *polis*, why not choose athletes in the same way?). A maxim (**2.21**) is a sort of enthymeme which is a generalised assertion (for example, "There is no man among us all is free" (1394b4) from Euripides's *Hecuba*): Aristotle notes that the audiences of speeches love these, because they can gleefully apply them to the particular case at hand. Aristotle then recaps on enthymemes (**2.22**), as shorter syllogisms which assume a shared premise, and then lists a huge number of these both real (**2.23**) and apparent (**2.24**). There is a thin line between folk wisdom and common sense, on the one hand, and spurious old saws and tired assertion, on the other. Aristotle was opposed to "sophistic phrase-mongering" which uses "the catchphrase and cliché" to win a debate.[21] However, in these chapters, Aristotle gives us a picture of what beliefs people shared: in short, an introduction to the everyday thought of a whole culture. He returns to the more technical discussion to point out that as the elements of any enthymeme are probability, example, proof and indication you can refute them (**2.25**) by showing their opposites or how they fail or can be amplified or diminished (**2.26**).

In the final book, having analysed the grounds of proof, Aristotle turns to style and arrangement (**book 3.1**). Poets used to perform their own works, he writes, and so previous writers have discussed dynamics, harmony and rhythm. But the style of talking must suit the audiences, since those are the people the speaker wants to influence. Aristotle writes that the sophists and rhetoricians of his time started to imitate the poets, and developed a kind of purple, highfalutin, poetic style of speaking, which people thought was impressive. But, he says, argument and poetry have different styles. Further, the poets and playwrights developed their style (changing their poetic metre to fit speech more naturally) and the orators who still used the high style now sound foolish. Instead (**3.2**) your style should be lucid. Your metaphors too should be clear, pleasant, and it is, he writes "well to give everyday speech an unfamiliar air: people like what strikes them" (1404b10–11). All must be in an appropriate tone for the subject. Bad or cold style (**3.3**) is made up of compound names, exotic words, epithets, silly or absurd or misplaced metaphors. Similes (**3.4**) are kinds of metaphors and your style should be grammatically correct and unambiguous (**3.5**) and both concise and accurate (**3.6**). Your style should match the subject matter (**3.7**) so don't be funny about serious things, or serious about funny ones, for example, and while you don't have to use strict metrical forms some sense of rhythm in speech is impressive. Your syntax must be good: concise is best, not too long, not too many sub-clauses. However, sometimes playing with sentence structure can be highly effective.

Metaphors and wit are important (**3.10**). While we make metaphors naturally, we can also be trained to become better at making them, and they are enjoyable. Aristotle starts logically: "we all naturally find it agreeable to get hold of new ideas easily; words express ideas, and therefore those words are the most agreeable that enable us to get hold of new ideas" (10140b9–11), and it is from "metaphor that we can best get hold of something fresh" (1014b12–13). When the poet "calls old age 'a withered stalk' he conveys a new idea, a new fact, to us by means of the general notion of 'lost bloom'" (1410b13–15). Clichéd (or dead) metaphors are unpopular (they're too obvious) and overly complex ones are not good because we can't understand them. New metaphors, drawing new parallels, are the best, if we 'get them' straight away (or almost) and, in doing this, learn something new. There are, Aristotle says, four types of metaphors of which analogy is the best (I discuss this in more detail in the next chapter). Metaphors should be vivid (**3.11**), 'bringing-things-before-the-eyes' in a way that indicates activity and our active engagement with the world. Metaphors draw together things that are related, but not too obviously related ("just as in philosophy also an acute mind will perceive resemblances even in things far apart" (1412a11–12)). Lots of jokes and proverbs rely on metaphors. And Aristotle reminds us that style must fit the genre (**3.12**).

Finally (**3.13**), Aristotle lays out the structure of a speech: introduction, presentation, proof and epilogue (conclusion). The introduction (**3.14**) lays out the theme and (**3.15**) the speaker can address there or elsewhere counter arguments or prejudice (literally 'pre-judgement' of an issue). The narration (**3.16**) lays out the events and the proofs (**3.17**) make the argument using the forms Aristotle has already outlined. He discusses how to deal with interrogation (**3.18**) (ideally, you make your questioner look a fool) and how to conclude: you (**3.19**) make the audience better disposed towards you (and hostile to your opponent), stress the importance (or unimportance) of the issues, create an emotional reaction in the audience and recap the key points of the argument.

As you can see from this brief summary, this is a complicated book, as if pulled in different directions by forces outside it. There's something in the traditional idea that the *Rhetoric* is a handbook, even if that's not its aim: after all, it's hard to explain the *why* without explaining the *how*. There's also something in Ricoeur's idea that the book concerns how philosophy disciplines, controls and delimits rhetoric. But the huge range of the book, the superfluity of what look like examples and even the very possibility of such a book, one which explains what we talk about, how we talk and the impact our words have, also suggest that Heidegger's account is deeply insightful. (Ironically, for a philosopher who is so often obscure and, later in his career, windily mystical, Heidegger notes in his lectures on everyday talking that he is "merely pointing out that it would perhaps be in order if philosophers were resolved to reckon what it actually means to speak to others".)[22]

Conclusion

The study of rhetoric is important in its own right, especially in a world which lacks an easily shared common 'town square'. In his defence of rhetoric in politics, Alan Finlayson argues that the

> practice of rhetoric—taking arguments to varied publics, taking time to develop ways of justifying propositions to the people with whom one

is talking—is a challenge, in form as well as content, to the continued development of a post-democratic anti-rhetorical political culture.[23]

There is a host of books, too, about 'post-truth', which advise the media, politicians and, most importantly, each of us how to respond. James Ball's *Post-Truth* says fact checking isn't fast enough; we've got to be media literate and sceptical of narratives. Matthew D'Ancona's *Post-Truth* argues that we must become our own editors, actively evaluating and judging all we read. Evan Davis's *Post-Truth* says we need to become discerning listeners, watch out for powerful narratives and be especially sceptical of claims that appeal to us. All these sound like demands to understand both rhetoric and something like Aristotle's science of rhetoric better.[24]

The *Rhetoric* is also important for literature as we've seen in its account of styles, its awareness of the importance of feelings and affects, and in its discussion of the working and impact of metaphors. But most of all, I think, the *Rhetoric* suggests the importance of *phronesis*, wisdom and deliberation. Michael Hyde argues that for Heidegger's Aristotle, "rhetoric, *phronesis* and collaborative deliberation go hand in hand" and "[c]ollaborative deliberation is a 'knowing together'".[25] As the role of rhetoric in collective decisions has declined, so the role of literature and art in collective deliberation has grown. Literature, especially, has this role, even in a 'post-truth' world, because it takes place in 'everyday language': the non-technical language that Aristotle's book is trying to foreground. While writing literature may be a specialized skill, reading and discussing it is not, necessarily (although it can be). Literature is part of the everyday deliberation that helps us figure out who we are and what we think, both individually and together. Again, *logos* and *polis* are also interwoven, because we are the political animal with *logos*. Language is how we are with each other, how we come to understand each other and our world. Poetry, plays, fiction and other works of literature are a patterned and intensified way of engaging with the world and everything in it, including ourselves. The next two chapters explore this in more detail.

Notes

1 Sam Leith, *Words like Loaded Pistols: Rhetoric from Aristotle to Obama* (New York: Basic Books, 2012), pp. 1–2.

2 For example, the "unity of the whole has often been questioned. Each of the three books hardly displays any continuity with the two others". Michael Meyer, *What is Rhetoric?* (Oxford: Oxford University Press, 2017), p. 20.

3 Paul Ricoeur, *The Rule of Metaphor*, trans. by Robert Czerny with Kathleen McLaughlin and John Costello, SJ (London: Routledge, 2003), p. 9, p. 10. Further citations in the text.

4 Daniel Gross, 'Introduction' in *Heidegger and Rhetoric*, eds. Daniel Gross and Ansgar Kemmann (Albany: SUNY Press, 2005), p. 5, p. 11.

5 Martin Heidegger, *Basic Concepts of Aristotelian Philosophy*, trans. Robert Metcalf and Mark Tanzer (Bloomington: Indiana University Press, 2009), p. 75. Page numbers in the text.

6 Martin Heidegger, *Being and Time*, trans. Joan Stambaugh, revised Dennis Schmidt (Albany: SUNY Press, 2010), p. 139.

7 Heidegger, *Basic Concepts of Aristotelian Philosophy*, p. 80.

8 Heidegger, *Basic Concepts of Aristotelian Philosophy*, p. 43.

9 Heidegger, *Basic Concepts of Aristotelian Philosophy*, p. 81.

10 Heidegger, *Basic Concepts of Aristotelian Philosophy*, p. 90.

11 Heidegger, *Basic Concepts of Aristotelian Philosophy*, p. 84.

12 Daniel Gross, 'Introduction' *Heidegger and Rhetoric*, eds. Daniel Gross and Ansgar Kemmann (Albany: SUNY Press, 2005), p. 4.

13 Ludwig Wittgenstein, *Philosophical Investigations*, trans. G. E. M. Anscombe (Oxford: Blackwell, 1963), p. 8e, paragraph 18.

14 Heidegger, *Basic Concepts of Aristotelian Philosophy*, p. 92.

15 Martha Nussbaum, *The Fragility of Goodness* (Cambridge: Cambridge University Press, 1986), p. 261.

16 Heidegger, *Being and Time*, p. 139.

17 Heidegger, *Being and Time*, p. 139.

18 The lectures in which Heidegger makes this case most clearly, from 1924, seem strikingly liberal, in some ways: it's no surprise that the ideas in them were picked up and further developed by those who heard them, like Arendt and Gadamer, who vehemently (and at no little personal cost and risk, in Arendt's case) opposed Heidegger's later Nazi politics.

19 Theodore Kisiel, 'Rhetorical Protopolitics in Heidegger and Arendt' in *Heidegger and Rhetoric*, eds. Daniel Gross and Ansgar Kemmann (Albany: SUNY Press, 2005), pp. 131–60, p. 146.

20 Leith, *Words like Loaded Pistols*, p. 58.

21 Theodore Kisiel, 'Rhetorical Protopolitics ...', p. 137. *Heidegger and Rhetoric*, eds. Daniel Gross and Ansgar Kemmann (Albany: SUNY Press, 2005).

22 Heidegger, *Basic Concepts of Aristotelian Philosophy*, p. 115.

23 Alan Finlayson, 'Rhetoric in Contemporary British Politics', *The Political Quarterly* 85:4 (2014), pp. 428–36, pp. 435–6.

24 James Ball, *Post-Truth: How Bullshit Conquered the World* (London: Biteback, 2017); Matthew D'Ancona, *Post-Truth: The New War on Truth and How to Fight Back* (London: Ebury Press, 2017); Evan Davis, *Post-Truth: Why We Have Reached Peak Bullshit and What We Can Do About It* (London: Little Brown, 2017).

25 Michael J. Hyde, 'A Matter of the Heart: Epideictic Rhetoric and Heidegger's Call of Conscience' in *Heidegger and Rhetoric*, eds. Daniel Gross and Ansgar Kemmann (Albany: SUNY Press, 2005), pp. 81–104, p. 91.

10

PATTERNS OF LITERATURE, PATTERNS OF LIFE

The *Poetics*

'Read our other works' before going back to the *Poetics* demanded Wayne Booth's version of Aristotle. We have followed a path from the most basic questions of philosophy though a discussion of how to live, the patterns of our universe and ourselves into Aristotle's concern for everyday talk. This has brought us to the *Poetics*. For Aristotle, poetry and drama, what we call literature, is an intensification of the patterns of our mortal life. It arises out of *telos*, from the interaction between people's aims, their circumstances, virtues and weaknesses, and presents itself in a unified way which grabs our attention and encourages practical wisdom and deliberation. Crucial to this, as we'll see, is story and metaphor.

The *Poetics* lays out how to understand, compose, respond to and judge plays, poems and poetic language (this means that it is a little like the work of the sophists, Stephen Halliwell points out).[1] It is a short book, 40 pages or so. That said, it's not straightforward to read. T. S. Eliot called it a "short and broken treatise".[2] Genevieve Liveley writes that it is "incomplete, contradictory, abstruse and sometimes simply garbled" and adds that the problematic text has led to a "great diversity of different translations and interpretations – several of which flatly contradict each other".[3] As I've said, without a wider and fuller sense of Aristotle's thought, it looks dull, disconnected and seemingly interested in obvious statements or classification. It's somewhere between a set of notes (or PowerPoint slides), an argument and a collection of insights.

I am going to discuss it over two chapters. In this chapter, I introduce the ideas through a summary. Unlike the rest of this book, I'm going to use the translation by Anthony Kenny, for its lucidity and because he brings out the relationship between Aristotle's analysis of literature and wider ethical ideas.[4] I conclude with the briefest history of the text and its influence and a dense account of what literature is, for Aristotle. In the next chapter and in more detail, I am going to discuss the importance and meaning of pleasure in literature, *mimesis* and *catharsis*, tragedy and metaphor.

DOI: 10.4324/9781003097914-13

Commentary: what is poetry?

Aristotle begins (**Chapter One**) like any good (but slightly dull) lecture, laying out the basic question:"what is poetry, how many kinds of it are there, and what are their specific effects?" (1447a7–9). Note how it is like a natural history – a kind of description – and we'll see that nature plays an important role in the *Poetics*. It's also concerned with the personal effect of poetry, and so its wider political impact, on what poetry *does*, and on the interaction of *polis* with *logos*. This was certainly the view of Ibn Rushd, who argued that

> Aristotle came to the opinion that this art was highly useful, because by means of it the souls of the multitude could be moved to believe in or not believe in a certain thing and towards doing or abandoning a certain thing. For that reason, he enumerated the matters which enable a man to devise an imaginative representation for any particular thing he wishes and to do so in the most complete manner possible for that thing. Thus, the art of poetics is that which enables a man to devise an imaginative representation of each particular thing in the most complete manner possible for it.[5]

Poetry is a representation, *mimesis* and the forms – epic, tragic, comedic and lyric – vary in medium, object or mode. (I'll suggest in the next chapter that this concept of *mimesis* is both more developed and a challenge to the one suggested by Socrates in *The Republic*.) The differences in *medium* mean, roughly, if the words are put into verse or music, and if so, which metre and rhyme-scheme they use. Just using verse, Aristotle points out, doesn't make one a poet (because, for example, medical texts could be in verse). There is no classical Greek word for creative writing in prose (he mentions that the Socratic dialogues don't have a generic name: they still don't, really). The difference of *objects* (**two**) concerns the actions of people represented: characters are either morally better, the same or worse than we are. Tragedy represents people as better, comedy as worse. The differences in *mode* (**three**) concern whether the action is simply narrated or dramatised by different voices, as we saw in *The Republic*. Aristotle says that this 'doing' is where the word 'drama' comes from (because it "is derived from a Greek verb for doing" (1448a30), *dran*) and he offers a brief history of the origins of the words for comedy and tragedy.

This leads Aristotle to address the origins of poetry itself (**four**). "Representation comes naturally to human beings from childhood, and so does the universal pleasure in representations" (1148b5–7). Through it, we learn our "earliest lessons" (1148b8). *Mimesis* is natural, pleasurable and educational. We enjoy learning from pictures (even horrible ones of dead people and weird animals) and working out who or what we are seeing ('oh, look, that's you!') or admiring the style of the representation ('nice photo!'). Our use of *mimesis*, like *logos*, marks us out from animals. Poetry arose as this natural ability for and pleasure in *mimesis* became more formalised. More serious poets made works which represented more noble people, while frivolous poets represented worse, and presumably funny, people. Aristotle acknowledges that there were poets before Homer, but his works are the first that can be identified (we know from fragments of Aristotle's lost work *On Poets* that he had more to say about Homer).[6] Tragedy, too, developed through increasing specialisation: Aeschylus increased the number of actors from one to two and reduced the singing of the chorus; Sophocles introduced a third actor and painted scenes; the plays became longer and the verse forms also became more like everyday speech in using iambic stress (the kind we use in normal speech, stressing one syllable and not stressing the next, rather than more complex stress and verse forms that you find in poems, raps and songs).

Comedy (**five**) is about inferior though not wicked people made ridiculous through "some error or embarrassment that is neither painful not life-threatening" (1148b34–5). Comedy is not about pain! The history of comedy is lost, Aristotle writes, because no one took it seriously.[7] Epic is like tragedy because it's about superior people. Tragic dramas are supposed to take place within a day, whereas epics can cover any length of time. (Taking place in a day is one of the celebrated 'unities' that became a 'rule' of drama in the seventeenth and eighteenth centuries: a rule more broken than kept, actually. That this minor comment became a rule shows the authority that Aristotle's work was given. What Aristotle is really concerned with is the 'unity' of an action, so that we can follow it through from start to finish.)

Aristotle then turns specifically to tragedy (**six**). Although he is discussing tragic plays, these core ideas about tragedy are, for Aristotle, the model for all narrative literatures. He defines tragedy as "an action of a superior kind – grand and compete in itself" (1449b24–5), performed by actors using language embellished with rhythm and melody, some parts with music, some without. The point of the completeness is that a tragedy offers the story of a whole action, its impact and consequences: this is satisfying in terms of the audience's emotions and intellect. Tragedy, through "pity and fear" (1449b27), leads to "the purification of the emotions" (1149b28), *catharsis*.

Catharsis is so important and contentious that I discuss it at length in the next chapter, but I want to discuss pity and fear here. Kenny makes a thought-provoking point when he suggests that while pity and fear are the emotions that arise from tragedy, *catharsis* might also arise from other emotions in relation to other forms of literature or drama: perhaps the lost volume on comedy explored "the relation of the emotions of amusement to the virtue of wittiness or conviviality" and he notes how Vàclav Havel's plays "circulated in samizdat served to purify the emotion of anger against communist tyranny, and a reading of *Anna Karenina* may teach us to love wisely rather than too well".[8] However, I am less convinced by this: pity and fear are not just some emotions amongst others. Rather, they are fundamental and revealing forms of our attunement to other people and ourselves: not feelings in a straightforward way but names for the very possibility of feelings, and so revealing of something important about who we deeply are.

The possibility of *pity* arises from the very fact that we exist with other people in the world. We are with others in sharing our world and our lives. Pity is a term to express this fundamental exposure to others. Heidegger calls this 'Being-with' and writes that it is "existentially constitutive" for us.[9] He means that 'being-with' is part of each of us. This doesn't mean actually being with a person, real or fictional, or that we have ethical responsibilities for them. Instead, for Heidgger, part of who you are is, simply, the inbuilt *capability* of being with others: this is integral to our own being. We might feel compassion or indifference (indeed, we don't feel compassion if people are comic, or wicked or too powerful or too good, for Aristotle) but pity names the possibility for feeling compassionate or indifferent, because it names this very fact of our being with others. Sometimes, we can forget this fundamental aspect of ourselves, thinking ourselves far from everyone: literature reminds us, draws our attention to it. Toni Morrison writes something analogous to this: language

> (saying, listening, reading) can encourage, even mandate, surrender, the breach of distances among us, whether they are continental or on the same pillow, whether they are distances of culture or the distinction and indistinction of age or gender, whether they are the consequences of social invention or biology.[10]

Literature reveals this deep and inalienable exposure to others. It does not suggest we are all the same, nor do we actually think a person from a novel or character from the stage is present. But 'pity' names the way that literature reminds us of our exposure, our 'being-with' others.

If pity reveals our 'being-with' others, so fear tells us something deeply important about ourselves. This is because fear, which leads to deliberation (as we have seen in the *Rhetoric*), is tied up with our care for ourselves. Heidegger argues that fear, or perhaps, better, anxiety or concern is how we come to individuate ourselves and pay attention to what concerns us.[11] Why? Because fear is about something (a tiger is attacking me!), is a physical feeling (we often say, 'in the pit of our stomachs') and is *for* something: we are afraid *for* our lives, we are afraid in case we die. In this way, fear makes us pay attention to our own life. Obviously, in literature, the tiger is not real, nor does the 'pit of the stomach' feeling last long, but paying attention to our life lasts (a little while, at least). Normally, we don't pay much explicit attention to our life: we are just thinking about what to make for lunch, or what we have to do at work tomorrow, or what he said about what she said (this *is* all a kind of *inexplicit* attention to our life, of course). But the intensity of a literary work throws us out of our normal run-of-the-mill daily life and can make us feel 'not at home', a stranger to ourselves, filled with anxiety or concern. This anxiety *does* make us pay explicit attention to ourselves: this is what Heidegger calls, roughly, care. Literature reveals this care to ourselves and leads us to think attentively and clearly about our lives. Again, Morrison says something analogous about narrative fiction: it is "an opportunity to be and to become Other. The stranger. With sympathy, clarity and self-examination".[12] Feeling 'not at home' in our lives, other in own lives, leads to self-examination. 'Pity and fear' are not just feeling sympathy and being frightened. They are ways into the very deepest parts of who we are, and the impact of literature makes us attentive to them.

To return to the sixth chapter of the *Poetics*: Aristotle stresses that tragedy represents actions. The agents of these actions have certain qualities (they are noble, for example) and we judge their actions by their qualities (whether the actions live up to or fail to live up to these qualities). It is because of their actions that the agents "succeed or fail in life" (1450a1–2). Tragedy is about action and action reveals character.

Each tragedy has six elements: "the story (*muthos*), the moral element (*ethos*), the style, the ideas (*dianoia*), the staging (*opsis*) and the music" (1450a8–10).[13] The most important element is the plot, which represents the events. Plot is the "soul of tragedy" (1450a38). Aristotle focuses so much on plot and so insistently that, for Halliwell, it becomes almost a technical term, something like 'plot-structure', the "formal organization which is purposefully produced and fashioned to coherence by the poet".[14] The elements which impact the audience most, "reversal and discoveries" (1450a35), are plot elements (plot twists we call them). Aristotle remarks that "novice poets" can "master style and moral character before they can compose plots" (1540a37–8) and many grizzled authors and screenwriters will tell you that 'story is the hardest thing to write'. Story is the foundation and all the other characteristics of tragedy depend on this.

The moral element, the *ethos*, describes the virtues and flaws of the agent. The ideas are "the power of expressing what is involved in or appropriate to a situation" (1450b5). The story is the most significant because actions reveal *who* people are through their choices; their *ethos*, their moral element creates their options about which they deliberate; their ideas are how far they understand, express and think through their position. This is why there "is no such thing", Aristotle writes, as "speeches in which the speaker reveals no choice or rejection" (1450b10–11). In tragedies, the key speeches (and in musicals, the big numbers) are moments of plot, in which character is revealed through choices made. Arendt observes that action and speech "are so closely related because the primordial and specifically human act must at the same time contain the answer to the question ... 'who are you?'.[15] While Heidegger writes that *ethos* "makes manifest, at the moment, the being-resolved of the speaker", you can only be resolved in a concrete, particular way, which depends on your circumstances, that is, your story, the world into which you are thrown.[16]

Character emerges from this. On the one hand is the external world, the protagonist's circumstances and events. On the other is their – what we might

156

call today 'inner' – dispositions or subjectivity. They are, of course, seeking happiness, *eudaimonia*, with their own combination of virtues and flaws, wisdom and ignorance about themselves, their situations and world. We see their deliberation, active choices and actions (or inability to act) as well as their thoughtlessness, errors and what they fail to see (as we'll see, this is *hamartia*). They make, and we can judge, their decisions. Their character is revealed to themselves, others and the audience, through their speeches and actions (in drama as in life). The drama is the play between their dispositions and their *eutuchia*, their 'good luck', 'prosperity', usually charting their change in circumstances and fortune. To return to Aristotle's list for the elements of tragedy, style means the expression of all these, music is a source of pleasure and the staging is important, but not vital, for Aristotle.

Because plot is so important, Aristotle turns to it next (**seven**). A plot is *complete* with a beginning, a middle and an end. It is of the right *scale*: not too huge and long, nor too small. The right length is enough to show a transformation from "adversity to prosperity or prosperity to adversity in a probable or necessary sequence of events" (1051a14–15). Again, the concern is for completeness, so we can see a whole action and all its implications worked through. This is why a plot (**eight**) has unity. This doesn't necessarily mean a focus on one person (because lots of things happen to anyone) but on an action "single and entire" (1051a34). An action is, if you like, the product of the tragedy. It's clear, writes Aristotle (**nine**), that a poet tells not "what actually happened" but rather "the kind of thing that *would* happen ... what is possible in term of probability and necessity" (1450b38). This is why "poetry is more philosophical and more serious than history; poetry utters universal truths, history particular statements" (1451b5–7).

This remark has led to a great deal of commentary.[17] He may mean something like this. Poetry, creative writing, deals with stories and in stories, one event must not just follow but inevitably develop from another: not, to reuse E. M. Forster, that the king dies, then the queen dies but that the queen dies *because* the king dies. This brings in *telos*, for-the-sake-of-which leads to deeper moments of understanding and simultaneously cuts out much extraneous information (recall the point of significant details: Chekhov's gun). In this intensification of everyday life and talk, poetry and tragedy draw attention to the profounder shape of the world. From the shaping of actions in their representation, we learn not facts but see more clearly the truths about how our lives and the world are formed for Aristotle. Paul Ricoeur adds that this forming is why *mimesis* gives us the "variety of the pleasure" we find in learning because what "pleases us in the poem is the sort of clarification, of total transparency, that the tragic composition achieves".[18] Aristotle goes on to say that even when poetry concerns real people or actual events – what we call history – a poet is still dealing with them as a poet. That is, historians are poets because they shape and select events for their narrative: they emplot actions. In so doing, they speak, implicitly perhaps, of (their view of) universal truths. Martha Nussbaum offers another angle on this remark: the identification of the audience with the pro-tagonist in tragedy, through which the pity and fear are generated, is a source for learning wisdom, finding universal truths. However, figures in history may be "so idiosyncratic that they prevent identification. Because Alcibiades is such a unique and unusual figure, we do not regard what happens to him as showing a possibility for ourselves".[19] While this reading draws out the impact on the audience of the difference between literature and history, it is still about seeing and understanding more clearly.

Aristotle continues and argues that poor-quality stories are episodic, just one-thing-after-another, with no profound connection, whereas tragedies are complete, connected accounts of events which evoke pity and fear. In the best of these, the unexpected things happen seemingly inescapably, as a necessary or inevitable surprise.

Stories of actions (**ten**) can be simple or complex. Simple, if the change in fortune is just one way; complex if there is a "reversal or a discovery or both" (1452a16–17). The Greek word for reversal is *peripeteia*, which also means wandering: happily, our term 'plot twist' keeps this sense of turning.[20] Discovery is *anagnorisis*, which means recognition. Writers and critics use both terms today. These need to grow out from the plot, and not simply be inserted. Reversals (**eleven**) change the course of events: in *Oedipus*, a messenger arrives bearing good news, but in telling it reveals Oedipus's true identity, and so unleashes calamity. Discovery is the movement from ignorance to knowledge, and works best with reversal, as in the Oedipus example, but can also happen in other ways. It is these which evoke the pity and fear and lead to a happy or unhappy ending. Tragedy also involves, perhaps obviously, suffering. There is (**twelve**) a prescribed order of scenes: a prologue (plus chorus, the parode), episodes (most of the tragedy, divided up by chorus), exode (the final episode, the opposite of the prologue, leading to the departure – *exodus* – of the chorus).

How does a tragedy arouse pity and fear (**thirteen**)? Tragedies must be com-plex (in the terms Aristotle has laid out), with pitiable and frightening events. But good men must not be shown to have bad fortune (this evokes outrage), nor bad men good fortune (we have no sympathy for them at all). And while we may feel sorry for wicked men who suffer, we don't feel pity or fear. I've discussed the deeper significances of these terms: pity names the deep sense of our 'being with' others. The character we feel for is neither, recalling the *Politics*, a 'beast or a god', but someone who shares our world. Fear comes from the sense that the person is like us, a form of identification, and so leads to self-examination. A tragedy involves someone like us, "not outstanding in virtue or justice" (1453a8) who is brought low "because he errs in some way" (1453a10). This erring is *hamartia* and I return to it in the next chapter: briefly, scholars argue over whether *hamartia* is a flaw in character or a mistake in calculation or an occasion of thoughtlessness. (In fact, of course, these may all be the same thing: the general who is too brave will not bother to check carefully the layout of their own and their enemies' forces, for example; the person who trusts too little may not work out that someone is genuinely offering to help.) The better kind of tragedies tells one story, but Aristotle notes that audiences love (and so authors write) stories with a 'double plot' in which the good end happily and the bad unhappily.

Pity and fear (**fourteen**) arise when you see a play. However, they should be integral to the plot, so just retelling the story ought to be enough to create this reaction (rather than making it horrific on stage). Aristotle goes on: there is nothing pitiable if enemies or strangers fight (that's expected, so in fact rather predictable). This means that plays should focus on relationships (brother with brother, son and father and so on) in which a terrible deed (a killing, for example) is done. He then lays out the dramatic interplay between knowing and doing.

You can know about the relationship and not do any terrible action ('I was thinking about shooting you, brother, but I decided not to': unimpressive because it's "monstrous without being tragic, since no one suffers" (1453b39)). You can know the relationship and still act. ('He was my brother and I shot him down': the third best twist). You could not know about the relationship, under-take the action and discover afterwards. ('Oh no, I discovered after the gunfight that it was my brother I killed!': this is the second best twist and creates the most impact.) Or, finally, you might discover the relationship at the last moment and so decide not to act. ('I worked out just in time that you are my brother! Good thing we didn't start shooting!'. This is the best twist for Aristotle.)

Aristotle turns next to moral character (**fifteen**). Characters should be *good*. This does not mean perfect, like a god or a famous invulnerable superhero but, Aristotle says, just a portrait painter makes the painting look like the subject but handsomer, they should be like us but a little better. Their moral character, their commitments (*prohairesis*) and choices will be revealed in their speech and actions: and this is true for everyone (including women and enslaved people). They should also be *appropriate*: for example, "it is no good for a character to be courageous if the courage or intelligence is expressed in a way that is not appropriate for a woman" (1454a23). They must be *plausible* and *consistent*. This means, for example, that the resolution of the plot must arise from the character and the story, and not be simply a *deus ex machina*.

Aristotle circles back to the idea of discovery (*anagnorisis*) (**sixteen**). Discovery can happen in a number of ways: through recognising some external sign (someone's scar or birthmark, say); when someone simply says who they are ('*I am your father*'); when someone is recognised by memory (a particularly moving example of this occurs when Odysseus, in disguise, hears a song about his own suffering and that of his comrades, and weeps under his cloak in *self*-recognition); when a character works out some discovery by themselves (some-times the audience can be misled, when, for example, we incorrectly assume that the obvious character is the murderer, when, of course, it is the one we least suspect), but the best form of discovery for Aristotle arises from the events themselves.

Bearing in mind that the *Poetics* is both a kind of natural history and a handbook, prescribing and describing, Aristotle next (**seventeen**) offers advice to playwrights. Visualise the events (to avoid 'continuity errors'). Act out and feel the events so that you are more persuasive: "to write tragic poetry, you must be either a genius who can adapt himself to anything, or a madman who lets himself get carried away!" (1455a 35–6). This remark, while suggesting writers are not quite right (too protean or not totally sane), is very different from Plato's idea that they are divinely inspired (and so both holy and not necessarily intelligent or skilled in a craft). Plan the overall structure before filling in the episodes: the completeness of the story is key. Tragedies (**eighteen**) have a set-up and a resolution. The set-up might include things that have happened before the play starts and go on until the reversal: the resolution goes from the reversal to the end. This means that there are four kinds of tragedy. The Greek text is uncertain at this stage, but it seems as if Aristotle wants to classify tragedies based on when the reversal and discovery happen.[21] Aristotle reminds playwrights that a play must focus on one story (and not several, like an epic); reversals should astonish us; the chorus, who sing between scenes, should be like one of the actors and part of the whole plot, not just added in (with a nice tune).

The next chapter (**nineteen**) turns to ideas and style. Ideas, he writes, are discussed in his *Rhetoric*: they include both the result of reason (proofs, refutations) and the impact of emotions, as well as the events in the plot, and how these are represented, either by words or by actions on stage (writers don't have to make characters say what can be shown, after all). Under style, Aristotle wonders about investigating the different kinds of "speech acts: command, prayer, statement, question, answer and so on" (1456b9–10). (This is part of directing for the stage, and perhaps underlies a technique known by directors as 'actioning': in this, actors apply one transitive verb to explain and underlie each line they say.) This last idea takes the *Poetics* into a very brief discussion of what we now call linguistics (**twenty**). He covers phonemes, vowels, syllables, particles, nouns, verbs and sentences.

It's through the discussion of nouns that Aristotle addresses metaphors (**twenty one**). A metaphor is "applying to something a noun that properly applies to something else", from "genus to species, from species to genus or from species to species" or by "analogy" (1457b8–9) from one field of speech to another. Aristotle then makes a classification of these depending on which:

> If someone says 'My ship stopped here', I call that a transfer from genus to species, because mooring is a kind of stopping. 'Odysseus wrought in truth ten thousand noble deeds' is transfer from species to genus, a specific large number is used instead of the generic 'many'. Examples of transfer from species to species are 'drawing off the life with bronze' and 'cutting off with sharp bronze': here 'drawing off' means 'cutting' and 'cutting' means 'drawing off' – both activities are a kind of removal.
> (1457b10–16)

This looks much harder than it need be. (1) *Stopping* is the overall category (genus): mooring, parking, anchoring are species of, subsets of or ways to describe stopping. (2) *Many* is the overall category: large numbers like 9,999 or 1,034 are subsets of 'many'. (3) Both 'drawing off' and 'cutting' are subsets of 'removal'. Analogy is best shown by example: old age is to life, as evening is to day, so you can call the evening 'the day's old age' or old age 'life's evening'. (Technically, "B is related to A as D is to C" (1457b17–18), so you can swop B and D.)[22] Aristotle's discussion of metaphor still grounds our contemporary thinking on this issue, as we'll see in the next chapter.

A little later, Aristotle writes that

> Above all the poet must be skilled in metaphor. This is one thing that cannot be learned from others, and it is a sign of genius, since it involves a keen eye for similarities.
>
> (1459a6–8)

An ability to make insightful metaphors cannot be learned, but it is the sign of a genius because it relies on a profound insight which finds similarities in different things. The key issue here is not really poetry. Aristotle is less interested in the beauty of a metaphor and more in explaining "how metaphor promotes to consciousness an awareness of relations that subsist between the objects and concepts that make up our universe".[23] For Aristotle, metaphors are ways in which we come to understand our world (and I discuss this in the next chapter, too).

Aristotle has some things to say about style (**twenty two**): working out good style is similar to working out what is virtuous: seeking the middle point. In terms of clarity, say, one extreme is vulgarity: the other is exotic, overly metaphorical and extraordinary language. It's true in drama too: the language must not sound too low or too high for the characters. A contemporary example to show the force of this: authors of historical fiction often talk of having to use language and grammar that is historical enough to sound as if it comes from the past, on the one hand, but not so authentic as to be actually quite hard to understand, on the other.[24]

Aristotle moves now from drama to epic (**twenty three**). Like drama, epic must be one single action, with a beginning, a middle and an end. Only then will epic "like a living organism, produce its own proper pleasure" (1459a20) (shades of the proper speech as a living creature in *Phaedrus*). An epic concerns one action and its consequences and is not a history (in which many different things happen during the same chronological period). Homer's *Iliad* concerns only one incident, the wrath of Achilles, not the whole Trojan War and all its many stories. Like tragedy (**twenty four**), epic can be "simple or complex, and based on character or suffering ... we need reversals, discoveries, and sufferings as well as intelligence and style" (1459b8–12). Epics can be longer than tragedies, with many simultaneous but related incidents, and so can be both grander and offer more variety. It should be in heroic meter, but welcomes "foreign words and metaphors, because narrative is an exceptional form of representation" (1459b34–5). Homer models excellence in epic: Aristotle gives five examples. Homer rarely speaks in his own voice but uses different and highly distinct and fully formed characters instead. Astonishing (and so pleasurable) events occur but these look neither ridiculous (as they might do acted out on stage) nor seem improbable. Homer "taught poets the right way to tell falsehoods" (1460b18): that is, by leading the audience to infer a fact from what looks like its consequence (we infer that the person holding the bloody knife over the dead body is the murderer ... but, of course, in literature, they are not). In Homer, even improbable things (monsters! coincidences!) are gently made to seem more likely. Finally, his style is not so strong as to overpower the story, even in the quieter passages.

The penultimate chapter (**twenty five**) is notoriously hard to follow, and is perhaps an abbreviated account of *Homeric Problems*, another lost work. He writes that "the criterion for correctness is not the same in poetry as in ethics, and not the same in poetry as in any other art" (1460b12–13). Some commentators have taken this to be declaration that poetry is utterly separate from ethical or political considerations ('art for art's sake') but I don't agree. Halliwell says (rightly) that for Aristotle, form can't be "detached and divorced from substance".[25] Aristotle argues that critics have five objections to literary texts: "impossibility, implausibility, immorality, self-contradiction and violation of artistic standards" (10461b23–4), and offers 12 responses. He begins by saying a poet (like a painter) imitates three kinds of things: those that were or are, are said to be, or ought to be, and that we judge these by different standards from ethics (and poetry differently again from painting). Mistakes might be intrinsic: the writing is just so poor that the representation is incompetent. Or they can be extrinsic: incorrectly describing (say) how a horse gallops. This is not a poetic mistake but, in the case of a horse, a zoological one.

Intrinsic errors which are improbabilities are to be forgiven if they serve the point of the work. Incidental errors, where the poet just does not know that a female deer has no horns, are not too serious a mistake.[26] Poets represent things that are not true: well, says Aristotle, perhaps they ought to be true (as Sophocles said to Euripides) or we have to go with what is generally assumed to be true: stories about the gods may not be "edifying" but they are "current" (1461a1–2). To judge if a speech or action is morally good in literature, you can't just take the words or action: you have to examine the speakers and the whole wider context (again, art and the impact of art are woven together for Aristotle). Errors in style might be caused by foreign words or a metaphor or caused by punctuation or normal use (wine usually means 'diluted wine') or accentuation or just ambiguity. Overall, Aristotle tells critics and philosophers, we need to read a text and work out how it might make best sense: critics who take up unreasonable positions about texts often find that the texts don't support those positions, and then blame the text.

Aristotle's point that "the criterion for correctness" (1460b12–13) for poetry is different from ethics and from other skills has led to some important discussions. Edith Hall, a classicist with an interest in Aristotle's historical context, asked a significant question: is there a *polis* in Aristotle's *Poetics*? She notes three particular silences in the *Poetics*: over "the political nature of the context of tragic perform-ance at the City Dionysisa", Athens's drama festival; over the "patently Athenian content" of very many of the tragedies: and about "the civic-didactic function of tragedy ... whose consumer is ... a citizen".[27] She argues that Aristotle seems to pass over the fact that tragedies were public performances, and so political by nature: they addressed the *polis*, Athens, its history, present and future. Aristotle, significantly, focuses on the impact not on the many but on the individual. More, Hall suggests that Aristotle's examples are, strikingly, not taken from Athenian writers. As a *metic*, a resident non-Athenian, he was in an ideal position to see a different trajectory for tragedy, less rooted in Athens. The point of these absences, she suggests, was to make tragedy (and the *Poetics*) more universal and so able to adapt and change through time: the cost was to sever the particular link between the tragedy and the *polis*. She makes a linked argument in an account of *cath-arsis*, suggesting that, at the time of writing the *Poetics*, tragedy was separating from both the Athenian state and religious festivals, and "had become a mass-market export consumed by audiences in colonies and new civic Macedonian foundations far afield": links to a particular city, in Aristotle's thought, would only hinder the spread of tragedy as an art form.[28]

In a long reply, 'Should There Have Been a *Polis* in Aristotle's *Poetics*?' Malcolm Heath argues that the ethics and politics in the *Poetics* lie in the shape and struc-ture of tragedy and epic, and in their effects, less than their content. More, because we are the 'political animal', politics and living in the *polis* underlie but do not necessarily dominate all activities. Aristotle's point about correctness means that an evil action in a tragedy does not mean that the tragedy itself is evil or poetically poor. Heath argues, too, that the account of *mimesis* as arising naturally means that the *Poetics* is, like a natural history, applicable to all humans.[29] More, the implication that plays lead to deliberation means that they must impact, too, on the *polis*.

As the conclusion (**twenty six**), Aristotle explains why he considers tra-gedy to be superior to epic. Epic, the older and less public form, is often taken to be superior but Aristotle disagrees. Of course, tragedy can be performed in a vulgar or clichéd way, overacted, with silly effects, but this is a criticism of the performance, not the form: the recitation of epics can be vulgar and overacted, too. Both forms can produce their effects without staging, although staging and music make tragedy more enjoyable. But overall, tragedies are usu-ally more concentrated and more unified, focused on a single event, and so achieve their purpose better: thus, they are superior to epic. This is why tragedy is the model of literature, for Aristotle, displaying what literature is in its most concentrated form.

The history and influence of the *Poetics*

Before concluding, I'm very briefly going to outline the textual history and influence of the *Poetics*. I've mentioned the complex intercultural histories of how the texts of Plato and Aristotle have come down to us. The case of the *Poetics* is an exemplary one and Leonardo Tarán and Dimitri Gutas explore it in painstaking detail.

The *Poetics* appears in the three ancient lists of Aristotle's writings: in Diogenes Laertius's *Lives of the Philosophers*; in the 'word collection' (*Onomatologos*) of Hesychius of Miletus, who lived in the sixth century AD; and in a biography of Aristotle by Ptolemy al-Gharib, 'the Unknown', in an Arabic translation. The earliest known surviving manuscripts are from the tenth to twelfth centuries.

The text's history is hard to trace. Aristotle left his library to his colleague Theophrastus, and he, in turn, to one Neleus, whose descendants buried the scrolls to keep them from being stolen. They were later sold to Apellicon of Teos. This library ended up in Rome where the text was copied (although unreliable copies were already in circulation). From the second century to the seventh, there is very little information. However, towards the end of the second century, the codex, our modern book form, came into use. Many ancient scrolls were transcribed but this

> change in the book form had the unintended consequence of causing the loss of many texts, since those works which happened not to be of interest at the time ceased to be copied. In the case of the *Poetics* it may have led to the loss of the second book.[30]

While there was great interest in Aristotelian philosophy, there is no evidence that *Poetics* was very much used. However, it is clear from the later copies that there was a sixth-century manuscript of the *Poetics* which was not included with Aristotle's main works and a version of the text was circulated in the Islamic world of Syria, northern Africa and Spain (as we've seen, Ibd Rushd commented on the *Poetics* in the twelfth century).

In the early Renaissance, the attempt to heal the division between the Greek Orthodox Church and Catholic Church as well as the fall of Constantinople in 1453 meant that "a great number of Greek scholars arrived in Italy" who "lectured, taught, and also explained Aristotle".[31] This wave of scholarship brought two of the four surviving texts of the *Poetics* to Western Europe. A Latin translation was published in 1498. The *Poetics* became more popular but, as Kenny suggests, was misunderstood, as scholars treated it as fundamentally about rhetoric.[32] More, the *Poetics* was read alongside and became intellectually amalgamated with Horace's *Ars Poetica*: this shaped the understanding of

Aristotle's arguments. Perhaps the most influential translation and commentary was by Lodovico Castelvetro in 1570 and in a posthumous edition of 1576. Castelvetro believed that the *Poetics* was the draft of a fuller work by Aristotle which had not survived (we know now from fragments that this is probably not correct: *On Poets* refers back to the *Poetics*, suggesting that the *Poetics* is a mature work and not a draft). Castelvetro's opinion led to him supplementing Aristotle's views from the text, arguing for a much stronger unity of action, location and time (roughly, that a tragedy had to be about one event, in one place, in one day) and that a poem could deal with the numerous events of a history.[33] Castelvetro's Aristotle is the source for the 'dramatic unities', an idea so influential that it became a dramatic and critical orthodoxy. While Aristotle's authority in many areas like science and medicine waned in the Renaissance and afterwards, his *Poetics*, or ideas based approximately on his poetics, grew in influence: we've seen a trace of this in Sidney, for example. These ideas went on to shape much of the literature of the European neo-classical movement. The German philosopher Dilthey summed this up in the mid-nineteenth century:

> The *Poetics* of Aristotle was the organon [tool] for all poetic technique
> through the second half of the eighteenth century, and the feared standard
> of critics … Together with grammar, rhetoric, and logic, the *Poetics* was a
> constituent of the curriculum of higher education.

However, he goes on to argue that "a new aesthetics" emerged and that now "anarchy rules the wide field of literature in every country. The poetics created by Aristotle is dead". (He adds that this "anarchy of taste always characterizes periods when a new way of feeling reality has shattered the existing forms and rules, and when new forms of art are striving to unfold": it is the ferment before a new age in art, not a sign of decline.)[34] While much fuller editions and translations of the *Poetics* were made in the last half of the nineteenth century, and are still being produced today, the influence of the book seemed to move from writers to critics.

Genevieve Liveley's excellent *Narratology* shows the influence of the *Poetics* on Russian formalism in the early twentieth century, especially through a concern for story, emplotment and the way poetic language 'defamiliarises' what we expect; on French and French-inspired structuralism in the mid-twentieth century, focusing on their quasi-scientific classifications of narrative and narration; and on the mid-to-late twentieth-century USA Neo-Aristotelians, the Chicago school formalists.[35]

Wayne Booth, who I discussed in Chapter 7, is the most well-known member of this school. His *The Rhetoric of Fiction* (1961) is a kind of rewriting of the *Poetics* with the novel in mind: it's called *Rhetoric* because it is interested in the impact on the reader of literary effects; it outlines, discusses, demonstrates and contextualises four 'general rules' of fiction; it analyses the authorial voice as dramatised, reliable or unreliable, and explores the many different forms of narration and their impact; it draws on very many examples to show "what good novelists have in fact done", as the *Poetics* does.[36] Further, in *The Company We Keep* (1988), Booth advances the very Aristotelian idea of *coduction*. Coduction is how we develop our opinions and judgements about a work of literature, comparing it with our experiences of other works. Coduction can never be "performed with confidence by one person alone" but occurs through conversation.[37] Coduction is a literary critical analogue to deduction and induction, although unlike them it will never offer a universally valid proof, because we do not deliberate about unchanging things (*episteme*) but about changeable human things (here, literary texts, their meaning and value) and we do this with others. If, in Aristotle's *Rhetoric*, an enthymeme is analogous to a deduction and an example is like an induction, then in discussions of poetics, a judgement or an informed opinion is a coduction, arising not from working alone like logic, or speaking *to* people, like rhetoric, but speaking *with* people and texts.

Another key Aristotelian inheritance in the Chicago school is the concern for making literature, as well as analysing it. Booth quotes Ronald Crane, the founder of the school, as saying what "pleases me most about the work of the Chicago school on the *Poetics* is the number of responses I get from novelists and playwrights thanking us for our help".[38] Indeed, Booth's work – and the work of the school – is closer to "the immediate compositional concerns of contemporary novelists".[39]

Conclusion: the intensified patterns of literature

Why is "the lover of stories" a "lover of wisdom"? (*Metaphysics* 982b19–20). Why is literature philosophical for Aristotle? As a form of *mimesis*, it is natural, educative and enjoyable, we wonder about it and learn from it. We know that Aristotle thinks it is *philosophical* in some degree because, he says, it is "more philosophical and more serious than history" and "poetry utters universal truths" (1451b5–7). One way of drawing this together is to suggest that we learn something like the pattern or form of mortal life from literature. For Aristotle, this means several things: we can break them down but they function all together, as he repeatedly argues.

We see *telos*, purpose, 'for the sake of which', in the completeness of a work and in the way that it is structured, through the story. We see people seeking for happiness or fulfilment and how their virtues, flaws, emotions, judgements and mistakes help or hinder that, through the moral element (*ethos*) and ideas. We see them deliberating in everyday speech about what to do, making choices and taking actions. At the same time, we see the impact on them of their families and others, of their society and of events in their world. These interactions, from 'within' and 'outside' them, form their character and show how our character is formed: human character as the meeting point between what is inside and outside of ourselves. Speech and actions, including responses to others' actions and the events of the world, reveal who people are, in literature and in life. In literature, we see the consequences of actions in events that are likely or possible. All this is presented in a unified way which seizes our attention through pity and fear, and through striking language: these feelings and the insight given through striking language are a kind of activity. Pity is the active recognition that others are with us in the world, this is part of who we are and we are bound to them by that: like them, we are exposed to others, the world and its fates. Fear is what makes us deliberate with ourselves or together: literature shows us our care for ourselves, others and the world, and our need for understanding in self-examination. Striking language, literary style and especially metaphors lead us to see new similarities between aspects of things and so our comprehension of the world and ourselves is expanded. All this is presented to us in everyday non-technical language which makes it easy for us to discuss and deliberate with others. Indeed, deliberation about what a text means, with yourself and others, is really part of the work itself, its interwoven role in teaching practical wisdom. This is how literature is an intensification of these patterns of our mortal life. This then is why, too, literature is philosophical.

The next chapter looks at pleasure, *mimesis*, tragedy and metaphor in more detail to develop these ideas.

Notes

1 Stephen Halliwell, *Aristotle's Poetics*, 2nd ed. (London: Duckworth, 1998), pp. 8–9, p. 46.
2 T. S. Eliot, *Selected Prose*, ed., Frank Kermode (London: Faber and Faber, 1975), p. 55.
3 Genevieve Liveley, *Narratology* (Oxford: Oxford University Press, 2019), p. 25. Halliwell lists the difficulties in the text really clearly, *Aristotle's Poetics*, pp. 32–5.
4 Aristotle, *Poetics*, trans. Anthony Kenny (Oxford: Oxford University Press), 2013, p. xxxviii.
5 Ibn Rushd, *Averroes' Three Short Commentaries on Aristotle's Topics, Rhetoric and Poetics*, ed. and trans. Charles E. Butterworth (Albany: State University of New York Press, 1977), p. 84.
6 See e.g. Richard Janko, ed., *Philodemus on Poems Books 3-4 with the fragments of Aristotle on Poets* (Oxford: Oxford University Press, 2010), p. 471.
7 Again, there was clearly more on this in *On Poets*, including the story that comedy was invented by Susarion, the first comic poet. Asked to perform while mourning his wife, he made a grieving version of the 'can't live with'em, can't live without'em' joke: it has dated. Dated to the origin of comedy, in fact Janko, *Philodemus* p. 427.
8 Kenny, *Aristotle's Poetics*, p. xxvii.
9 Martin Heidegger, *Being and Time*, trans. Joan Stambaugh, revised Dennis Schmidt (Albany: SUNY Press, 2010), p. 118.
10 Toni Morrison, *The Origin of Others* (Cambridge, MA: Harvard University Press, 2017), pp. 35–36.
11 Heidegger hardly ever mentions the *Poetics*, but discusses 'Being-with' in sections 26 and 27, and fear in sections 30 and 40 of *Being and Time*.
12 Morrison, *The Origin of Others*, p. 91. Using Morrison's words is not meant to exonerate the beliefs on race or slavery that Heidegger or Aristotle held: rather, they show that part of literature's power is that it can be turned against wicked ideas held by those who claim to defend or explain it.

13 Kenny points out that *muthos* just means story and *ethos* is often translated as 'character': but this isn't helpful here as everyone in a play is a character and Aristotle is interested in the specifically moral element in the tragedy. Kenny, *Poetics*, p. xix.

14 Halliwell, *Aristotle's Poetics*, p. 24.

15 Hannah Arendt, *The Human Condition* (Chicago: University of Chicago Press, 1998), p. 178.

16 Martin Heidegger, *Basic Concepts of Aristotelian Philosophy*, trans. Robert Metcalf and Mark Tanzer (Bloomington: Indiana University Press, 2009), p. 114.

17 Silvia Carli's discussion 'Poetry and *historia*' is especially clear: see in Pierre Destrée, Malcolm Heath, Dana L. Munteanu, eds., *The Poetics in Its Aristotelian Context*, (London: Routledge, 2020), pp. 202–23.

18 Paul Ricoeur, *The Rule of Metaphor*, trans. by Robert Czerny with Kathleen McLaughlin and John Costello, SJ (London: Routledge, 2003), p. 44.

19 Nussbaum, Martha, *The Fragility of Goodness* (Cambridge: Cambridge University Press, 1986), p. 386.

20 "One of the most frequent forms of peripeteia, or 'reversal', is actually peripeteia of status. Numerous characters, especially in plays treating the fall of Troy, lose previously aristocratic status and become slaves, a fate regarded in the tragic universe as particularly hard to bear". Edith Hall, 'The Sociology of Greek Tragedy' in *The Cambridge Companion to Greek Tragedy*, ed. P. E. Easterling (Cambridge: Cambridge University Press, 1997), pp. 93–126, p. 111.

21 Perhaps something like: discovery then reversal; reversal then discovery; reversal before the play begins (so the play concerns the discovery or recognition which comes from that reversal of fortune: what happens to a family who have, say, lost all their wealth and prosperity before the story begins, and have to move to the back of beyond); discovery before the play (the play's action concerns the reversal that comes from the discovery which occurs before the play begins).

22 For a really clear account, see Thomas Cirillo, 'Taxonomic Flexibility: Metaphor, *genos*, and *eidos*' in *The Poetics in Its Aristotelian Context*, eds. Pierre Destrée, Malcolm Heath, Dana L. Munteanu (London: Routledge, 2020), pp. 185–201.

23 Samuel R. Levin, 'Aristotle's Theory of Metaphor', *Philosophy & Rhetoric* 15:1, (1982), 24–46, p. 25.

24 See, for example, Martin Paul Eve's use of computation methods to investigate where, precisely, anachronistic language has been used by David Mitchell in *Cloud Atlas* (2004). Martin Paul Eve, *Close Reading with Computers* (Stanford: Stanford University Press, 2019).

25 Halliwell, *Aristotle's Poetics*, p. 5.

26 In the fragments of *On Poets*, there is a fully worked example of this kind of error in Euripides. Janko, *Philodemus*, p. 461.

27 Edith Hall, 'Is there a *polis* in Aristotle's *Poetics*?' in *Tragedy and the Tragic: Greek Theatre and Beyond*, ed. M. S. Silk (Oxford: Oxford University Press, 1996), pp. 295–309, p. 296. Simon Goldhill argues that much work in the last 30 years has been to counteract the impact of this separation and "relocate tragedies within a local and national socio-political space" 'Generalising about Tragedy' in *Rethinking Tragedy*, ed. Rita Felski (Baltimore: Johns Hopkins University Press, 2008), pp. 45–65, p. 54.

28 Edith Hall, 'Aristotle's Theory of Catharsis in its Historical and Social Contexts' in *Transformative Aesthetics*, ed. Erika Fischer-Lichte, Benjamin Wihstutz (London: Routledge, 2017), pp. 26–47, p. 41.

29 Malcolm Heath, 'Should There Have Been a *Polis* in Aristotle's *Poetics*?', *The Classical Quarterly* 59:2 (2009), pp. 468–85. See also the essays by Pierre Destrée and Thornton Lockwood in *The Poetics in Its Aristotelian Context*, eds. Pierre Destrée, Malcolm Heath, Dana L. Munteanu (London: Routledge, 2020).

30 Leonardo Tarán, and Dimitri Gutas, *Aristotle's Poetics* (Leiden: Brill, 2012), p. 33.
31 Tarán and Gutas, *Aristotle's Poetics*, p. 39.
32 Kenny, *Poetics*, p. xxxvi.
33 Tarán and Gutas, *Aristotle's Poetics*, pp. 55–6.
34 Wilhelm Dilthey, 'The Imagination of the Poet: Elements for a Poetics', trans. Louis Agostaand and Rudolf A. Makkreel in *Selected Works* vol. V (Princeton: Princeton University Press, 1985), pp. 29–31.
35 Genevieve Liveley, *Narratology* (Oxford: Oxford University Press, 2019). See also for the influence of Aristotle, Shlomith Rimmon-Kenan's *Narrative Fiction: Contemporary Poetics* (London: Routledge, 1990); Gérard Genette, *Narrative Discourse*, trans. Jane E. Leavis (Oxford: Blackwell, 1980). Or, online, *The Living Handbook of Narratology* www.lhn.uni-hamburg.de/index.html.
36 Wayne Booth, *The Rhetoric of Fiction* (Chicago: University of Chicago Press, 1961), preface n.p.
37 Wayne Booth, *The Company We Keep* (Berkeley: University of California Press, 1988), p. 73.
38 Wayne Booth, 'The Poetics for a Practical Critic', *Essays on Aristotle's Poetics*, ed. Amélie Oksenberg Rorty (Princeton: Princeton University Press, 1992), pp. 387–408, p. 405.
39 Mark McGurl, *The Program Era: Postwar Fiction and the Rise of Creative Writing* (Cambridge, MA: London: Harvard University Press, 2009), p. 232.

11

BUT WHAT, AFTER ALL, IS ENTERTAINMENT?

The pleasures of literature (the *Poetics*)

The *Poetics* is about making as well as understanding poetry and drama. In his own Aristotle-influenced handbook, *Story*, the celebrated screenwriter and teacher of screenwriting Robert McKee argues that we read literature, watch film and television,

> in such quantities and with such ravenous hunger that the story arts have become humanity's prime source of inspiration, as it seeks to order chaos and gain insight into life. Our appetite for story is a reflection of the profound human need to grasp the patterns of living, not merely as an intellectual exercise, but within a very personal, emotional experience. In the words of the playwright Jean Anouilh, 'Fiction gives life its form'. Some see the craving for story as simply entertainment, and escape from life rather than an exploration of it. But what, after all, is entertainment?

This is his answer:

> To be entertained is to be immersed in the ceremony of a story to an intellectually and emotionally satisfying end. To the film audience, entertainment is the ritual of sitting in the dark, concentrating on a screen in order to experience the story's meaning and, with that insight, the arousal of strong and, at times even painful emotions, and as the meaning deepens, to be carried to the ultimate satisfaction of those emotions.[1]

For literature, too, and the other forms, entertainment is experiencing the story's meaning to an intellectually and emotionally satisfying end.

Throughout the *Poetics*, Aristotle stresses the pleasure of literature. Stephen Halliwell usefully draws out three different levels of pleasure in the *Poetics*.[2] The first, and relevant to drama (and film and games), is a pleasure in spectacle for its own sake. The second is a pleasure in the *mimesis*, in the form of imitation: the technical qualities of a poem, for example, or when we admire the intricate cleverness of a plot or a well-drawn character. The highest form of pleasure,

 DOI: 10.4324/9781003097914-14

the most intellectually and emotionally satisfying, is in understanding meaning (as when we declare, 'oh, I get what this poem is *saying* ...'). This is why literature can lead to knowledge. This is why, too, the delight in *mimesis*, story and understanding is, at its best, akin to the pleasure we get in learning, and why it is that people enjoy and are struck by powerful metaphors. This chapter will focus on story and on metaphor.

You'll recall that Socrates says that he'd listen to a defence of poetry "graciously" (*The Republic* 607d). These forms of pleasure and what we learn from literature are at the core of Aristotle's response.[3] The pleasure in literature for Socrates is to be feared: for Aristotle, it is to be welcomed, as natural, educational and vital for us and our deliberations. I'll begin with *mimesis* and its major instance in the *Poetics*, tragedy.

Mimesis, The Republic **and the** Poetics

Mimesis in classical Greek had a range of meanings: an imitation of what something looked like; imitations of behaviour and speech (we saw how Socrates was anxious about the guardians copying behaviour); and the way that what we do here on earth imitates or echoes the divine world.[4] While Plato's work introduces ideas and concerns about *mimesis*, Aristotle's describes and analyses it, as well as develops and challenges the views expressed in *The Republic*. Socrates admits that representation is pleasurable (too pleasurable!) and, properly controlled, has some limited role in learning. By contrast, in his discussion of *mimesis* in Chapters 1–4 of the *Poetics*, Aristotle embraces the naturalness, pleasure, educational quality and range of *mimesis*. More, while for Socrates, imitation made us closer to our lower 'animal' selves, for Aristotle, it differentiates us from them.

Most importantly, as we've seen, for Socrates, *mimesis* is a form of deception that stops us being ourselves. By contrast, for Aristotle, *mimesis* is a form of comprehension and understanding of the world: not reality itself but a way to make reality intelligible. As Halliwell explains,

> the plot of a dramatic poem, which is its essential structure of action, is not to be understood as simply corresponding to reality past or present (though certain aspects of it may do so) but as representing a heightened and notional pattern of possibility, and as therefore more accessible to rational apprehension than are the events of ordinary experience.[5]

Paul Ricoeur draws out the significance of this. He argues that in the *Poetics*, the structure of plot constitutes *mimesis*: "quite a strange brand of imitation, which composes and constructs the very thing it imitates!"[6] His point is that *mimesis* for Aristotle is not the duplication but the *ordering* of reality (and recall for Aristotle reality and its ordering match: thus the way his text seems both to describe and prescribe). For Ricoeur's Aristotle, our reality has a kind of deep narrative form, which literary works intensify and so foreground.

This sense of *mimesis* as our active human ordering of reality is why Aristotle emphasises the *techne*, the human skill of composing poems and plays, rather than suggesting that it is inspired by the Muses and gods (as Plato does, in *Ion*, for example). Despite this, as Curran points out, for Aristotle, poets need not "have an explicit grasp of the reason why" poems work: they do not need "theoretical knowledge of what makes good poems good in order to succeed at their craft" unlike other makers of products.[7] This is because understanding literature, the intellectual and emotional responses asked for, belongs to all of us and is not, in itself, a specialised skill. However, like any natural human ability – running, eating, even breathing – we can work to refine and improve our receptiveness and skill at deliberation, for Aristotle: part of the point of the *Poetics*.

Catharsis, tragedy and the impact of *mimesis*

Pleasure, the effect of poetry and drama on the individual, gives a way into thinking about *catharsis*, one of the most famous and most argued over ideas from *Poetics*.[8] As we've seen, *catharsis* from tragedy comes from pity and fear (I discussed these in the previous chapter). The word *catharsis* had a range of linked meanings in classical Greek: clarification, medical purgation, religious and ritual purification (that is, purgation of the soul).[9] A key issue for commentators on Aristotle is which of these nuances Aristotle is seeking to draw out. Because there are so many different views on this, before I discuss it further, take a leaf from Nietzsche's book, and think classical scholarship "through the prism of the artist" and "art through the prism of life".[10] Think about how you felt at the end of a great work of art, a novel, a film, a play that really spoke to you. Not one which just looked impressive or beautiful, nor one which, through its well-crafted plot, gripped you until the last revelation, but one which you felt you were almost living through, at the end you felt wrung out, and that stayed with you, occupied your thoughts, put you at a distance somehow to your daily life. We feel and think *catharsis*.

Venting: blowing off steam

The most influential view of *catharsis* came from a commentator called Jacob Bernays who argued, in a book published in 1857, that *catharsis* was best understood by comparing it to "pathological bodily phenomena".[11] "Let no one primly wrinkle his nose and allege that this reduces aesthetics to medicine", he wrote, as he suggested that the effect of a tragedy was the same as a medical purgative.[12] A bodily purgative makes you excrete: an emotional purgative does the same for your feelings. We might say it helps *vent* your feelings. Bernays was influenced by Aristotle's many medical metaphors and by an account from *Politics* in which Aristotle suggests that music can work as a "relief of the passions" (*Politics* 1341a22–3). Pent-up feelings are released by literature.

This is why some thinkers, who focus on the links between art and society, suggest that *catharsis* is a sophisticated form of repression. The German philosopher Theodor Adorno, for example, declared that Aristotle's theory (that is: Bernays's version of Aristotle's theory) served the ruling class interests because the "surrogate satisfaction" of art was a substitute for the "bodily satisfaction" of the "public's instincts and needs": catharsis "*imputes* to art the principle task" which "the culture industry appropriates and administers".[13] Venting at films, music, theatre, books and art meant that oppressed people did not vent on the social system that oppressed them but just 'let off steam'.

This idea implies that 'pity and fear' are shitty emotions which need to be evacuated, and that the audiences of tragedy need emotional healing. Jonathan Barnes is blunter: "philosophical readers have found it strange of Aristotle to suggest that tragedy is, by definition and essentially, a form of rhubarb", a food which helps us 'vent'.[14]

However, of course, there is more to this idea. Angela Curran in her very clear introductory account suggests a modified version: experiencing pity and fear in art works to "diminish" these feelings in our real life, and so does not vent excess emotion but helps us cope with it.[15] Similarly, Kenny argues that *catharsis* helps us "calibrate the emotions of pity and fear when felt in real life … helps us put our own sorrows and worries into proportion".[16]

Closure: please release me

Responding to the repeated insistence on the idea of unity and on the importance of plot-construction, G. R. F. Ferrari argues that fear and pity are "the emotions engaged by tragic suspense" and not "an audience being braced with a sense of its own tragic vulnerability".[17] This means that the "pleasure of *catharsis* is the pleasure that the audience feels when the suspense that has been tightening throughout the play is suddenly released. It is the pleasure of relief".[18] Lear makes a similar argument, and notes too that the audiences were not children, who needed education in the virtues, but adults.[19] This is a kind of pleasure in closure, in finding out 'whodunnit' or what happens at the end. This desire is very gripping, relies on well-made plots, but it doesn't really explain why we go to see a play, say, in which we already *know* the ending. Nor does it explain why we find ourselves so involved with literary texts afterwards (apart from the satisfaction of admiring the cogs of the plot). Further, Aristotle often reminds his audience that they (and we) have constantly and practically to work at being virtuous (it's not a kind of finished state). Who, after all, is not a person 'in between', "not outstanding in virtue or justice" (*Poetics* 1453a8)? Narrative is gripping and closure is pleasurable, but perhaps *catharsis* is more profound than this.

Clarification: I can see clearly now

Martha Nussbaum offers another nuance of the meaning of *catharsis*: the non-technical meaning of catharsis is "roughly one of 'clearing up' or 'clarification', i.e. of the removal of some obstacle (dirt or blot or obscurity)": the word is used for "water that is clear and open, free of mud or weeds; of a space cleared of objects; of grain that is winnowed, and so clear of chaff".[20] The medical and moral senses stem, she argues, from this. For her, then, *catharsis* is "the clearing up of the vision of the soul by the removal of these obstacles" (389). For Aristotle, "the viewing of pitiable and fearful things, and our responses of pity and fear themselves, can serve to show us something of importance about the human good" (388) and the experience of *catharsis* leads to a form of knowledge, a kind of understanding crucial for *phronesis*.

Similarly, for Halliwell, *catharsis* is part of Aristotle's response to Plato's Socrates. In *The Republic*, emotions evoked by literature nourished the worst part of ourselves. But through *catharsis*, Halliwell suggests, through clarification or seeing clearly in our thoughtful, "conscious, cognitive experience of a work of mimetic art" (200), we put our feelings and our reason into "an ethical alignment" (201).[21] For Halliwell and Nussbaum, *catharsis* is the drawing of emotions into ourselves, rather than expulsion of them, and so vital for coming to clearer, more insightful knowledge of our world, our fate and ourselves.

This understanding of *catharsis* aligns too, with the everyday feelings of fear and pity from the *Rhetoric*, discussed in the last chapter. Fear leads us to deliberation (*Rhetoric* 1383a6) and pity is for "one who does not deserve" their suffering and who is like us in vulnerability to suffering "which we might expect to befall ourselves" (1385b13–15).

This is the sense, too, given above, by Robert McKee. Entertainment, pleasure, is both intellectual and emotional, and concerns 'the story's meaning'. His book *Story* is a guide to constructing good plots but these are not just a peg on which to hang beautiful cinematography or amazing special effects, nor only to keep the audiences gripped by the next twist or turn. The point (the *telos*) is the satisfying unification of intellect and emotion in meaning. The meaning of the story gives insight: clarification of our feelings and thoughts. It seems to me that *catharsis* is the state you are in during or after a great work of art, when you feel both wrung out and elated, where somehow your feelings and thoughts give you a clearer sense, if only for a few moments, of reality.

Tragedy and fate

Catharsis in the *Poetics* arises from tragedy. As I've suggested, tragedy is the core literary art for Aristotle, and from discussions of this, we can learn a great deal about literature in general. The influential literary critic Peter Szondi draws a distinction: since Aristotle, "there has been a poetics of tragedy" but only since "Schelling has there been a philosophy of the tragic".[22] The German idealist philosopher Friedrich von Schelling (1775–1854) began an extraordinarily significant tradition of debating the meaning of tragedy which has since expanded across the humanities. As Miriam Leonard writes, "tragedy has repeatedly provided a common lexicon for arguments between philosophers, political theorists and literary critics".[23] These ideas far exceed the reach of this

174

book. Indeed, even the most prominent example, Hegel's reading of Sophocles's *Antigone*, has created a huge bibliography.[24] The literary and philosophical discussions circle around the idea of our fate as humans, what we can and what we can't control, and what that means: this seems a lot to lay on 'goat songs', which is what the word *tragoidia* originally meant. I'm only going to look at four discussions that draw on Aristotle's ideas.[25]

Bernard Williams, in *Shame and Necessity*, contrasts the views of the great Greek tragedians with those of Plato and Aristotle. For the tragedians, there is a sense of fate, of 'supernatural necessity', that the "structure of things is purposive: that it is, so to speak, playing against you".[26] This does not mean that you are powerless: you can act but not escape; you can think, regret, be bewildered by the necessity under which you have suffered. This inevitability, William writes, is in the "operations of tragedy" (145) itself: the "supernatural and dramatic necessity cannot be ... separated" (145). When the idea that we humans lived under a 'supernatural necessity' faded – when the gods died – it became clear that we are "metaphysically free" (152): but, he warns, "this news is less exciting than it may sound" (152). This freedom means that "there is nothing in the structure of the universe that denies" our power "to intend, to decide, to act" (152) – no fate – but we are still unfree because of "psychological, social and political" obstacles, because of the "constraint exercised by the power of others" (152). "To lack freedom", he writes, is "not simply to be short on choices but to be subjected to the will of another" (154), which is the same, really, as being limited by the external 'supernatural necessity' of fate. This is why, when we think about what these tragedies might mean to us, these 'supernatural necessities' might find some modern-day and not supernatural equivalents.

For Williams, Plato's work is an attempt to make people free: not politically but through the "inner freedom of the soul" (154), free from the rhetoric and persuasion that can lead us to put ourselves under the will of another. Indeed, for Plato, through reason, we can become free from the necessities of our own nature. Opposed to Plato's models of reason, knowledge and philosophy are desire, belief, politics and art: sometimes, Plato presents these as merely shadowy illusions, and sometimes as terrifying powerful forces (the hydra-headed monster within us in **book 9** of *The Republic*, for example). But these ideas lead, Williams says, to the rule of the philosopher-kings and their attendant brainwashing, an idea which makes us feel, shall we say, uncomfortable. Returning to Aristotle's ideas (as, say, MacIntyre suggests) is also not an option for Williams. Aristotle's version of Plato's 'ethical psychology' may be more "helpfully realistic" (162) but Williams traces links between it and Aristotle's defence of slavery and views of women: "among the things that modernity has most conspicuously, and justifiably, learned to distrust" (162). He argues that for Aristotle, "a person whose life fails to be the life of reason is a spoiled or, imperfect or incomplete human being" (161). Again, this might make us feel deeply uneasy, to say the least, about Aristotle.

The tragedians offer 'supernatural fate', while the beliefs of philosophers have unacceptable political consequences, for Williams. Underneath this lies an even deeper question: apart from what we humans have made, is there "anything at all that is intrinsically shaped to human interests, in particular human beings' ethical interests" (163)? Is there a shape or pattern to the moral universe? He says that Plato, Aristotle and more modern philosophers like Kant and Hegel all believed that "in one way or another that the universe or history or the structure of human reason can, when properly understood, yield a pattern that makes sense of human life and aspirations" (163). Tragedians like Sophocles and writers and historians like Thucydides "by contrast are alike in leaving us with no such sense" (163). They present us with a world "only partially intelligible to human agency and in itself not well adjusted to ethical aspirations" (164). This is the case, thinks Williams, whether the forces that oppose people are 'super-natural' or embedded in the "social reality of a world" (165). Your view on these most fundamental issues will determine where you stand.

Williams lays out his view in a powerful conclusion, which relies upon a universal and magisterial 'we'.[27] If we accept that there is no shape or pattern to the moral universe, that "the world was not made for us, or we for the world, that our history tells no purposive story, and that there is no position outside the world or outside history from which we might hope to authenticate our activities" (166), then, he writes,

> In important ways, we are, in our ethical situation, more like human beings in antiquity than any Western people in the meantime. More particularly, we are like those who, from the fifth century and earlier, have left us traces of a consciousness that had not been touched by Plato and Aristotle's attempts to make our ethical relations to the world fully intelligible.
>
> (166)

Classical tragedy has a lot to teach us philosophically, but not if we go through Aristotle.

Simon Critchley builds on Williams in his account of tragedy. Tragedy disorients us and makes us ask "what shall I do?"[28] It presents us with a way of thinking that voices suffering, "partial agency, limited autonomy, deep traumatic affect, agonistic conflict, gender confusions, political complexity and moral ambiguity" (11). Full of "rage" (17) and the "irreducible facticity of violence and the fragile necessity of reasoning in a world of conflictual force" (27), tragedy is a "dialectical mode of experience" (28), a kind of "bracing sceptical realism that heavily qualifies what we think of as hope, but also perhaps deepens it into a form of courage" (29). In all this, Aristotle is not our ally: while he seems more open to tragedy than Plato, he also – Critchley writes with irony – "described tragedy from the unquestionably superior rational vantage point of scientific or theoretical discourse" (248). Aristotle, says Critchley, is not "troubled" (247) by tragedy. Instead, he calmly analyses and dissects, and so controls it, reducing it to both a skill to be learned and a specimen to be measured by pre-given standards (unity of action, beginning, middle and end) and so presents a "theory of tragedies, not a theory of the tragic" (Critchley glosses classicist Simon Goldhill).[29] At least Plato's Socrates took drama seriously enough to be seriously worried by it. Critchley's Aristotle is not a philistine. Much worse for Critchley, he is an *optimist* who lacks a sense of the tragic. Like Lear and Ferrari, Critchley thinks that *catharsis* is really, simply, the enjoyment we get from closure (the thrill of a well-made plot) and neither the venting of pent-up feelings nor the Nussbaum/Halliwell view that it is a form of clarification. But he thinks that there is more to tragedy than this: "Art is not moral tutorial" (191) and again, tragedy is "another way of thinking" from "philosophy, conventionally understood, which tends to confuse art with moral tutorial" (284). His emphasis falls as much on the 'tutorial' as 'moral' since, after all, the very many characteristics he ascribes to tragedy are at least roughly tied into how we find ourselves in the world and make choices, something to do with 'moral'. But a tutorial implies a simple telling or teaching, handed down from the fobbed belly of time. It implies something safe, controlled, taken away from the movement of the theatre into the sedate world of the coolly rational educational institute. Williams and Critchley's accounts are on the side of tragedy against philosophy, as Nietzsche seemed to be, and find something in tragedy that is both 'beyond' us as mortals and yet can teach us about our lives.

By contrast, drawing on rather than opposing Aristotle, both Nussbaum and Halliwell set tragedy on a human scale. Nussbaum's book, *The Fragility of Goodness*, has as its special concern the interplay between *eudaimonia* as a state within our own power and as something at risk in the chances of the world. Nussbaum's argument is that Plato sought to put human goodness beyond mere chance. The happiness of contemplation can be achieved through reason alone: she points out, for example, that Socrates attacks poets for representing good and just people being upset by terrible events (*The Republic* 392a–b). However, this is not the lesson of Greek tragedy, as her Aristotle shows. Unlike Plato, Aristotle believes that a "good person can be dislodged from *eudaimonia*" by bad luck, chance events and material conditions.[30] In the *Nicomachean Ethics*, for example, Aristotle does say you need external things for prosperity (1099a32). Our *eudaimonia* must best be understood in the light of these, and so is fragile. This means that for Aristotle, she argues, the "great tragic plots explore the gap between our goodness and our good living, between what we are (our character, intentions, aspirations, values) and how humanly well we manage to live": that is, the gaps between *eudaimonia*, us and our actual lives.[31]

For Nussbaum's Aristotle, reversals of luck happen to people 'like us', not divine or invulnerable figures. We see how people fall short of *eudaimonia* in the play of reversal and recognition and in *hamartia*, which she translates as 'missing the mark', "a mistake in action that is causally intelligible, not simply fortuitous, done in some sense by oneself", not some terrible flaw but a recognisable aspect of human character or even just an error.[32] We identify with 'people like us' and we see the impact of that falling short on their character: the

world can make us unvirtuous (although Aristotle does believe that the properly virtuous person will be able to bear best the turning of fortune's wheel
(*Nicomachean Ethics* 1100b20)). We feel pity for someone's suffering, when
they don't deserve it. (In a later essay, Nussbaum concludes that, while pity
does prompt us to action, it is also "fickle and in league with hierarchy", and
so the moral good in pity needs to be drawn out and cultivated.)[33] We fear
for ourselves as similarly fragile. Pity and fear are how our vulnerability is
illuminated: our emotional responses help us understand, and this is why *catharsis* is a kind of clarification. All this is why "Aristotle's ethical views make him
hospitable to tragedy and its style as a source of illumination".[34] *Eudaimonia*
may be the result of the virtues and within the scope of the individual, but
prosperity and good fortune (*eutuchia*) are not. Tragedy concerns our interaction with the world.

Similarly, Halliwell argues that "tragedy should deal with the essential fabric
of life" which is why Aristotle gives a "quasi-philosophical" status to poetry.[35]
He locates this even more clearly in *hamartia*, 'failing' or 'going wrong' which is
"somewhere in the space between guilt and vulnerability to misfortune" (220).
For Halliwell, *hamartia* is a *human* failing. Tragedy does not show our lives as
some divine game with human beings as chess pieces because an account of
random events makes a bad play: "pity and fear will best be elicited by events
which happen unexpectedly but on account of one another" (209). The need
for unity rules out the representation of chance. Further, the representation of
chance events in life is the focus of history, not tragedy. For Halliwell's Aristotle,
"poetry's portrayal of human life approximates ... to philosophy" because tragedy presents "some order and pattern in the transformation of fortune" (210),
the patterns of 'reversal' (*peripeteia*) and 'recognition' (*anagnorisis*). Both these
depend upon our human ignorance: reversal is caused by some kind of ignorance and recognition (obviously) depends on ignorance. The role of ignorance
means that *hamartia* lies in us as active agents (it is *our* ignorance), and tragedy explores the interplay between us, our character, virtues and actions in
the world in which we find ourselves. Tragedy is intelligible and not beyond
comprehension. This accounts for the "paradoxical strand of optimism" (235)
in the *Poetics*, writes Halliwell, recalling that the best tragedies are those in
which recognition happens just before some catastrophic action. This optimistic
intelligibility also means that we can learn from tragedy, by recognising "the
mechanisms of human error and their consequences in the heightened form
made available by myth" (236). This takes pleasure as its most demanding for
thought, and invokes our emotions as well as our intellectual cognition.

Much is at stake in these various views of tragedy which grow through or in
opposition to Aristotle. Whether the universe is, in some profound way, good
or indifferent or inhospitable; whether what we learn from tragedy is amenable
to reason, or even to speech, and so human, or whether we just have to 'gaze
into the terrors of individual existence'; whether philosophy, and thought more
generally, is capacious enough not merely to be (and fail at) 'moral tutorial' but

to allow tragedy to become part of our deliberations about our lives. The inter-action of philosophy and literature has taken us to wonder about and puzzle on these questions: the answers only you can decide.

The gift of metaphor: tools and more than tools

In Aristotle's work, metaphors of health (perhaps unsurprisingly for a doctor's son) and building occur often. However, for me, one of his most striking metaphors neither of these. In a very short work, he writes: dream images are "analogous to the forms reflected in water" and so if the water is turbulent, then the images are "scattered and distorted fragments" (*On divination in sleep* 464b9–14). A beautiful and productive metaphor of the mind as water, calm or tempes-tuous, and dreams mirrored on its surface, in the water but somehow not of it.

The *Poetics* and the *Rhetoric* repeatedly stress that metaphor, in particular, and striking language, in general, are a source of pleasure: for example, metaphors give "clearness, charm and distinction" (*Rhetoric* 1405a88) and their "liveli-ness" (*Rhetoric* 1412b18) impresses and pleases. As we've seen, the books classify metaphors, explain how they work and demonstrate that metaphor is a tool in persuasion. "But the greatest thing by far" says the standard transition of the *Poetics*, is for a poet to be "a master of metaphor": this cannot be learnt from others and its insightful use is also a mark of genius, since a good metaphor implies "an intuitive perception of the similarity in dissimilars" (*Poetics* 1059a5–9). Metaphors, then, are pleasurable; are a special sort of language that can be classified; their technical working is explained; they are a tool and also some-thing more profound and important, not merely decoration added to speech.

Many contemporary scholars agree that metaphors are not merely ornament. Indeed, Lakoff, Johnson and Turner, leading cognitive researchers, show that metaphor "is pervasive in everyday life, not just in language but in thought and action. Our ordinary conceptual system, in terms of which we both think and act, is fundamentally metaphorical in nature".[36] We all use metaphors all the time to address emotions, the *polis*, ourselves and our lives. Indeed, metaphor "is a primary tool for understanding our world and ourselves".[37] This is why it can be a tool in rhetoric.

An example: recall Aristotle's example of a metaphor, "old age 'a withered stalk'" (*Rhetoric* 1410b13–15). As we saw, metaphor is "applying to some-thing the name that properly applies to something else" (1457b8–9).[38] The English 'metaphor' comes from the classical Greek which means something like 'to carry over' or 'to transfer'. In Aristotle's example, the sense from one area, human life, is 'carried over' to another, plant life, and some similar pattern understood between these two dissimilar domains. But actually, this is a very common metaphor, what Lakoff and Turner call a 'basic conceptual metaphor', one of the fundamental ideas through which we understand ourselves. They call this one 'PEOPLE ARE PLANTS' (their capitals). Aristotle's example maps human beings onto vegetation. In ordinary speech, we say that people can flower, bloom, have roots, wither, be green, be a petal, branch out, our days are as grass. Once we have made that mapping, we can structure the thought, develop it, evaluate, reason and persuade people with it: a person and an acorn need the right nutrients and environment to bloom, or, say, just as leaves have a *telos*, to shade the fruit, so our lives have a *telos*. Both these rely on intuiting some deep similarities between people and plants.[39] Because of this, metaphors are powerful tools to help our reasoning: Daniel Dennett writes, for example, that "metaphors are not just metaphors; metaphors are the tools of thought ... so it is important to equip yourself with the best set of tools available".[40] They can also be dangerous and manipulative, as we've seen.

The invisible made visible in the metaphor

However, metaphors only work as tools for a deeper reason, because of what Aristotle calls 'the greatest thing' for a poet. (Or, to put this another way, we can judge that 'tool' is not an apt enough metaphor for metaphor.) Metaphors make the invisible world of thought visible and pattern meaning, just as literature itself does, for Aristotle. For Aristotle, metaphor is a way of seeing and so understanding the world and its fundamental patterns of meaning. Most profoundly, this means that metaphor is a link between us and the world.

Hannah Arendt explains in her Aristotelian-inflected account of meta-phor: "mental activities, invisible themselves and occupied with invisible things, become manifest only in speech" and "thinking beings have an urge to speak, speaking beings have an urge to think".[41] Speaking and thought in Aristotle are bound together. She notes, too, that Aristotle does not "decide whether thinking is the origin of speaking, as though speech were merely an instrument of communicating our thoughts, or whether thought is the consequence of the fact that man is a speaking animal" (99). Arendt goes on to argue that speech, *logos*, is first about meaning and then next about truth or falsity. Arendt suggests that Aristotle draws a subtle but important distinc-tion between meaning and truth. At the start of *De Interpretatione*, Aristotle writes that

> Falsity and truth have to do with combination and separation. Thus names and verbs by themselves – for instance 'man' or 'white' when nothing is added – are like the thoughts without combination and sep-aration; for so far they are neither true nor false. A sign of this is that even 'goat-stag' [he means: a centaur] signifies something but not, as yet, anything true or false – unless 'is' or 'is not' is added.
>
> (*De Interpretatione* 16a11–18)

The word 'Centaur' has a meaning, but it is not true or false unless it's combined with '... does/doesn't exist'. Propositions can be true or false, but before that they are meaningful: a prayer, Arendt says, "is a *logos*, but neither true or false" (99). Arendt draws from this that "implicit in the urge to speak is the quest for meaning, not necessarily the quest for truth" (99). Metaphors are speech which shape or reflect the profoundest patterns of meaning. Aristotle does not decide whether thought or speech is primary, and for him thinking and the world's intelligibility mirror each other, so metaphors are ways of expressing and understanding that profound intelligibility, even between things that seem dissimilar. This is why metaphors are so powerful.

However, the patterns of meaning, how things relate to each other, which is established with thought, are invisible. There is no "ready-made vocabulary for mental activities" (102). So to make meaning philosophers and poets "borrow their vocabulary from words originally meant to correspond either to sense experience or to other experiences of ordinary life" (102). (As Gadamer writes, Plato and Aristotle "created a conceptual language from the living flexible language of their contemporary Athens".)[42] This means that philosophical and poetic language *can only* be fundamentally metaphorical: this is *why* all "philosophical terms are metaphors, frozen analogies" (104). Terms are taken from one field, sense experience or ordinary life, and applied to another, the invisible patterning of meaning, and so make manifest the "unapprehended relations of things" (102) (Arendt quotes Shelley).[43] Some metaphors find similarities in things we can see: old age is like the evening of the day. Some are even more conceptual: Arendt's example is from Kant: a despotic state is like a hand mill (a kind of grinder). In these analogies, the metaphor has become a tool for philosophical insight which bridges the gap "between inward and invisible mental activities and the world of appearance" (105). These metaphors are not true or false but convey and shape meaning and this is why metaphors, discovered by poets, were "certainly the greatest gift language could bestow on thinking and hence on philosophy" (105).

Metaphors, too, extend to convey a "hidden story" (107) or a larger pattern of meaning. Arendt gives a beautiful and moving example (and one that draws on her own 'frozen analogy' metaphor), a dialogue between Penelope and Odysseus. He is disguised as a beggar and invents a story about how he, the beggar, had looked after her husband, Odysseus, in Crete. Arendt writes that

> 'her tears ran' as she listened 'and her body was melted, as the snow melts along the high places of the mountains when the West Wind has piled it there, but the South Wind melts it, and as it melts the rivers run full flood. It was even so that her beautiful cheeks were streaming tears, as Penelope wept for her man, who was sitting there by her side'. Here the metaphor seems to combine only visibles; the tears on her cheek are no less visible than the melting snow. The invisible made visible in the metaphor is the long winter of Odysseus' absence, the lifeless frigidity and unyielding hardness of those years, which now, at the first signs of hope for a renewal of life, begin to melt away. The tears

181

themselves had only expressed sorrow; their meaning – the thoughts that caused them – became manifest in the metaphor of the snow melting and softening the ground before spring.

(107)

For Arendt, the invisible meaning behind, for example, Plato's myth of the cave is made visible through the metaphor of the cave. There is no 'non-metaphorical language' for thinking and speaking about meaning.

However, this does not mean that all metaphors are just or appropriate: we judge them but not by the standards of truth or falsity, but by a profounder sense of how life is, of the patterns of life. It is not factually true that an old man is like a withered reed, or that human hope is like spring blossom, but these images are still revealing in the most significant way and we can judge the aptness or unsuitability. This is the importance of judgement, which, in turn, is part of *phronesis* and occurs through deliberation. Judging metaphors is judging our sense of life itself and the patterns of meaning within it.

Arendt is also well aware how metaphors can mislead: in pseudoscience, in science and in philosophy as well. Arendt's example is the way that the Greeks took sight as a model of understanding (we often do too in English: 'insight', 'vision', 'picture this', 'we see that …'). This has profound implications: what you see in understanding and how you speak about it will be different, because you can't speak about what you see except by metaphor, while you can repeat exactly, for example, words you hear. (Imagine if hearing was our metaphor for understanding: what is the difference between being *seen* and being *heard*?)

Jacques Derrida offers a similar example in his essay 'White Mythology', a discussion of "metaphor in the text of philosophy".[44] Like Arendt, he argues that many of the founding concepts of philosophy themselves are analogies and metaphors ("Concept is a metaphor, foundation is a metaphor, theory is a metaphor").[45] Like Arendt on the primacy of the sight metaphor in Greek thought, he extends the idea and reveals a more sinister turn. The title of his essay comes from a dialogue in a philosophical text book, in which one character says

> I have at last made you realize one thing … any expression of an abstract idea can only be an analogy. By an odd fate, the very metaphysicians who think to escape the world of appearances are constrained to live perpetually in allegory. A sorry lot of poets, they dim the colours of the ancient fables, and are themselves but gatherers of fables. They produce white mythology.[46]

That is, philosophers are like poets in that they have to use metaphors to think. Poets, however, take the colours from your mind and, in showing them to you, make them shine. Philosophers imagine that they have escaped metaphors and their vibrant colours, bleaching or freezing them out to the white of the page or ice. For Derrida, this is the way that Western thought has set up one myth, one set of metaphors, forgotten that they are metaphors and assumed that they are universally true. By paying attention to the way philosophers uses metaphors, to how their language was originally coloured and vivid, we not only make it live but also see it for one metaphorical choice among others. We can 'unfreeze' metaphors and analogies. (Is this philosophical? Derrida would argue that to decide whether it is or is not is already a philosophical choice.)

Arendt offers a final thought about the power of metaphors. Metaphor for Aristotle is about relation and not substitution, seeing-as, finding similarities in dissimilar, not seeing-instead-of or poetic ornament. This means that metaphors, especially when extended and applied, are how "the mind holds onto the world" and "guarantee the unity of human experience" (109). If the language of thought is "essentially metaphorical" (110), it means that the "world of appearances" is already inside our thinking and the thinking I "never leaves the world of appearances altogether" (110). Language "by lending itself to metaphorical usage, enables us to think, that is, to have traffic with non-sensory matters, because it permits a carrying-over, *metapherein*, of our sense experiences" (110). Metaphor shows that we do not have an inner and outer world but rather one united by metaphor.

Lakoff and Turner write that because metaphors are a "primary tool for understanding our world and ourselves", engaging with "powerful poetic metaphors" is grappling with "what it means to have a human life".[47] This is so, but for a deeper reason, as we have seen. For Aristotle, metaphors are a patterning, a reaching out of our thought and a model of our unity. They make the invisible patterning of meaning manifest in the *logos* and are the gift given by poetry to thought. Further, in "this respect, metaphor epitomizes or recapitulates in itself all of language – that mysterious, miraculous means by which we mirror the whole world around us".[48] We may not choose to accept this idea of mirroring. However, thinking about metaphors, beginning with our pleasure in their use, their power as tools, what they seem most profoundly to imply and the possibility of 'unfreezing' them, has, again, led us to profound existential questions.

Conclusion

In this chapter, I've followed Aristotle's idea that literature is pleasurable entertainment, but pleasure not just in what it looks like or how it works. Pleasure lies in thinking about, grasping towards what a work of poetry, drama or literature means. In striving towards this, in paying attention and discovering meaning, literature can help us in how to live. For Aristotle, *mimesis* is how we naturally and enjoyably comprehend the world. A literary work draws its audience in and has an impact on them. I looked at four different views of tragedy and at what metaphor means for Aristotle. Both discussions, by revealing patterns, led to the profoundest questions we can ask ourselves.

The *Poetics*, and this enquiry, began with what looks like a literary crit-ical question "what is poetry, how many kinds of it are there, and what are their specific effects?" (1447a7–9). This expanded into a much wider exploration. The critic I. A. Richards noted that this was typical of literary questions: "questions in literary history and criticism" grew, he wrote, so that they took on a "new interest and a wider relevance to human needs". "In asking how language works", he suggested, "we ask how thought and feeling and all the other modes of the mind's activity proceed, about how we are to learn how to live".[49] Taking what Aristotle says *for* and *about* literature, and approaching a range of his work *as* literature, has drawn out some of his most significant ideas.

Aristotle *for* and *as* literature

In this half of the book, I have told a story about Aristotle and his importance both *for* and *as* literature. Because this is an introduction, I took an interpretive path through his work. I began with his insistence on doing, and the way this shaped the most fundamental questions, on through the idea of *telos* and then *eudaimonia*, and how the moral and intellectual virtues help us work at happiness. At each step, I paid attention to the consequences of each of these for literature: teleology and the sense of an ending; the role of literature in demonstrating behaviour and the importance (and problems) of stories and traditions for cultures; the role of literature for wisdom and in deliberation. I arrived at the *Rhetoric*, and suggested it was an investigation into the everyday language of people, and so, really an investigation into what people are really like. I then came to the *Poetics*. For Aristotle, poetry and drama (and I will add: literature) are an intensification of our everyday language. Through the careful and emplotted representation of action and using striking language, lit-erature reveals the shape of ourselves and our world, and so our characters and the consequences of choices. In this, it reveals, for him, the patterns of our exist-ence. It's not a surprise that for Aristotle, language, both in 'large-scale' plot and in 'small-scale' metaphor, reveals these patterns because how we are and how the world is reflect each other in the profoundest ways. This is why, too, we find intellectual and emotional pleasure in the meanings we find in literature. It is entertainment. The pleasure it gives moves from how it looks and sounds, to the grip and release of an exciting story, to the profounder sense of what it means for us: it is, in this regard, and a companion to philosophy. How different this is from the view of Plato's Socrates, but also, how interestingly this illuminates the challenges and impact of the dialogues. Aristotle's work shows us something we may have already known. Literature is wonderful. In puzzling at that wonder, with others and with ourselves, we learn to love wisdom and see the patterns of our existence.

Notes

1 Robert McKee, *Story* (London: Methuen, 1999), p. 12.
2 Stephen Halliwell, *Aristotle's Poetics*, 2nd ed. (London: Duckworth, 1998), pp. 62–81.
3 Halliwell lists very clearly many points where Aristotle responds to Plato, *Aristotle's Poetics*, pp. 331–6.
4 Halliwell, *Aristotle's Poetics*, p. 111ff.
5 Halliwell, *Aristotle's Poetics*, p. 135.
6 Paul Ricoeur, *The Rule of Metaphor*, trans. by Robert Czerny with Kathleen McLaughlin and John Costello, SJ (London: Routledge, 2003), p. 44.
7 Angela Curran, *The Routledge Philosophy Guidebook to Aristotle and the Poetics* (London: Routledge, 2016), p. 26.
8 The term is so contentious that some scholars even suggest that it is a later interpolation to Aristotle: a clear discussion and opinion about this idea is Stephen Halliwell, *Between Ecstasy and Truth* (Oxford: Oxford University Press, 2011), pp. 260–5.
9 Halliwell, *Aristotle's Poetics*, pp. 185–90, p. 197.
10 Friedrich Nietzsche, *The Birth of Tragedy and Other Writings*, ed. Raymond Geuss and Ronald Speirs, trans. Ronald Speirs (Cambridge: Cambridge University Press, 1999), p. 5.
11 Jacob Bernays, 'Aristotle on the effect of tragedy', trans. Jennifer Barnes, intr. Jonathan Barnes, in *Ancient Literary Criticism*, ed. Andrew Laird (Oxford: Oxford University Press, 2006), 158–77, p. 166.
12 Bernays, 'Aristotle …', p. 166.
13 Theodor Adorno, *Aesthetic Theory*, trans. Robert Hullot-Kentor (London: Athlone, 1997), p. 238.
14 Bernays, 'Aristotle …', p. 159.
15 Angela Curran, *The Routledge Philosophy Guidebook to Aristotle and the Poetics* (London: Routledge, 2016), p. 231, p. 232. See also her (really useful) ch. 11 'The Distinct Pleasure of Tragedy'.
16 Kenny, *Poetics*, p. xxvi.
17 G. R. F. Ferrari, 'Aristotle's Literary Aesthetics', *Phronesis* 44:3 (1999), 181–98, p. 194.
18 Ferrari, 'Aristotle's Literary Aesthetics', p. 196.
19 Jonathan Lear, 'Katharsis', *Essays on Aristotle's Poetics*, ed. Amélie Oksenberg Rorty (Princeton: Princeton University Press, 1992), pp. 315–40.
20 Martha Nussbaum, *The Fragility of Goodness* (Cambridge: Cambridge University Press, 1986), p. 389; further references in the text.
21 Halliwell, *Aristotle's Poetics*, p. 200, p. 201.
22 Peter Szondi, *An Essay on the Tragic* (Stanford: Stanford University Press, 2002), p. 1.
23 Miriam Leonard, *Tragic Modernities* (Cambridge, MA: Harvard University Press, 2015), p. 13.
24 In *Antigone*, Creon has taken the throne of Thebes from Antigone's brothers, leaving the corpse of one, Polynices, on the battlefield. Creon forbids his burial. Hegel argues that Antigone, his sister, has to choose between two conflicting ethical commands: the demand of family and divine law, to bury her brother or the law of the state, commanding her not to.
25 Tragedy has the most demanding bibliography of any literary genre. Even within only relatively recent literary criticism, there are too many significant books to list. However, they include *Rethinking Tragedy*, ed. Rita Felski (Baltimore: Johns Hopkins University Press, 2008); Terry Eagleton, *Sweet Violence* (Oxford: Wiley-Blackwell, 2002); George Steiner, *The Death of Tragedy* (London: Faber and Faber, 1974); Ato Quayson, *Tragedy and Postcolonial Literature* (Cambridge: Cambridge University Press, 2021); Raymond Williams, *Modern Tragedy* (London: Chatto & Windus, 1992).

26 Bernard Williams, *Shame and Necessity* (Princeton: Princeton University Press, 2008), p. 14. Further page numbers in the text.

27 When Williams writes that "We live in an ethical condition that lies not only beyond Christianity but beyond its Kantian and Hegelian legacies" (p. 166), the 'we' sounds deeply European and universalist. Perhaps some of this critique that once seemed so acute has aged in face of the increased globalised understanding of our species.

28 Simon Critchley, *Tragedy, The Greeks and Us* (London: Profile Books, 2019), p. 4.

29 Simon Goldhill, 'Generalising about Tragedy' in *Rethinking Tragedy*, ed. Rita Felski (Baltimore: Johns Hopkins University Press, 2008), pp. 45–65, p. 49.

30 Martha Nussbaum, 'Tragedy and Self-sufficiency' in *Essays on Aristotle's Poetics*, ed. Amélie Oksenberg Rorty (Princeton: Princeton University Press, 1992), pp. 261–90, p. 273.

31 Martha Nussbaum, *The Fragility of Goodness: Luck and Ethics in Greek Tragedy and Philosophy* (Cambridge: Cambridge University Press, 1986), p. 382.

32 Nussbaum, *Fragility*, p. 383.

33 Martha Nussbaum, 'The Morality of Pity', *Rethinking Tragedy*, ed. Rita Felski (Baltimore: Johns Hopkins University Press, 2008), pp. 148–69, p. 167.

34 Nussbaum, *The Fragility of Goodness*, p. 391.

35 Halliwell, *Aristotle's Poetics*, p. 157, p. 202.

36 George Lakoff and Mark Johnson, *Metaphors We Live By* (Chicago: Chicago University Press, 1987), p. 3. A more fully cognitive version is George Lakoff, *Women, Fire and Dangerous Things* (Chicago: Chicago University Press, 1987).

37 George Lakoff and Mark Turner, *More than Cool Reason: A Field Guide to Poetic Metaphor* (Chicago: University of Chicago Press, 1989), p. xi.

38 On the precise language of this definition, see John T. Kirby, 'Aristotle on Metaphor', *American Journal of Philology* 118:4 (1997), pp. 517–54, pp. 531–3.

39 Lakoff and Turner, *More than Cool Reason*, pp. 64–5.

40 Daniel Dennett, *Consciousness Explained* (London: Penguin, 1991), p. 455.

41 Hannah Arendt, *The Life of the Mind* (Harvest: New York, 1978), p. 98, p. 99. Further references in the text.

42 Hans-Georg Gadamer, *Heidegger's Ways*, trans. John W. Stanley (Albany: State University of New York Press, 2004), p. 26.

43 Heidegger puts it like this: we have the "the inclination to be entangled in the world" and to interpret ourselves "in terms of that world by its reflected light". Martin Heidegger, *Being and Time*, trans. Joan Stambaugh, revised Dennis Schmidt (Albany: SUNY Press, 2010), p. 20.

44 Jacques Derrida and F. C. T. Moore, 'White Mythology: Metaphor in the Text of Philosophy', *New Literary History* 6:1 (1974), pp. 5–74, p. 6. See on this: Duncan F. Kennedy, 'Aristotle's Metaphor' in *Derrida and Antiquity*, ed. Miriam Leonard (Oxford: Oxford University Press, 2010).

45 Derrida, 'White Mythology', p. 23.

46 Derrida, 'White Mythology', p. 11.

47 Lakoff and Turner, *More than Cool Reason*, p. xi.

48 Kirby, 'Aristotle on Metaphor', p. 547.

49 I. A. Richards, *The Philosophy of Rhetoric* (Oxford: Oxford University Press, 1936), p. 94, p. 95.

CONCLUSION

Starting

This book has introduced what the work of Plato and Aristotle can tell us *about* literature and has also looked at what happens when we read their work *as* literature. The philosophy illuminates the literature as the literature illuminates the philosophy. In so doing it's revealed that the difference between philosophy and literature is harder and harder to distinguish. What are the differences? What do they have in common?

Both philosophy and literature are involved with wonder. Wonder can mean: simply awestruck. For Plato's Socrates, the philosopher is awestruck and silenced by the contemplation of the true, the good and the beautiful. But, as Socrates says,

> I feared my soul would be altogether blinded if I looked at things with my eyes and tried to grasp them with each of my senses. So I thought I must take refuge in discussions and investigate the truth of things by means of words.
>
> (Phaedo 99e)

This returns him, and us, to words, *logos*, to wondering about philosophical and literary questions to do with speech and writing. For Aristotle, philosophy begins in wonder, too, at the stars and the moon, and at stories, composed of wonders. His wonder turns to the activity of understanding, puzzling out.

These two linked responses to wonder lead me to the cover image for this book. One of a series called *Ephemeris*, it's by the British artist Darren Almond. For me, the image tells us something important about wonder and understanding. The picture is composed of an intense stroke of indigo and blue, dark at the top, fading and becoming more ragged as it descends: the rest of the space is a calm, monochrome not-quite-white background with ruled gridlines. In ancient Greek *ephemeris* just meant 'a calendar'. In English, it is an obsolete word for a daily journal, a record of our mundane, everyday life. The word is also the stem of *ephemeron*, a mayfly that lives for only a day once it has developed wings: Aristotle noted that this creature was "exceptional ... in regard to the duration of its existence, whence it received its name" (*History of*

DOI: 10.4324/9781003097914-15

Animals 490a33–4). Our word 'ephemera' derives from this insect's name, and means something transitory and unimportant. Applied to written or printed material, ephemera means it is of 'no lasting value except to collectors': "writing is of little worth" says Socrates, writes Plato (*Phaedrus* 278c). All these associations make us wonder about our daily life, our mortality and how we record or reflect this.

The word *Ephemeris* also has a current usage: an astronomical, technical word meaning a chart which shows where a heavenly body will be for each period during a set time. Beginning in wonder "about the phenomena of the moon and … the sun and the stars" (*Metaphysics* 982b14–17), this chart is a rational mapping out and delineation of those phenomena, as the gridlines in the picture suggest. The ruled lines on the paper are gentle and do not dominate the blue shape: they give us a way to follow, describe and, through measurement, share with others the sweep of the ink. By contrast, the blue stroke is another kind of working out, a sudden creative response to the same movements in the heavens, vivid but finite. The indigo is composed, smooth, slightly curving, as if a single brushstroke. It tracks in colour the movement of a star, and so links the heavens with the beauty of the mundane, the passing of a mortal life and, because it's ink, writing. To me, this picture is an image of a companionable meeting of two responses to wonder: the inspired artistic, the rationally geometrical, both differently creative. Together, they remind us that one thoughtful understanding should not dominate another. Each complements the other, and in turn, both can orient us towards the object of wonder and so towards understanding.

Three more images from this book.

A path: at the beginning of this book, I used the metaphor of a path through unfamiliar terrain as way of describing an introductory work. There are very many introductions to Plato and Aristotle: for philosophers, political theorists, historians, classicists, for screenwriters, but rarely for people specifically interested in literature. This still seems odd to me, until I remember that literature is, somehow, always already there. Whatever path you wish to make for yourself through these thinkers will involve the literary. That path will, can only, travel through questions of form, style, character, meaning, direction. This is why questions of the literary reach so quickly the central themes in these two thinkers. The literary also invokes (perhaps often inexplicit) questions about traditions, contexts and how these thinkers are given to our world today.

A gift: Plato and Aristotle are sometimes described as a legacy: the "legacy of Greece to Western philosophy is Western philosophy", for example.[1] A legacy is an inheritance, something bequeathed to you in a will or from the past. We know from stories that gifts of this sort may be important but are not always pleasant or safe. If Socrates's arguments are taken at face value, his wider political solutions are unpalatable and literature is something between a distraction and a disease. If the dialogues are read as more literary, perhaps they warn about the very possibility of political solutions. Williams is right to point out that for all the talk of virtue, flourishing and a shared common world, Aristotle posits a view that a person is devalued by what might be innate to them or by some terrible circumstance occurring their world. This is surely, at best, an opening or, at worst, an invitation to prejudice and other forms of hate (and I recall the words of Simone Weil cited in the introduction, that 'man who takes the trouble to draw up an apology for slavery' does not love justice and those who follow his ideas will have a 'decrease in powers of discernment'). Linked with this is the idea that we can all speak equally in the *agora*: this is lovely in theory but we do not all have equal access to, status in or the disposition for, speech in a shared forum. Perhaps this metaphor itself fails to address our contemporary world. But this gift, the legacy of Plato and Aristotle, is already given and has shaped the Western tradition: in order to rewrite or reject it, develop it, interleave it with others, discern and draw from it what we judge to be good and abandon what is not, we need to understand and recognise it.

Companions: finally, in the introduction, I contrasted the way literature brings strands together (character, ideas, themes, form, style, ambiguity, subtext) while philosophy makes finer and finer distinctions. Literature fuses (perhaps it confuses?): philosophy divides (perhaps so small as to make thinking impossible?). You'll recall that the movement of the dialectic is to take things apart and put them back together. The witty Socrates of *Phaedrus* says he is a "lover of these processes of division and bringing together, as aids to speech and thought" (*Phaedrus* 266b). However, perhaps as *Ephemeris* shows, literature and philosophy both have a role to play in this dialectic, as companions, taking apart, bringing together.

A chart. A path. A dangerous gift. Companions. Where better to start?

Note

1 Bernard Williams, *The Sense of the Past* (Princeton: Princeton University Press, 2006), p. 156.

BIBLIOGRAPHY

Abbott, H. Porter, *Narrative* (Cambridge: Cambridge University Press, 2002).

Abensour, Miguel and Martin Breaugh, 'Against the Sovereignty of Philosophy over Politics: Arendt's Reading of Plato's Cave Allegory', *Social Research* 74:4 (2007), 955–82.

Alighieri, Dante, *Inferno*, Canto IV, l. 131–3, *The Divine Comedy*, trans. C. H. Sisson (Oxford: Oxford University Press, 1993).

Allen, Danielle S., *Why Plato Wrote* (Oxford: Wiley-Blackwell, 2013).

Arendt, Hannah, *The Origins of Totalitarianism* (London: Harvest, 1958).

Arendt, Hannah, *The Life of the Mind* (Harvest: New York, 1978).

Arendt, Hannah, *Essays in Understanding* (New York: Schocken Books, 1994).

Arendt, Hannah, *The Human Condition* (Chicago: University of Chicago Press, 1998).

Arendt, Hannah, *The Promise of Politics* (New York: Schocken Books, 2005).

Arendt, Hannah, *Between Past and Future: Eight Exercises in Political Thought* (London: Penguin, 2006).

Arendt, Hannah, *Reflections on Literature and Culture*, ed. Susannah Young-Ah Gottlieb (California: Stanford University Press, 2007).

Aristotle, *The Complete Works of Aristotle: The Revised Oxford Translation*, ed. Jonathan Barnes (New Jersey: Princeton University Press, 1984).

Aristotle, *The Metaphysics*, trans. Hugh Lawson-Tancred (London: Penguin, 1998).

Aristotle, *Poetics*, trans. Anthony Kenny (Oxford: Oxford University Press, 2013).

Aristotle's Ethics, revised, ed., trans. Jonathan Barnes and Anthony Kenny (Princeton: Princeton University Press, 2014).

Assman, Jan, *Cultural Memory and Early Civilisation: Writing, Remembrance and Political Imagination* (Cambridge: Cambridge University Press, 2011).

Badiou, Alain, *Plato's Republic*, trans. Susan Spitzer (Cambridge: Polity, 2015).

Ball, James, *Post-Truth: How Bullshit Conquered the World* (London: Biteback, 2017).

Barnes, Jonathan, *Method and Metaphysics* (Oxford: Oxford University Press, 2011).

Bhabha, Homi, *The Location of Culture* (London: Routledge, 1994).

Blondell, Ruby, *The Play of Character in Plato's Dialogues* (Cambridge: Cambridge University Press, 2002).

Booth, Wayne, *The Rhetoric of Fiction* (Chicago: University of Chicago Press, 1961).

Booth, Wayne, *The Company We Keep* (Berkeley: University of California Press, 1988).

Booth, Wayne, 'The Poetics for a Practical Critic' in *Essays on Aristotle's Poetics*, ed. Amélie Oksenberg Rorty (Princeton: Princeton University Press, 1992), pp. 387–408.

Brand, Russell, *Revolution* (London: Century, 2014).

Brogan, Walter, *Heidegger and Aristotle* (Albany: State University of New York Press, 2005).

Brooks, Peter, *Reading for the Plot* (Cambridge, MA: Harvard University Press, 1984).

Burkert, Walter, *Babylon Memphis Persepolis; Eastern Contexts of Greek Culture* (Harvard: Harvard University Press, 2004).

Carli, Silvia, Discussion 'Poetry and *historia*' in *The Poetics in Its Aristotelian Context*, eds., Destrée, Pierre, Malcolm Heath, Dana L. Munteanu (London: Routledge, 2020), pp. 202–23.

Carson, Anne, 'How Not to Read a Poem: Unmixing Simonides from "Protagoras"', *Classical Philology* 87:2 (1992), 110–30.

Chamberlain, Charles, 'The Meaning of Prohairesis in Aristotle's Ethics', *Transactions of the American Philological Association* 114 (1984), 147–57.

Chappell, Sophie, Grace *Knowing What to Do: Imagination, Virtue and Platonism in Ethics* (Oxford: Oxford University Press, 2014).

Chroust, Anton-Hermann, *Aristotle: New Light on His Life and Some of His Lost Works* (London: Routledge & Kegan Paul, 1973).

Cirillo, Thomas, 'Taxonomic Flexibility: Metaphor, *genos*, and *eidos*' in *The Poetics in Its Aristotelian Context*, eds., Pierre Destrée, Malcolm Heath, Dana L. Munteanu (London: Routledge, 2020), pp. 185–201.

Cline, Eric H., *1177 B. C.: The Year Civilisation Collapsed*, rev. ed. (Princeton: Princeton University Press, 2021).

Cooper, John M., ed., *Plato: Complete Works* (Indianapolis: Hackett Publishing, 1997).

Cornford, F. M., *From Religion to Philosophy: a Study in the Origins of Western Speculation* (London: Edward Arnold, 1912).

Cornford, F. M., *The Unwritten Philosophy and Other Essays* (Cambridge: Cambridge University Press, 1950).

Critchley, Simon, *Tragedy, The Greeks and Us* (London: Profile Books: 2019).

Curran, Angela, *The Routledge Philosophy Guidebook to Aristotle and the Poetics* (London: Routledge, 2016).

D'Ancona, Matthew, *Post-Truth: The New War on Truth and How to Fight Back* (London: Ebury Press, 2017).

D'Angour, Armand, *Socrates in Love* (London: Bloomsbury Publishing, 2019).

Davis, Evan, *Post-Truth: Why We Have Reached Peak Bullshit and What We Can Do About It* (London: Little Brown, 2017).

De Crescenzo, Luciano, *The Dialogues*, trans. Avril Bardoni (London: Picador, 1985).

Derrida, Jacques, *Of Grammatology*, trans. Gayatri Chakravorty Spivak (London: Johns Hopkins University Press, 1976).

Derrida, Jacques, *Writing and Difference*, trans. Alan Bass (London: Routledge and Kegan Paul, 1978).

Derrida, Jacques, *Dissemination*, trans. Barbara Johnson (London: The Athlone Press, 1981).

Destrée, Pierre Malcolm Heath, Dana L. Munteanu, eds., *The Poetics in Its Aristotelian Context* (London: Routledge, 2020).

Detienne, Marcel, *The Masters of Truth in Archaic Greece*, trans. Janet Lloyd (New York: Zone Books, 1999).

Dilthey, Wilhelm, 'The Imagination of the Poet: Elements for a Poetics', trans. Louis Agostaand and Rudolf A. Makkreel in *Selected Works Vol. V* (Princeton: Princeton University Press, 1985).

Doody, Margaret, *Aristotle: Detective* (London: Arrow, 2002).

191

Eliot, T. S., *Selected Prose*, ed. Frank Kermode (London: Faber and Faber, 1975).

Eve, Martin Paul, *Close Reading with Computers* (Stanford: Stanford University Press, 2019).

Felski, Rita, *Hooked: Art and Attachment* (Chicago: Chicago University Press, 2020).

Ferrari, G. R. F. 'Aristotle's Literary Aesthetics', *Phronesis* 44:3 (1999), 181–98.

Finlayson, Alan, 'Rhetoric in Contemporary British Politics', *The Political Quarterly* 85:4 (2014), 428–36.

Folch, Marcus, *The City and the Stage* (Oxford: Oxford University Press, 2015).

Forster, E. M., *Aspects of the Novel*, ed. Oliver Stallybrass (London: Penguin, 2000).

Frank, Jill, *Poetic Justice: Rereading Plato's* Republic (Chicago: Chicago University Press, 2018).

Frede, Michael, 'Plato's Arguments and the Dialogue Form' in *Methods of Interpreting Plato and His Dialogues: Oxford Studies in Ancient Philosophy: Supplementary Volume*, eds., James C. Klagge and Nicholas D. Smith (Oxford: Oxford University Press 1992), pp. 201–19.

Fuss, Diana, *Identification Papers* (London: Routledge, 1995).

Gadamer, Hans-Georg, *Truth and Method*, 2nd ed. trans. Joel Weinsheimer and Donald G. Marshall (London: Sheed and Ward, 1989).

Gadamer, Hans-Georg, *Heidegger's Ways*, trans. John W. Stanley (Albany: State University of New York Press, 2004).

Gagarin, Michael, 'The Purpose of Plato's Protagoras', *Transactions and Proceedings of the American Philological Association* 100 (1969), 133–64.

Genette, Gérard, *Narrative Discourse*, trans. Jane E. Leavis (Oxford: Blackwell, 1980).

Geuss, Raymond, 'Russell Brand, Lady T, Pisher Bob and Preacher John', *Radical Philosophy* 190 (March/April 2015), 2–7.

Goldhill, Simon, *Rethinking Tragedy*, ed. Rita Felski (Baltimore: Johns Hopkins University Press, 2008), pp. 45–65.

Goldstein, Rebecca, *Plato at the Googleplex* (London: Atlantic Books, 2014).

Gonzalez, Francisco J., "The Virtue of Dialogue, Dialogue as Virtue in Plato's Protagoras" *Philosophical Papers* 43:1 (2014), 33–66.

Gordon, Jill, *Turning Toward Philosophy: Literary Device and Dramatic Structure in Plato's Dialogues* (Pennsylvania: Pennsylvania State University Press, 1999).

Gordon, Jill, *Poetic Justice: Rereading* Plato's Republic (Chicago: Chicago University Press, 2018).

Gross, Daniel, 'Introduction' *Heidegger and Rhetoric*, eds. Daniel Gross and Ansgar Kemmann (Albany: SUNY Press, 2005), pp. 1–48.

Haden, James, 'On Socrates, with Reference to Gregory Vlastos', *The Review of Metaphysics* 33:2 (1979), 371–89.

Hadot, Pierre, *Philosophy as a Way of Life*, ed. Arnold Davidson, trans. Michael Chase (Oxford: Blackwell, 1995).

Hall, Edith, 'Is There a *polis* in Aristotle's *Poetics*?' in *Tragedy and the Tragic: Greek Theatre and Beyond*, ed. M. S. Silk (Oxford: Oxford University Press, 1996), pp. 295–309.

Hall, Edith, 'The Sociology of Greek Tragedy' in *The Cambridge Companion to Greek Tragedy*, ed. P. E. Easterling (Cambridge: Cambridge University Press, 1997), pp. 93–126.

Hall, Edith, 'Aristotle's theory of *catharsis* in its historical and social contexts' in *Transformative Aesthetics*, eds. Erika Fischer-Lichte, Benjamin Wihstutz (London: Routledge, 2017), pp. 26–47.

Halliwell, Stephen. *Aristotle's Poetics*, 2nd ed. (London: Duckworth, 1998).

Halliwell, Stephen, *The Aesthetics of Mimesis: Ancient Texts and Modern Problems* (Princeton: Princeton University Press, 2002).

Halliwell, Stephen, *Between Ecstasy and Truth: Interpretations of Greek Poetics from Homer to Longinus* (Oxford: Oxford University Press, 2011).

Havelock, Eric A., *Preface to Plato* (Cambridge, MA: Harvard University Press, 1963).

Heath, Malcolm, 'Aristotle on Natural Slavery', *Phronesis* 53:3 (2008), 243–70.

Heath, Malcolm, 'Should There Have Been a *Polis* in Aristotle's *Poetics*?', *The Classical Quarterly* 59:2 (2009), 468–85.

Heidegger, Martin, *Pathmarks*, ed. William McNeill (Cambridge: Cambridge University Press, 1998), pp. 155–82.

Heidegger, Martin, *Plato's Sophist*, trans. Richard Rojcewicz and André Schuwer (Bloomington: Indiana University Press, 2003).

Heidegger, Martin, *Basic Concepts of Aristotelian Philosophy*, trans. Robert Metcalf and Mark Tanzer (Bloomington: Indiana University Press, 2009).

Heidegger, Martin, *Being and Time*, trans. Joan Stambaugh, revised Dennis Schmidt (Albany: SUNY Press, 2010).

Hesiod, *The Homeric Hymns and Homerica with an English Translation* by Hugh G. Evelyn-White (Cambridge, MA: Harvard University Press, 1914) via Perseus Digital Library www.perseus.tufts.edu/hopper/

Howland, Jacob, 'Re-Reading Plato: The Problem of Platonic Chronology', *Phoenix* 45:3 (1991), 189–214.

Hughes, Bettany, *The Hemlock Cup* (London: Vintage, 2011).

Hyde, Michael J., 'A Matter of the Heart: Epideictic Rhetoric and Heidegger's Call of Conscience' in *Heidegger and Rhetoric*, eds. Daniel Gross and Ansgar Kemmann (Albany: SUNY Press, 2005), pp. 91–104.

Hyland, Drew A., *Finitude and Transcendence in the Platonic Dialogues* (Albany: SUNY Press, 1995).

Hyland, Drew A. and Johan Panteleimon Manoussakis, eds., *Heidegger and the Greeks* (Bloomington: Indiana University Press, 2006).

Janaway, Christopher, *Images of Excellence: Plato's Critique of the Arts* (Oxford: Oxford University Press, 1995).

Janko, Richard, ed., *Philodemus on Poems Books 3–4 with the Fragments of Aristotle on Poets* (Oxford: Oxford University Press, 2010).

Joyce, James, *Ulysses* (London: Penguin, 1986).

Kennedy, Duncan F., 'Aristotle's Metaphor' in *Derrida and Antiquity*, ed. Miriam Leonard (Oxford: Oxford University Press, 2010), pp. 267–88.

Kermode, Frank, *The Sense of an Ending* (Oxford: Oxford University Press, 2000).

Keynes, John Maynard, *The General Theory of Employment, Interest and Money* (London: Macmillan, 1936).

Kierkegaard, Søren, *Writings, II, Volume 2: The Concept of Irony, with Continual Reference to Socrates/Notes of Schelling's Berlin Lectures*, eds. Hong, Howard V., and Edna H. Hong (Princeton: Princeton University Press, 1989).

Kirby, John T., 'Aristotle on Metaphor', *The American Journal of Philology* 118:4 (1997) 517–54.

Kisiel, Theodore, 'Rhetorical Protopolitics in Heidegger and Arendt' in *Heidegger and Rhetoric*, eds. Daniel Gross and Ansgar Kemmann (Albany: SUNY Press, 2005), pp. 131–160.

Kisiel, Theodore and John van Buren, eds., *Reading Heidegger from the Start* (Albany: State University of New York Press, 1994).

Klein, Liam and Daniel Schillinger, 'Entangling Plato: A Guide through the *Political Theory* Archive', *Political Theory* (2021), 1–15 https://doi.org/10.1177/0090591721998073.

Kołakowski, Leszek, *Metaphysical Horror* (London: Penguin, 2001).

Kosman, L. A., 'Silence and Imitation in the Platonic Dialogues' in *Methods of Interpreting Plato and His Dialogues: Oxford Studies in Ancient Philosophy: Supplementary Volume*, eds. James C. Klagge and Nicholas D. Smith (Oxford: Oxford University Press, 1992), pp. 73–92.

Lavery, Jonathan, 'Plato's Protagoras and the Frontier of Genre Research: A Reconnaissance Report from the Field', *Poetics Today* 28:2 (2007) 191–246.

Layne, Danielle A., 'The Anonymous Prolegomena to Platonic Philosophy' in *Brill's Companion to the Reception of Plato in Antiquity*, eds. Harold Tarrant, François Renaud, Dirk Baltzly, and Danielle A. Layne (Boston: Brill, 2017), pp. 533–54.

Lazarus, Micha, 'Sidney's Greek Poetics', *Studies in Philology*, 112:3 (2015), 504–36.

Lear, Jonathan, *Aristotle: The Desire to Understand* (Cambridge: Cambridge University Press, 1987).

Lear, Jonathan, 'Katharsis', *Essays on Aristotle's Poetics*, ed. Amélie Oksenberg Rorty (Princeton: Princeton University Press, 1992), pp. 315–40.

Leavis, F. R., *Education and the University* (London: Chatto and Windus, 1948).

Ledbetter, Grace M. M., *Poetics Before Plato: Interpretation and Authority in Early Greek Theories of Poetry* (Princeton: Princeton University Press, 2002).

Leith, Sam, *Words Like Loaded Pistols: Rhetoric from Aristotle to Obama* (New York: Basic Books, 2012).

Lemoine, Rebecca, *Plato's Caves: The Liberating Sting of Cultural Diversity* (Oxford: Oxford University Press, 2020).

Leonard, Miriam, *Athens in Paris: Ancient Greece and the Political in Post-War French Thought* (Oxford: Oxford University Press, 2005).

Leonard, Miriam, *Tragic Modernities* (Cambridge, MA: Harvard University Press, 2015).

Leroi, Armand-Marie, *The Lagoon: How Aristotle Invented Science* (London: Bloomsbury, 2014).

Levin, Samuel R., 'Aristotle's Theory of Metaphor', *Philosophy & Rhetoric* 15:1 (1982), 24–46.

Liveley, Genevieve, *Narratology* (Oxford: Oxford University Press, 2019).

Lyotard, Jean-François, *The Postmodern Condition*, trans. Geoff Bennington (Manchester: Manchester University Press, 1986).

MacIntyre, Alasdair, *After Virtue* (London: Duckworth, 1985).

Marx, William, *The Hatred of Literature*, trans. Nicholas Elliott (Cambridge: MA, Harvard University Press, 2018).

Mazzoni, Guido, *Theory of the Novel* (Cambridge, MA: Harvard University Press, 2017).

McGurl, Mark, *The Program Era: Postwar Fiction and the Rise of Creative Writing* (Cambridge, MA: London: Harvard University Press, 2009).

McKee, Robert, *Story* (London: Methuen, 1999).

Meyer, Michael, *What Is Rhetoric?* (Oxford: Oxford University Press, 2017).

Miller, Paul Allen, *Diotima at the Barricades* (Oxford: Oxford University Press, 2016).

Moi, Toril, Amanda Anderson, and Rita Felski, *Character: Three Inquires in Literary Studies* (Chicago: Chicago University Press, 2019).

Moller, Violet, *The Map of Knowledge: How Classical Ideas Were Lost and Found: A History in Seven Cities* (London: Picador, 2020).

Moore, A. W., *The Evolution of Modern Metaphysics: Making Sense of Things* (Cambridge: Cambridge University Press, 2012).

Moore, John D. 'The Dating of Plato's *Ion*', *Greek, Roman, and Byzantine Studies* 15:4 (1974), 421–39.

Morrison, Toni, *The Origin of Others* (Cambridge, MA: Harvard University Press, 2017).

Murdoch, Iris, *Metaphysics as a Guide to Morals* (London: Allen Lane, 1992).

Murdoch, Iris, *Existentialists and Mystics* (London: Penguin, 1997).

Myers, D. G., *The Elephants Teach: Creative Writing Since 1880* (Chicago: University of Chicago Press, 2006).

Nails, Debra, 'The Dramatic Date of Plato's *Republic*', *The Classical Journal* 93:4 (1998), 383–96.

Nails, Debra, *The People of Plato* (Indianapolis: Hackett Publishing Company, 2002).

Nails, Debra, 'The Life of Plato of Athens' in *A Companion to Plato*, ed. Hugh H. Benson (Oxford: Blackwell, 2006), pp. 1–12.

Naas, Michael, *Derrida from now on* (New York: Fordham University Press, 2008).

Natali, Carlo, *Aristotle: His Life and School* (Princeton: Princeton University Press, 2013).

Nehamas, Alexander, *Virtues of Authenticity* (Princeton: Princeton University Press, 1999).

Ngũgĩ wa Thiong'o, *Decolonising the Mind* (Nairo bi: East African Educational Publishers, 1986).

Nietzsche, Friedrich, *On the Genealogy of Morals*, trans. Carol Diethe (Cambridge: Cambridge University Press, 1989).

Nietzsche, Friedrich, *The Birth of Tragedy and Other Writings*, eds. Raymond Geuss and Ronald Speirs, trans. Ronald Speirs (Cambridge: Cambridge University Press, 1999).

Nussbaum, Martha, *The Fragility of Goodness* (Cambridge: Cambridge University Press, 1986).

Nussbaum, Martha, *Love's Knowledge: Essays on Philosophy and Literature* (Oxford: Oxford University Press, 1990).

Pappas, 'Nickolas Socrates' Charitable Treatment of Poetry', *Philosophy and Literature* 13:2 (1989), 248–61.

Peters, F. E., *Aristotle and the Arabs: The Aristotelian Tradition in Islam* (New York: New York University Press, 1968).

Plato, *Protagoras*, trans. Benjamin Jowett, revised Martin Ostwald, ed. and intro Gregory Vlastos, (Indianapolis: Bobbs-Merrill Company, 1956).

Plato, *Complete Works*, ed., into, notes John M. Cooper, associate D. S. Hutchinson (Indianapolis: Hackett Publishing Company, 1997).

Popper, Karl, *The Open Society and Its Enemies* (London: Routledge, 2011).

Quayson, Ato, *Tragedy and Postcolonial Literature* (Cambridge: Cambridge University Press, 2021).

Ralkowski, Mark A., *Plato's Trial of Athens* (London: Bloomsbury, 2019).

Renault, Mary, *Fire from Heaven* (London: Virago, 2014).

Richards, I. A., *Principles of Literary Criticism* (London: Routledge, 2001).

Ricoeur, Paul, *The Rule of Metaphor*, trans. by Robert Czerny with Kathleen McLaughlin and John Costello, SJ (London: Routledge, 2003).

Rimmon-Kenan, Shlomith, *Narrative Fiction: Contemporary Poetics* (London: Routledge, 1990).

Rosen, Stanley, *Plato's Republic: A Study* (New Haven: Yale University Press, 2005).

Ross, W. D., *Aristotle*, 5th ed. (London: Methuen, 1949), p. 190.

Rowe, Christopher, *Plato and the Art of Philosophical Writing* (Cambridge: Cambridge University Press, 2007).

Rushd, Ibn, *Averroes' Three Short Commentaries on Aristotle's Topics, Rhetoric and Poetics*, ed. and trans. Charles E. Butterworth (Albany: State University of New York Press, 1977).

Rushdie, Salman, *Imaginary Homelands: Essays and Criticism 1981–1991* (London: Granta Books in association with Penguin, 1992).

Rutherford, R. B., *The Art of Plato* (London: Duckworth, 1995).

Ryle, Gilbert, *Critical Essays: Collected Papers Volume 1* (London: Routledge, 2009).

Saxonhouse, Arlene, 'The Socratic Narrative: A Democratic Reading of Plato's Dialogues', *Political Theory* 37:6 (2009), 728–53.

Scott, Dominic, *Levels of Argument* (Oxford: Oxford University Press, 2015).

Scott, Gary Alan ed., *Philosophy in Dialogue: Plato's Many Devices* (Evanston: Northwestern University Press, 2007).

Shakespeare, William, *Coriolanus (The Arden Shakespeare Third Series)*, ed. Peter Holland (Bloomsbury: London, 2013).

Sheehan, Thomas, *Making Sense of Heidegger* (London: Publisher: Rowman & Littlefield International, 2014).

Shelley, Percy Bysshe, *Selected Poems and Prose*, eds. Jack Donovan and Cian Duffy (London: Penguin, 2016).

Shields, Christopher, ed., *The Oxford Handbook of Aristotle* (Oxford: Oxford University Press, 2012).

Shields, Christopher, *Aristotle*, 2nd ed. (London: Routledge, 2014).

Sidney, Philip, *Sidney's 'The Defence of Poesy' and Selected Renaissance Literary Criticism*, ed. Gavin Alexander (London: Penguin, 2004).

Smith, Nicholas, 'Editorial Afterword: Platonic Scholars and Other Wishful Thinkers' in *Methods of Interpreting Plato and His Dialogues: Oxford Studies in Ancient Philosophy: Supplementary Volume*, Oxford University Press. James C. Klagge and Nicholas D. Smith (1992) pp. 245–60.

Sorabji, R., ed., *Aristotle Transformed: The Ancient Commentators and Their Influence* (London: Duckworth, 1990).

Sorabji, R., ed., *Aristotle Re-Interpreted: New Findings on Seven Hundred Years of the Ancient Commentators* (London: Bloomsbury, 2016).

Stone, I. F., *The Trial of Socrates* (New York: Anchor Books, 1989).

Strauss, Leo, *The City and Man* (Chicago: University of Chicago Press, 1964).

Tarán, Leonardo and Dimitri Gutas, *Aristotle's Poetics* (Leiden: Brill, 2012).

Taylor C. C. W., ed., Plato, *Protagoras*, trans. C. C. W. Taylor (Clarendon Press: Oxford, 1976).

Thucydides, *History of the Peloponnesian War*, trans. Rex Warner (London: Penguin Book, 1972).

Trapp, M. B., ed., *Socrates in the Nineteenth and Twentieth Centuries* (London: Routledge, 2016).

Turner, James, *Philology: The Forgotten Origins of the Modern Humanities* (Princeton: Princeton University Press).

Vernant, Jean-Pierre, *The Origins of Greek Thought* (New York: Cornell University Press, 1982).

Vlastos, Gregory, ed., *Plato, Protagoras*, trans. Benjamin Jowett, revised Martin Ostwald, ed. and intro Gregory Vlastos (Indianapolis: Bobbs-Merrill Company, 1956).

Vlastos, Gregory, *Socrates: Ironist and Moral Philosopher* (Cambridge: Cambridge University Press, 1991).

Volpi, Franco, 'In Whose Name? Heidegger and "Practical Philosophy"', *European Journal of Political Theory* 6:1 (2007), 31–51.

Wallace, Jennifer, 'Shelley, Plato and the Political Imagination' in *Platonism and the English Imagination,* eds. Anna Baldwin, Sarah Hutton (Cambridge: Cambridge University Press, 1994).

Wallace, Jennifer, *Tragedy Since 9/11: Reading a World Out of Joint* (London: Bloomsbury, 2020).

Weil, Simone, *Gravity and Grace*, trans. Emma Crawford and Mario von der Ruhr (London: Routledge, 2002).

Weil, Simone, *The Need for Roots*, trans. Arthur Wills (London: Routledge, 2002).

Williams, Bernard, *The Sense of the Past* (Princeton: Princeton University Press, 2006).

Williams, Bernard, *Shame and Necessity* (Princeton: Princeton University Press, 2008).

Wittgenstein, Ludwig, *Philosophical Investigations*, trans. G. E. M. Anscombe (Oxford: Blackwell, 1963).

Wittgenstein, Ludwig, *Culture and Value*, ed. G. H. von Wright, trans. Peter Winch (Oxford: Blackwell, 1998).

Woolf, Virginia, *The Common Reader* (London: Hogarth Press, 1948).

Xenophon, *Conversations of Socrates*, trans. Hugh Tredennick and Robin Waterfield (London: Penguin, 1990).

Zuckert, Catherine, *Plato's Philosophers: The Coherence of the Dialogues* (Chicago: University of Chicago Press, 2012).

Zuckert, Catherine and Michael Zuchert, *The Truth about Leo Strauss: Political Philosophy and American Democracy* (Chicago: University of Chicago Press, 2006).

INDEX

Spartan wit 95
Speaking animal, humans as 16, 141–2, 180
Speech-as-living-thought 35–6, 39, 49, 76,
    80–1, 84–5, 87, 96
Spitzer, Susan 48, 57, 58
Stagira 2, 106
Stalin 59
Steiner, George 185
Stephanus numbers (in Plato) 7
Stone, I. F., 39, 42, 94, 102
Strauss, Leo 41, 59, 61–2, 74–5, 80, 88
Syllogisms 144–5, 148
Syracuse 12–13
Syria 164
Szondi, Peter 174, 185

Tarán, Leonardo 164, 168
Techne (craftsmanship or skill) 54, 77, 90–1,
    112, 129–30, 133, 135, 138, 141, 143, 171
Telos 109–10, 112–5, 118, 125, 131, 133,
    145, 152, 157, 166, 174, 180, 184;
    meaning 112–3
Thales of Miletus 55
Thamus 78, 82–4
Theagenes 145
Theatrocracy 51
Thebes 13, 68, 185
Theophrastus 164
Thessaly 30
Theuth 78, 82–4
Thirty, the 13
Thrasymachus 11, 44, 53
Thucydides 11, 12, 17, 176
Tierno, Michael 117
Timocracy 53
Tradition 3, 86, 100, 126; Characteristics
    of healthy traditions 126–7; impact of
    traditions on literature 127–8

Tragedy 4, 43, 46–7, 65–6, 78, 100, 128,
    147, 152–4, 156–8, 160–8, 170–9, 183–5
tragoidia 175
Troy, Trojan 10, 161
Turner, Mark 179, 183, 186
Twist, Oliver 49
Tyranny, tyrants 53, 145

Ulysses (James Joyce) 44, 57
USSR 59

Van Buren, John 117
Vernant, Jean-Paul, 9, 17
Virgil 106
Virtue ethics 120, 124
Vlastos, Gregory 22, 24, 30, 40–1, 102
Volpi, Franco 117
Von Schelling, Friedrich 174

wa Thiong'o, Ngũgĩ 127–8, 136
Wallace, Jennifer 7, 71, 75
Walton, Jo 33
Weil, Simone 3, 7, 58, 188
Wilamowitz-Moellendorff, Ulrich von
    75
Williams, Bernard 6, 7, 14, 17, 41, 50, 58,
    74, 175–7, 185–6, 188–9
Williams, Raymond 185
Wittgenstein, Ludwig 64, 75, 141, 151
Woolf, Virginia 3, 7

Xanthippe 63
Xenophon 17, 38–41

Zeus 94
Zoology 15, 27, 140–1
Zuckert, Catherine, 23, 40, 74, 101
Zuckert, Michael 74

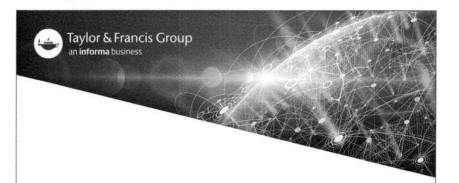